I0032111

The Fusion of Law and Economics

With Foreword from Gerald Alain P. Chen-Young

Woody R. Clermont

The Fusion of Law and Economics by Woody R. Clermont

With Foreword from Gerald Alain P. Chen-Young

Copyright © 2025 by Woody R. Clermont

All rights reserved.

No part of this publication may be reproduced, distributed, or transmitted in any form or by any means, including photocopying, recording, or other electronic or mechanical methods, without the prior written permission of the publisher, except in the case of brief quotations embodied in critical reviews and certain other noncommercial uses permitted by copyright law. For permission requests, write to wclermont2004@gmail.com.

Legal and Tax Disclaimer: This book is for educational and informational purposes only. It does not constitute legal, tax, accounting, or financial advice, and no attorney-client or other professional relationship is created by reading it. Many laws vary by state, county, city, and even nation and change over time; consult a qualified attorney and an economics, finance, or accounting professional in your jurisdiction before taking action. The author and publisher disclaim any liability for actions taken or not taken based on this work.

Trademarks: Product and company names mentioned herein may be trademarks of their respective owners. Use of such names is for identification only and does not imply endorsement.

All rights reserved. No part of this book may be reproduced in any form or by any electronic or mechanical means, including information storage and retrieval systems, without written permission from the publisher, except in the case of brief quotations embodied in critical articles or reviews.

Limitation of Liability: This publication is provided "as is" without warranty of any kind, either express or implied. Neither the author, editor, nor publisher shall be liable for any damages arising from the use of this book. Readers should exercise independent judgment and verify information where applicable.

Acknowledgments: My deepest gratitude is offered to the Most High God, the source of all light, clarity, and strength. I honor the ancestors who crossed oceans, tilled stolen soil, built nations, and whispered wisdom into the marrow of future generations. Their presence was with me throughout this journey, urging me to speak truth without fear.

This book is dedicated to my family, past, present, and yet to be, whose love steadies my spirit and whose legacy fuels my work. Everything I write begins and ends with them.

Preface

Woody R. Clermont

I have spent over twenty years as an attorney immersed in the world of civil litigation. Part of that involves the field of complex business litigation. My legal practice has exposed me to the intricate interplay between law, markets, and data. Parallel to my legal career, I have pursued an academic path grounded in quantitative rigor: a Bachelor of Science in Mathematics from Mayville State University, a Bachelor of Science in Business and a Master of Science in Data Analytics from Western Governors University, a Master of Business Administration and a terminal[1] Master of Science in Economics from Florida Atlantic University.[2]

That combination of professional experience and academic inquiry ultimately led to this book. Years earlier, I wrote *Foundations of Data Science and Statistics: Analytics Made Simple*, a text that gave readers an accessible path into quantitative methods. Even then, I found myself fascinated by the overlap between legal reasoning and statistical inference. I still recall a spirited discussion with a teaching assistant during a statistics course at Harvard Extension School, taught by Michael Parzen. I defended an answer she believed was incorrect; after I showed her the exact language from a lecture slide, she restored the points and conceded the dispute. That moment, seemingly unremarkable on its face, reminded me how much precision, clarity, and rigor matter when stakes are high and judgment depends on correct interpretation.

The Fusion of Law and Economics is the product of that lifelong convergence between legal practice and quantitative thinking. It is written for attorneys, judges, students, and analytically minded readers who recognize that modern

---

[1] A terminal master's degree is the highest degree achievable in a specific field of study, even if it's not a doctorate. In some disciplines, like fine arts or library science, a master's degree can be considered the terminal degree, meaning it's the final academic credential needed for professional practice in that field.

[2] Florida Atlantic is one of only 21 institutions in the nation to earn both Carnegie Classifications of R1, a top-tier research university, and an Opportunity University, as a model for student success.

litigation, regulation, and legal policy increasingly require fluency in economic logic. The goal is not to turn lawyers into economists, nor to strip law of its normative commitments, but to show how the two disciplines strengthen one another. When legal rules are understood as structures that allocate risk, shape incentives, and influence behavior, economics becomes indispensable. When economics is applied with sensitivity to doctrine, fairness, and institutional limits, it becomes a powerful partner to law.

Originally, this work began as a text in forensic economics. In time, however, the scope grew far beyond expert testimony and damages calculations. Through expanded research, collaboration, and many late-night conversations with my brother and friend Gerald Alain P. Chen-Young, whose mastery of economics and finance elevates every discussion, the project evolved into a broader and more ambitious treatment of the discipline. Gerald's Foreword is a generous contribution from someone who has thought deeply about the intellectual marriage between the rational agent of economics and the reasonable person of law. Our partnership began in the Moot Court competition twenty years ago and continues here, in these pages.

The expanded edition now covers not only forensic economics but the full architecture of law and economics. The book opens with a general introduction explaining why law and economics belong together: how legal systems structure incentives, why efficiency matters as an analytical lens, and how transaction costs, externalities, and information shape institutional design. It proceeds into new chapters that ground the reader in the economic logic of the rule of law itself, showing why predictability, stability, and procedural fairness are economic assets—not simply moral ideals.

Chapters on contract, tort, property, and criminal justice reflect the core domains of legal doctrine through an economic lens. Contract law emerges as a system for reducing transaction costs and encouraging efficient cooperation. Tort law becomes a mechanism for minimizing the social cost of accidents through incentives for care and risk management. Property law reveals itself as the foundation of markets, transforming scarcity into structure by defining rights, reducing information costs, and preventing waste. Even criminal law, which might seem least compatible with economic reasoning, takes on new dimensions when viewed through the logic of deterrence, error costs, and incentives for compliance.

One of the most substantial additions to this expanded edition is a full chapter on asset management and its law-and-economics underpinnings. The management of large-scale capital: pensions, endowments, sovereign wealth, insurance reserves, cannot be understood without integrating behavioral finance, portfolio theory, fiduciary law, agency costs, and market structure. The chapter presents an interdisciplinary synthesis that connects psychology, regulation, market design, and economic incentives into a coherent framework for understanding modern finance. Whether the subject is judicial oversight, securities regulation, or institutional governance, the management of capital is now inseparable from the economic logic that underlies legal rules.

The later chapters return to the book's original core in

forensic economics: valuation, damages estimation, econometric testing, antitrust and market analysis, and the role of experts in shaping evidentiary outcomes. They provide practical tools for practitioners while linking those tools to the larger economic principles developed earlier in the text.

My hope is that this book serves as both a conceptual map and a practical guide. It is intended for legal professionals who wish to understand the economic forces behind doctrine; for economists seeking insight into how law channels behavior; for students who want a clear and accessible introduction to a growing interdisciplinary field; and for judges and policymakers who must design or interpret rules in a world where incentives drive outcomes.

Finally, I remain grateful to the professors, mentors, and colleagues who shaped the work behind these pages. I extend special thanks to Professor Ky Hyang Yuhn of Florida Atlantic University, whose econometrics instruction pushed me toward precision and whose patience helped sharpen my own learning. For readers seeking the quantitative foundations that underlie the modeling in this book, I again recommend my earlier text on data science and statistics.

A complete listing of my books is available at https://woodycbooks.com. My hope is that this volume, expanded, sharpened, and enriched, continues the mission I began years ago: to make complex ideas accessible, to bridge disciplines, and to illuminate how law and economics together help us understand a world governed by both human judgment and the quiet mathematics of incentives.

Woody R. Clermont

Foreword

Gerald Alain P. Chen-Young

Section I: Background & Overview

The twin fields of law and economics have always fascinated
me albeit for reasons I did not understand especially being a
budding, precocious undergraduate student at the American
University. That inchoate understanding began to take form
in the graduate schools first at the London School of
Economics & Political Science and then even more so at York
University. What those studies shaped in my mind was the

idea that the discipline of economics, as a social science, was predicated upon certain axiomatic assumptions about human nature, behaviour, etc. as it pertained to the allocation of resources, be it for consumption or investment purposes. Those axiomatic assumptions, I concluded, could be summed up, defined, refined and eventually reduced to a simple concept, the rational agent.

Economics

However that characterisation was not enough for me or my still-developing mind. I came to that conclusion when I realised that without that bedrock rational agent assumption, many of the outcomes concerning behaviour, interactions, incentives and exchanges – i.e., trade – would not hold true with any degree of certainty or predictability. That meant that modelling human behaviour as rational agents could be next to impossible. Constructs such as indifference curves that established a locus of points reflecting "utility-maximising" preferences" between any two X, Y pair of choices would (a) not necessarily be ordered in terms of a trade-off and thus (b) never be smooth, let alone convex to the origin, in strict Cartesian terms.[3] Similarly, neat notions of categorical syllogisms would break down, the most classical of which (and the one that virtually all students learnt when they took Introduction to Logic) as follows in Aristotelian terms:[4]

---

[3]René Descartes, *Discourse on Method, Optics, Geometry and Meteorology*, Hackett Publishing Company (Revised Edition), Indianapolis/Cambridge (2001).

[4]Aristotle, *Prior Analytics* (ca. 4th c. BC).

Socrates is a man;
All men are mortal;
Ergo, Socrates is a mortal.

In brief, I had begun to question whether human behaviour was truly reduceable to a series of difference v. differential equations. My gripe with this "dismal science," to use an ugly, overtly racist term from the 19th c., was that economics as a discipline based on an admixture of entitlements, profit motives, investment incentives and self-interested pursuits had become too rigid and too mathematical.[5]

Upon completion of my M.A. (Spring 1993), I had a decision to make: whether to pursue a Ph.D. in economics, or, whether to pursue another field of interest that was complementary. Whether it was intuition or instinct, I immediately thought of law.

Law

After finishing at York University, I worked a couple of years with a family start-up, boutique investment bank, then a small regional securities firm and then eventually with a major global wire house, PaineWebber. I started the J.D. programme at the University of Miami School of Law, working full-time during the day and attending full-time

---

[5]Thomas Carlyle, *Past and Present*, Chapman & Hall, London (1843). Carlyle derided economics because of its quasi-philosophical/moral position on slavery. Carlyle's contention was pro-slavery based on pure property rights grounds. As dreadful as that was, such positions in antebellum USA were both used and defensible. The landmark case *Dred Scott v. Sanford*, 60 U.S. 393 (1856) made this clear.

school at night, and completed that programme in 1998.
There I had two great, life-altering encounters. The first
occurred somewhere between a slate of so-called first-year
("1L") courses in Elements, Property Law, Constitutional Law
and Civil Procedure, and included a competitive experience
involving something called The Moot Court; the second
involved meeting a true giant of a man and mind, and
someone for whom I developed a tremendous amount of
respect, admiration and fraternal love. This was a first-class
gentleman, single-father and fellow full-time night law school
student named Woody R. Clermont whom (a) I happened to
share partial Haitian & Caribbean (Jamaican in my case)
ancestry and (b) I now refer to as Hon. Woody R. Clermont,
Esq. Where the result of my first encounter was an
introduction to someone called the reasonable person for
reasons referenced above, the result of my second was the
formation of a life-long friendship that endures to this day.[6]

Not much needs to be said about the latter encounter for
obvious reasons. However the same is not true regarding the
former, especially bearing in mind that this was after my
introduction to the aforementioned rational agent from my
training in economics. What was an epiphany was realising
that these two creatures – viz., the reasonable person in law
and the rational agent in economics – were and still are close
kin. The cozy relationship was reinforced in later years when

---

[6]I would be remiss if I did not modestly point out that the giddy-eyed
team of Messrs. Clermont & Chen-Young actually won that Moot Court
competition as "1Ls" arguing a case under the Americans with Disabilities
Act of 1990, 42 U.S.C. § 12101 et seq.

I finished the LL.M. programme at AU Washington College of Law in 2001. What is important to note is that the realisation of the "cozy kinship" between the rational agent and reasonable person literally shook my intellectual foundation. Here's why.

Section II: Type of Marriage: Economics & Law

The prospect of a marriage between those two (2) axiomatic "agents" – viz., the "rational agent" & the "reasonable person" – had profound implications on many levels. Look at these parallels. In economics, if we do not have "ordered pairs" between X & Y outcomes, based on "utility-maximisation," then we will not have optimality in terms of economic outcomes. In law, if we assume away reasonableness in expectations of behaviour &/or conduct, then we will not have so-called "ordered liberties,"[7] meaning there will be borderline anarchy in society as standards of decorum and expectations break down.

The great late 18th c. Baron de Montesquieu commonly referred to concepts such as tranquility, peace of mind, etc., that stem from a safe, civil society where there is a minimum standard of care towards others. But these are nothing more than attributes of a reasonable person. More succinctly, there must be recognition of the fact that the rule of law must prevail at all times, uniformly and without caprice. The

---

[7]Baron de Montesquieu, *The Spirit of the Laws* (1748).

corollary to that follows: there is no such thing as absolute freedom in society. In that context, it is plain to see that the reasonable person is always confronted with a set of "constraints" – i.e., behavioural – not dissimilar to those that always confront the rational agent, albeit in a different context. Where the reasonable person is constrained by what is permissible, acceptable and normative, the rational agent is constrained by what is in his/her economic & pecuniary interests.

But therein lies the rub. Clearly, law & economics go hand-in-hand just as humanities & social sciences go hand-in-hand. Both are complementary disciplines and both require certain axiomatic assumptions regarding human behaviour, conduct & habits to ensure the functioning of a civil society with free markets for the exchange of goods, services and ideas in an equitable and profitable way. These complementary sets of assumptions give gumption to matters of both discord and dispute that will inevitably arise. And that is where arbiters come into play and those involve adjudication of so-called "rules of the game." It is also where myriad theories abound concerning both what & how those "rules" should be adjudicated. Let us examine a few of the most prominent in both spheres of economics and law.

Section III: Brief Analysis

A. Economics

Four (4) Grand Theories

One of the most prominent theories was given by Adam Smith. Prof. Smith argued that, if "markets" are efficient and freely functioning, with perfect information & with neither monopolies, barriers to entry nor externalities, then an "invisible hand" will naturally settle on a price that will clear buyers v sellers, meaning demand and supply.[8] That theory provided a solid, sound, sensible theoretical foundation for the efficient allocation of resources based literally on the idea of laissez-faire. Similarly, another famous 18th c./19th c. British classical economist, David Ricardo, had an equally succinct idea in the context of mercantilism – i.e., countries with different skills, natural resources, etc. should concentrate on those areas where they had the best "comparative advantage" in certain fields and then trade with other countries that had superior skills, natural resources, etc. in other fields. Proverbial "guns v butter" was Prof. D. Ricardo's famous example of contrasts.

Thirdly, enter Prof. K. Marx.[9] Prof. Marx directly criticised classicists like Prof.(s) A. Smith and D. Ricardo by introducing another interesting notion. Whenever there is a change in the underlying "forces of production" (i.e., basic underlying substructural technology), there is a corresponding change in the accompanying "relations of production" (i.e., ownership, management, specialisations, skillsets, etc. and

---

[8]Smith, Adam, *An Inquiry into the Nature and Causes of the Wealth of Nations*, Modern Library Edition, New York, NY (1994).

[9]Marx, Karl, *A Contribution to the Critique of Political Economy*, Franz Duncker (Berlin) (1859).

superstructures). Here are a few simple examples – i.e., when modes of transportation shifted from horse-and-buggy to railroads; when the shift occurred from railroads to automobiles was another; and when automobiles were replaced by air travel was also another; and so on. Each change in the underlying technology, what Marx called "forces of production" resulted in a corresponding change in the accompanying "relations of production". These changes, according to Marx, were (and some could easily make the argument are) inevitable.

The fourth giant in economics theory is Lord J.M. Keynes and his early 20th c. idea of "general equilibrium".[10] Keynes contended that, private markets alone, no matter how efficient and freely functioning, would not be sufficient to bring an economy into full employment. Government spending would necessarily be required to fill what Keynes termed an "output gap". Very simply, and formulaically as is fairly commonly known,

$$GNP = NI = C + I + G + (X - M).$$

Few would dispute that A. Smith's "markets" under the "invisible hand", D. Ricardo's "comparative advantage" and "mercantilism & trade", K. Marx's "forces- v. relations- of production" and J.M. Keynes' "general equilibrium" all made common sense, of sorts, and each in their own way. Fewer would even contend that these four (4) historical literary economics giants were somehow grossly mistaken or just

---

[10]Keynes, John Maynard, *The General Theory of Employment, Interest & Money*, Macmillan (London) (1936).

off-point, intellectually speaking. That said, unfortunately and as the old adage goes, common sense is not common.

In other words, there are inherent problems with all 4 of these theorems. First, take Prof. A. Smith. "Markets" are generally not freely functioning, nor is there perfect information and there are almost always monopolies, barriers to entry & externalities. That means the elegance of the "invisible hand" must come face-to-face with realities. Next, take Prof. D. Ricardo's "comparative advantage". Here, too, ordinary life's realities factor in when it comes to "mercantilism & trade". Impediments like tariffs, quotas, capital constraints, average wage differentials, productivity differentials, contractual issues, etc. all come into play. Trading proverbial "guns for butter" is not as simple as trading commodity A v. B.

K. Marx's elegant "forces- v. relations of production" has its own stumbling blocks. The 5th c./ 4th c. (BCE) classical Greek philosopher, Democritus, expounded the twin theories of "materialism and (atomistic) motion".[11] All change is constant and the only constant is change to use two applicable pleonasms to Democritus's twin theories. However, suggesting that change in humankind's evolution is somehow anything profound is mere hyperbole. It is just economic development plain-and-simple.

Finally, consider Lord J.M. Keynes's "general equilibrium".

---

[11]Original sources from Democritus are widely accepted as being in fragmented form only. Many cite his works simply by referring to these compendium sources such as: *Democritus: Early Greek Philosophy*, Penguin (1987).

Governmental intervention, to Prof. J.M. Keynes, in no way guarantees full employment. Issues like taxation, waste, misallocation of resources, indebtedness all creep into the calculation of national output &/or income given by

$$GNP = GI = C + I + G + (X - M).$$

Nevertheless, fiscalism, as some dubbed Lord J.M. Keynes' theory, managed to hold its own. And, arguendo, still does. This is even notwithstanding a strong antithesis to "fiscalism" that popped-up called "monetarism". Equally giant contemporary economics luminaries like Prof.(s) Milton Friedman, Irving Fisher et al. argued that monetary variables (e.g., fiddling with the money supply &/or tweaking, rejiggering, etc. benchmark interest rates) can only cause (and affect) monetary variables.[12]

In sum, this synopsis may be construed as some as being an over-brief that canopy that is designed by sketches using a very broad brush. Simplism or not, this picture of differing and, at times, competing, economic theories have shaped the modern world of economics in one way or another. From this, I can only draw one modest conclusion. Regardless of which school(s) of economic thought one gravitates towards, there are no perfect solutions or answers that economics, alone, can fully capture or explain.

B. Law

---

[12]Friedman, Milton and Schwartz, Anna J., *A Monetary History of the United States: 1867–1960*, Princeton University Press (1963); Fisher, Irving, *The Purchasing Power of Money*, The Macmillan Company (New York, NY) (1911).

Four Equally Grand Legal Theories

Law, like economics, addresses a lot of the shortcomings that
human conduct not so much as a rational agent, but more so
as a reasonable person. Over time, a few erudite legal scholars
rebut a lot of the aforementioned economic dogma and even
proffer a few of their own. Some of these reasonable person
theories provide an alternative narrative that could lead to
different courses of remedy and even possibly repair that a
mere rational agent could not do. That said, these are
obviously not mutually exclusive propositions despite coming
across as being so. Let's begin by examining a few major legal
treatises.

A decent starting point involves the legendary A. Smith. Prof.
Smith gave us the "invisible hand" for determining "markets"
success or failure, U.S. jurisprudence had the wisdom of a
brilliant jurist called Justice B. Learned Hand who skillfully
applied a very economics- and transactions-based
"cost-benefit test" for determining the same sort of market
success or failure. According to Justice B. Learned Hand's
theory, the test for determining success or failure "markets"
success v. failure, can be gleaned by whether the respective
parties had taken sufficient care to avoid damages through
their negligent conduct.[13] That was his standard. Under his
construct, the question boiled down very narrowly to whether
a rational agent took sufficient care as a reasonable person to
avoid causing injury &/or damage. A bare-bones monetary
test of this sort places the onus on the injuring party – i.e.,

---

[13]Judge Billings Learned Hand, opinion in *United States v. Carroll
Towing Co.* (1947).

presumably now the defendant – to strictly scrutinise their own behaviour & conduct.

If true, then clearly one could apply and extend this same test of marginal-cost v. cost-benefit to not just the "invisible hand" model of markets, but also to the D. Ricardo's "comparative advantage" model and standard for "markets" involving international trade – i.e., mercantilism. One could, as it definitely has a place by similar reasoning. A rational agent in Country A has an affirmative duty not to injure or cause damages to its counterpart rational agent in Country B. Granted differences in international law will factor in, but the basic principles elucidated by Justice B. Learned Hand are fairly universal in scope. By that I mean rational agents have an affirmative duty to behave in such a way that minimises the probability of causing injury &/or damage. Basic principles of civility, goodness and prudence apply, in other words.

Now, let's consider another giant field of law that has substantial overlaps with economics – viz., "contracts". Better yet consider one of history's most famous jurists the great Justice Oliver Wendell Holmes Jr. The same parallel analysis used above for Justice B. Learned Hand could be applied to Justice OW Holmes Jr.'s famous quip stating that a contract, roughly translated, is a promise to perform or pay damages.[14] Where Justice B. Learned Hand used the rubric of a "cost-benefit" analysis, Justice O.W. Holmes Jr. very deftly used a combination of old common law notions of "mirror

---

[14]Holmes Jr., Oliver Wendell, "The Path of the Law," 10 *Harvard Law Review* 457, 462 (1897).

image rule" regarding (a) the ex ante formation of a contract, on the one hand, versus (b) a "meeting of the minds" to confirm the ex post formation of said contract, on the other. Justice O.W. Holmes Jr.'s standard of perform-or-pay could (and can) just as easily be applied to any transaction involving any pair of i v. j persons, be they natural (humans) or legal (partnerships, companies, countries, etc.).

By the way, after "contracts", and how fittingly after OW Holmes on "contracts", perhaps I should have raised the seminal works from the bench done by Justice Richard Posner who, arguendo, is another legendary mind in this space. Justice Posner, in truth and as a 20th c. brilliant jurist, went further than virtually all of his contemporaries like B.L. Hands & O.W. Holmes, and R.H. Coase (discussed later). Posner argued that optimisation in economic terms – i.e., an exercise in "constrained economics where max Π s.t. constraints" is the de facto rule where the objective function, Π, is actually "wealth maximisation".[15] Note that the same basic principle concerning the above-referenced "utility maximisation" obviously applies. So here, once again, we have a parallel cozy relationship between rational agent and reasonable person manifesting itself.

Now, and finally, consider the equally gigantic idea in jurisprudence promulgated by the great legal academician Prof. Ronald H Coase ca. 1960 in more detail. What Prof. R.H. Coase did was specifically address the aforementioned problem of "externalities" and, in so doing literally took on

---

[15]Posner, Richard, *Economic Analysis of Law*, Little, Brown (3rd ed.), Boston (1973).

the economic purists head on.[16] Prof. Coase's argument was very simple: if we assume zero transaction costs, then any resulting externalities will be settled via privately-negotiated terms. The fairly obvious gist of Prof. R.H. Coase's argument is that reasonable persons behaving as rational agents will come to a solution &/or settlement that is (a) privately-negotiated, (b) obviously in their mutual interests and (c) better & more efficient for society as a whole.

Section IV: Conclusion

Arguments touting reasonable persons vs. rational agents are equally valid and have an equally unique place in the taxonomy of desired outcomes. Neither is superior and neither is infallible. What these twin disciplines of law and economics do is provide a respectable framework for attempting to understand the most fallible, capricious and inconsistent economic creature of all: man.

Gerald Alain P. Chen-Young

---

[16]Coase, Ronald H., "The Problem of Social Cost," *Journal of Law & Economics*, v. 3, pp. 1–44 (1960).

Contents

Chapter 1

A General Introduction to the Fusion of Law and Economics

Introduction

Law and economics, once considered distinct intellectual domains, have grown into an integrated discipline that examines legal rules through the lens of economic reasoning. The idea is simple but profound: legal rules create incentives, and those incentives shape human behaviour. When law is understood as a system that allocates rights, organizes responsibilities, and structures the cost of choices, economics

1

becomes an indispensable tool for evaluating whether those
rules promote or hinder social welfare.

This chapter introduces the foundational principles of the
fusion between law and economics. It outlines how the two
fields complement one another and why modern legal systems
cannot be fully understood without economic insight.

1.1 Why Law and Economics Belong Together

The legal system is, at its core, a framework that structures
human behavior in a world of scarcity. Laws determine:

- who may use resources,

- what obligations parties owe one another,

- how risks are allocated,

- and how disputes are resolved.

Economics, meanwhile, studies choices under scarcity. It asks
how individuals respond to incentives, how markets allocate
resources, and how cooperation or conflict arises when
interests diverge. When law imposes rules, rights, penalties,
or remedies, it changes the relative price of behaviour.
Economics provides the analytical structure to understand
those price changes and predict their effects.

Thus, law and economics intersect wherever rules influence:

- decision-making,

- resource allocation,

- risk distribution,

- or the costs of harmful behaviour.

The fusion of these fields does not diminish the normative aims of law—justice, fairness, legitimacy—but enhances our ability to evaluate whether legal systems achieve those goals effectively.

1.2 The Role of Incentives in Legal Systems

Every legal rule creates incentives. A rule requiring drivers to stop at red lights incentivises compliance by threatening sanctions. A rule enforcing private contracts incentivises parties to rely on promises. A liability rule incentivises manufacturers to design safer products.

Economics evaluates these incentives by asking:

- Does the rule promote socially beneficial conduct?

- Does it discourage harmful or wasteful behaviour?

- Does it minimize the total social cost of accidents, disputes, or transaction failures?

Incentive analysis does not assume that individuals are perfectly rational, only that they respond predictably to costs and benefits. Whether through strict liability, negligence standards, contract enforcement, or property rights, law shapes behaviour by altering the payoff structure of decisions.

1.3   Efficiency as a Legal Value

Economic analysis often evaluates legal rules according to their efficiency; in other words, whether they maximize the total welfare of society. This lens does not replace moral or constitutional constraints; rather, it complements them by offering a methodical way to compare the consequences of legal policies.

Two central concepts illustrate this:

1. Pareto Efficiency

A situation is efficient when no one can be made better off without making someone worse off.

2. Kaldor–Hicks Efficiency

A rule is efficient when the gains to the winners could, in principle, compensate the losers, regardless of whether compensation actually occurs.

Legal systems routinely adopt rules that align with these principles:

- Negligence rules minimize accident costs.
- Contract remedies encourage efficient performance or breach.
- Property rights reduce conflicts over scarce goods.
- Criminal penalties deter harmful externalities.

Efficiency is not the sole value of law, but it is an essential lens
for evaluating the real-world consequences of legal structures.

1.4 Transaction Costs and the Structure of Legal Rules

Ronald Coase's insight, that the allocation of rights affects
behavior only when transaction costs exist, is central to the
fusion of law and economics. Transaction costs include:

- search and information costs,

- negotiation and bargaining costs,

- enforcement and litigation costs,

- and strategic behaviour that impedes agreement.

Legal systems evolve to reduce these costs. For example:

- Contract default rules eliminate the need for exhaustive
  negotiation.

- Property registries reduce information costs in land
  transactions.

- Tort regimes allocate the burden of precautions to the
  least-cost avoider.

- Liability rules substitute for bargaining when
  negotiation is infeasible.

Without a legal structure minimizing transaction costs,
markets cannot coordinate efficiently.

1.5 Externalities and Legal Architecture

An externality arises when one party's actions impose costs or
benefits on others without compensation. Pollution is the
classic negative externality; innovation is a classic positive
one.

The fusion of law and economics evaluates how legal rules
internalize these externalities through:

- property rights,

- tort liability,

- regulatory schemes,

- and contractual solutions.

By internalizing costs and benefits, the law ensures that
parties face the true economic consequences of their actions.

1.6 The Domains of Law Through an Economic Lens

Nearly every major domain of law can be illuminated through
economic reasoning:

- **Contract Law**: encourages efficient cooperation and
  exchange.

- **Tort Law**: minimizes the cost of accidents and harmful

behaviour.

- **Property Law**: structures incentives for investment
  and allocates scarce resources.

- **Criminal Law**: deters socially destructive conduct by
  raising its cost.

- **Regulatory Law**: intervenes when markets fail due to
  externalities, monopolies, or asymmetric information.

- **Evidence & Procedure**: reduces adjudication costs
  and the risk of erroneous outcomes.

In each field, the legal rule is not merely a command from
authority—it is an economic instrument.

1.7   Law, Fairness, and the Limits of Economics

While economics provides powerful insights, legal systems
cannot rely exclusively on efficiency. Issues of fairness, dignity,
justice, and constitutional constraint remain essential.
Economic reasoning helps identify consequences, but it does
not dictate values.

The fusion of law and economics respects these boundaries by:

- integrating economic analysis without overriding moral
  commitments,

- evaluating rules for both fairness and efficiency,

- acknowledging distributional consequences,

- and balancing optimal outcomes with societal norms.

The goal is not to reduce law to economics, but to enrich law
with the analytical clarity economics provides.

1.8 Conclusion

The fusion of law and economics transforms the way we
understand legal systems. It reveals hidden incentive
structures, exposes inefficient doctrines, and uncovers the
underlying logic of legal rules. By analyzing how individuals
and institutions respond to costs, benefits, and risks, this
integrated discipline offers a unified framework for
understanding—and ultimately improving—the law.

In a world where resources are limited and human behavior is
complex, the marriage of law and economics is not optional; it
is essential. It provides both scholars and practitioners with
the tools to interpret legal rules with precision, evaluate
consequences with rigor, and design institutions that advance
the prosperity and fairness of society.

Chapter 2

The Rule of Law, the Economics of Litigation, and the Legal Process

Introduction

The legal system does more than resolve disputes; it structures incentives for all participants in society. The rule of law provides the foundation upon which markets function, contracts hold meaning, property rights retain stability, and individuals can predict the consequences of their actions. Litigation and the legal process are not merely procedural mechanisms but economic institutions that influence behaviour, allocate risk, and shape the cost of enforcing rights.

This chapter explores the economic logic behind the rule of law and examines how litigation, adjudication, and procedural rules create incentives for parties to behave efficiently—or inefficiently—within the justice system.

2.1 The Rule of Law as an Economic Institution

The rule of law comprises the bedrock principles that govern society: generality, predictability, stability, transparency, and impartial enforcement. These principles are not only moral commitments but economic necessities that reduce uncertainty and transaction costs.

Economically, the rule of law provides:

- **Predictability**: allowing individuals and firms to plan long-term investments.

- **Reliability**: ensuring that agreements and rights will be enforced.

- **Security**: reducing the risk of arbitrary government intervention.

- **Uniformity**: preventing differential treatment that distorts incentives.

When these principles hold, economic actors face a stable environment in which the costs of compliance, investment, and innovation are known. When the rule of law breaks down, uncertainty increases, investment declines, and resources shift toward protection, evasion, or rent-seeking.

Thus, the rule of law is not merely a legal ideal—it is an economic asset.

2.2 Litigation as an Economic Activity

Litigation is often perceived as a reactive process, but in reality it is a strategic decision influenced by expected costs and benefits. A party chooses to sue when:

$$\text{Expected Recovery} \times \text{Probability of Success} > \text{Cost of Litigation}.$$

Similarly, defendants choose whether to settle, fight, or counterclaim by comparing the expected costs of each strategy.

Litigation is therefore an economic game shaped by:

- filing costs,
- evidentiary burdens,
- attorney's fees,
- procedural rules,
- discovery obligations,
- risks of adverse judgment.

The legal system's rules influence behaviour long before a complaint is filed.

2.3   The Economics of Settlement

Most disputes never reach trial; they settle. Settlement is not a product of weakness but of rational bargaining.

Settlement occurs when:

$$\text{Plaintiff's Minimum Acceptable Amount}$$
$$\leq \text{Defendant's Maximum Willingness to Pay.}$$

The size of this bargaining range depends on:

- **probability of plaintiff success**,

- **magnitude of damages**,

- **legal costs for both sides**,

- **uncertainty in adjudication**,

- **risk tolerance of the parties**.

Procedural rules can either widen this bargaining range (encouraging settlement) or narrow it (promoting adjudication). For instance, fee-shifting rules, class actions, and discovery burdens dramatically affect negotiation strategies.

2.4 The Cost of Litigation and Procedural Design

Procedural rules distribute the costs of litigation and influence how many disputes enter the legal system. The economic question is: how should these rules be structured to minimize total social cost?

Key components include:

1. Pleading Standards

Higher pleading thresholds reduce frivolous litigation but may screen out meritorious claims. Economically, the optimal standard balances the cost of false positives (unjustified cases) with false negatives (legitimate claims never brought).

2. Discovery

Discovery is both essential and expensive. It reduces information asymmetry but can be abused to increase opponents' costs. Procedural rules must control costly fishing expeditions while ensuring access to necessary information.

3. Burden of Proof

Allocating the burden of proof to the party best positioned to produce evidence reduces administrative costs. For example, defendants often bear burdens regarding affirmative defenses because they possess superior information.

4. Standards of Review

Appellate standards influence the stability of legal rules. Deference reduces litigation and increases predictability; de novo review increases accuracy but invites more appeals.

2.5 Judicial Decision-Making and the Economics of Error Minimization

Courts do not seek perfect accuracy—that would be prohibitively expensive. Instead, the legal system attempts to balance the cost of errors with the cost of avoiding errors.

Two types of errors dominate economic analysis:

- **Type I Error (False Positive)**: imposing liability on an innocent party.

- **Type II Error (False Negative)**: failing to impose liability on a wrongdoer.

Procedural rules, evidentiary standards, and appellate review balance these errors to produce outcomes that, on average, minimize social costs.

For example:

- Civil law adopts a preponderance standard because a stricter standard would under-deter harmful behaviour.

- Criminal law uses "beyond a reasonable doubt" because

false positives are especially costly.

Each rule reflects an economic trade-off.

2.6 The Role of Judges and Judicial Discretion

Judges operate under constraints of limited information, finite time, and institutional legitimacy. Judicial discretion influences:

- how rules evolve,

- how standards are applied,

- how precedents adapt to changing circumstances,

- how disputes are resolved efficiently.

Economically, judicial reasoning promotes stability by creating predictable legal rules, while judicial flexibility allows adaptation to novel fact patterns. Good judging balances these competing imperatives: consistency vs. responsiveness.

2.7 Litigation Externalities

Litigation generates externalities—costs or benefits not borne by the direct parties. For instance:

- a damages award may deter others from engaging in harmful conduct,

- a precedent may guide future disputes,

- frivolous claims may clog dockets, increasing delay for others,

- large verdicts may raise insurance premiums for entire industries.

The legal system must account for these externalities when designing rules governing access, sanctions, burdens, and remedies.

2.8   The Economics of Access to Justice

Economic analysis must also address distri- butional concerns. Barriers to litigation — financial, informational, or procedural — may prevent injured parties from enforcing rights. This distorts incentives and weakens deterrence.

Law-and-economics frameworks examine:

- contingency fees,

- legal aid,

- fee-shifting statutes,

- class actions,

- arbitration agreements.

Each mechanism affects who can afford to litigate and how enforcement resources are allocated.

2.9   Conclusion

The rule of law and the legal process are inseparable from
their economic consequences. Litigation is not merely a forum
for dispute resolution—it is a system of incentives and
information that shapes behaviour throughout society. By
understanding litigation as an economic activity, we uncover
the hidden forces that drive settlement, shape judicial
outcomes, and determine the real-world effectiveness of legal
rights.

A legal system that aligns incentives properly reduces the cost
of disputes, promotes efficient behaviour, strengthens the rule
of law, and enhances overall social welfare. In this way, the
economics of litigation is as essential to justice as the
substantive law itself.

Chapter 2. The Rule of Law, the Economics of Litigation, and the Legal Process   18

Chapter 3

The Economics of Contract Law

Introduction

Contract law is the quiet architecture behind modern
economic life. Markets do not function merely because parties
wish to cooperate; they function because promises can be
relied upon, enforced, and priced. At its core, the economic
analysis of contract law concerns itself with three central
questions: (1) how contracts reduce transaction costs; (2) how
liability rules create incentives for efficient performance or
breach; and (3) how legal doctrines allocate risk in ways that
promote welfare-enhancing exchanges.

The law of contracts, far from being a mere doctrinal catalogue, is a system of incentives. Each rule, presumption, default term, and remedy shapes how rational agents behave ex ante and how reasonable persons are treated ex post.

3.1   Contracts Reduce Transaction Costs

A contract transforms uncertainty into structure. Parties incur search costs, negotiation costs, drafting costs, and information costs before any agreement is made. The economic function of contract law is to lower these frictions by:

- **Providing predictable default rules** that save parties from having to negotiate every contingency;

- **Enforcing voluntary exchanges** so parties need not invest in costly self-enforcement mechanisms;

- **Reducing opportunism** by deterring strategic behaviour such as shirking, renegotiation, or hold-up;

- **Clarifying property rights** in intangible or future goods.

Coasean bargaining hinges on the ability of parties to negotiate without oppressive transaction costs. Contract law is the institutional scaffolding that makes such negotiation possible.

3.2   Efficient Breach

One of the most intellectually provocative ideas in the economic analysis of contracts is the concept of the *efficient breach*. A breach is efficient when:

1. the breaching party's gain from breach exceeds the non-breaching party's loss, and

2. the remedy ensures the injured party is fully compensated.

Under this framework, the law should not compel performance at all costs. Instead, it should compel the breaching party to internalise the cost of non-performance. Expectation damages, the dominant remedy in American contract law, accomplish this by placing the injured party in the position they would have occupied had the contract been performed.

This damages structure incentivises parties to breach only when doing so increases total societal welfare. Performance is encouraged when it is efficient; breach is allowed when it is more efficient than performance.

3.3   Information Asymmetry

Many contractual exchanges occur under conditions of asymmetric information. Economic analysis identifies several recurring problems:

Adverse Selection

When one party possesses superior knowledge (e.g., quality of goods), markets may unravel unless legal rules mitigate the information imbalance. Warranty law, disclosure duties, and doctrines like misrepresentation serve this economic function.

Moral Hazard

When parties shift risk to others (e.g., through insurance or indemnification), they may behave differently. Contract law responds through:

- carefully drafted risk-allocation clauses,
- performance standards,
- liquidated damages,
- and conditions precedent.

Signaling and Screening

Contracts often embed mechanisms—performance bonds, deposits, earnest money—that signal commitment or screen for reliability. These are not merely legal instruments; they are microeconomic filters.

3.4   Default and Mandatory Rules

Economic theory distinguishes between **default rules** and **mandatory rules**.

Default Rules

Defaults fill gaps where parties are silent. Their economic purpose is to approximate what the majority of similarly situated parties would have wanted. Examples include:

- the implied warranty of merchantability,
- the obligation of good faith,
- the UCC's gap-fillers on price and delivery.

Some defaults are **majoritarian defaults**: designed to mirror the preferences of most parties. Others are **penalty defaults**: intentionally unfavourable terms used to force disclosure or negotiation of hidden information.

Mandatory Rules

Mandatory rules cannot be waived. Their economic rationale includes:

- preventing exploitation,
- controlling externalities,
- protecting vulnerable parties,
- establishing minimum standards in markets with systematic power imbalances.

Examples include unconscionability, usury limits, and certain consumer-protection statutes.

3.5 The Pricing of Promises

Contract remedies are the economic "price tags" attached to various forms of behaviour.

Expectation Damages

The gold standard for measuring loss; incentivises efficient performance.

Reliance Damages

Restore parties to their pre-contractual positions; relevant when expectation damages are too speculative.

Restitution

Prevents unjust enrichment; encourages trade by ensuring value is not expropriated.

Specific Performance

Economically justified when:

- goods are unique,
- markets are thin,
- or substitution costs are prohibitively high.

3.6 Strategic Behavior

When investments are relationship-specific, parties may behave strategically to extract concessions after the other has invested. This is known as the *hold-up problem*.

Economically rational contract structures used to mitigate hold-up include:

- long-term relational contracts,

- option contracts,

- staged performance,

- liquidated damages clauses,

- vertical integration.

Contract law's intervention aligns incentives to prevent parties from exploiting their counterpart's sunk costs.

3.7   Conclusion

The economics of contract law reveal a system built not simply on doctrine but on incentives. By evaluating rules through the lens of efficiency, welfare maximisation, and behavioural prediction, the field illuminates why courts enforce some promises, refuse others, and calibrate remedies so carefully.

Contract law is, at its core, an economic institution—one that shapes human cooperation, governs exchange, and stabilises expectations in a world defined by scarcity and choice.

Chapter 4

The Economics of Tort Law

Introduction

Tort law is the legal system's tool for managing accidents, deterring harmful behaviour, and allocating the costs of injury in a world where perfect safety is neither possible nor economically justified. In essence, tort law answers two fundamental economic questions: (1) how should society allocate the costs of accidents, and (2) how should incentives be structured to minimize the total social cost of harmful activities?

Economic analysis views tort law not as a moral inquiry into fault, but as an incentive mechanism. Every doctrine—negligence, strict liability, duty of care, proximate cause, joint and several liability—shapes decisions about precaution, risk-taking, and resource allocation.

4.1   The Social Cost of Harm

Accidents create three types of economic cost:

1. **Precaution Costs**: measures taken to reduce the probability or severity of harm.

2. **Accident Costs**: losses suffered when harm occurs.

3. **Administrative Costs**: the costs of running the tort system (litigation, enforcement, insurance).

The economic goal of tort law is to minimize the *sum* of these costs. A world with zero accidents would require infinite precautions; a world with zero precautions would produce unacceptable harm. Tort doctrine seeks an optimal middle ground.

4.2   The Learned Hand Formula

The classic starting point is Judge Learned Hand's economic test for negligence. Under this framework, a party is negligent when:

$$B < P \times L$$

where:

- B = the burden or cost of taking precautions,
- P = the probability of harm,
- L = the magnitude of the loss if harm occurs.

This creates a simple but powerful rule: take precautions when the cost of prevention is less than the expected cost of harm.

Economically, the Hand formula induces individuals and firms to choose *efficient precautions*—no more, no less. Excessive precautions waste resources; insufficient precautions shift external costs onto victims. Negligence bridges the gap.

4.3   Strict Liability

Where negligence focuses on *care*, strict liability focuses on the *activity level*. Even if a party meets all reasonable standards of care, some activities impose unavoidable risks (e.g., blasting, ultrahazardous operations).

Under strict liability:

> The injurer internalizes the cost of accidents regardless of fault.

This rule has two major economic effects:

1. It incentivises injurers to adopt optimal precautions, because they bear the accident cost either way.

2. It encourages injurers to consider the optimal *activity*

level—whether to engage in the activity at all, or how intensively.

Negligence regulates *how carefully*; strict liability regulates *how much*.

4.4 Economics of Uncertainty

Causation doctrines—both factual and legal—play a powerful economic role:

- They prevent infinite liability where actions have remote or unpredictable consequences.
- They balance fairness with administrability.
- They allocate the burden of proof to the party best positioned to avoid or insure against the risk.

Res ipsa loquitur, loss-of-chance theories, market-share liability, and alternative liability are all doctrinal adaptations to informational gaps. Economic analysis treats these doctrines as efforts to achieve the best possible incentives under uncertainty.

4.5 Comparative Negligence

Traditionally, tort law used contributory negligence—a rule where any fault by the plaintiff barred recovery. Economically, this created perverse incentives: plaintiffs had no incentive to take care, since any misstep eliminated compensation.

Modern systems adopt **comparative negligence**, which

apportions damages according to fault shares.

The economic benefits:

- Both parties face incentives to take optimal care.

- Accident costs are divided proportionally, reducing moral hazard.

- Courts reduce over- or under-deterrence produced by all-or-nothing rules.

Comparative negligence aligns incentives on both sides of the market for safety.

4.6   Tort Damages as Price Signals

Damages in tort law are not merely compensation—they are price signals that shape behaviour. Each type carries different economic implications:

Compensatory Damages

Restore the victim to their pre-injury state. They align the injurer's incentives with social cost by making the injurer internalize the harm caused.

Punitive Damages

Serve as multipliers in cases of recklessness or egregious misconduct. Their economic purpose is:

- to account for underdetection,

- to deter intentional or highly careless harm,

- to correct situations where injurers would otherwise treat liability as a "cost of doing business."

Pain & Suffering

Although sometimes criticized, these damages recognize intangible harms and incentivize avoidance of conduct that causes them.

Statutory Caps

Caps reduce uncertainty and litigation costs but may blunt deterrence by limiting recovery below the true social cost of harm.

4.7   The Insurance Market

Insurance plays a parallel economic role alongside tort law. It spreads losses across time and populations, but also introduces moral hazard. Premium structures, deductibles, and exclusions operate as economic tools to counteract excessive risk-taking.

Key insights include:

- Tort liability and insurance must be coordinated to avoid double deterrence or zero deterrence.

- Experience rating pushes parties toward efficient care levels.

- Subrogation ensures the true injurer ultimately bears the loss.

Tort law creates incentives; insurance distributes risk. Together, they shape behaviour in complex but predictable ways.

4.8   The Economics of Class Actions

Large-scale harms—environmental disasters, pharmaceutical injuries, data breaches—present collective-action and information problems. Economically, mass-tort procedures address:

- high administrative costs,
- underdeterrence due to diffuse individual harms,
- the free-rider problem,
- the difficulty of proving causation in complex systems.

Class actions and multidistrict litigation reduce duplication, lower costs, and allow courts to impose damages that reflect the true scale of harm, restoring proper deterrence.

4.9   Conclusion

Economic analysis reveals tort law as an intricate system of incentives, designed to minimize the total social cost of accidents. Whether through negligence rules, strict liability, comparative fault, or damage schemes, tort law channels behaviour toward efficient outcomes. It shapes how individuals and firms invest in safety, manage risk, and internalize the external costs of their actions.

Tort doctrine is, at its core, an economic institution—one that governs the cost of harm in a world where accidents are inevitable and resources are scarce.

Chapter 5

The Economics of Property Law

Introduction

Property law forms the foundation of all market-based systems. Without clearly defined and enforceable property rights, voluntary exchange becomes costly, investment becomes uncertain, and resources risk overuse or abandonment. Economically, property rights answer three essential questions:

1. Who has the right to use a resource?

2. Who controls how the resource is used?

3. Who keeps the benefits (and bears the costs) of that use?

The economic analysis of property law focuses on how legal rules allocate rights in ways that minimize transaction costs, prevent waste, and promote efficient resource use.

5.1 Property Rights

Property rights create value not merely by assigning ownership but by reducing uncertainty. Clear, enforceable rights allow individuals and firms to:

- plan long-term projects,
- invest in improvements,
- trade, lease, or subdivide interests,
- prevent harmful interference,
- and internalize both the costs and benefits of their actions.

As Harold Demsetz famously observed: property rights develop when the gains from internalizing externalities exceed the costs of establishing and enforcing them. In other words, property systems evolve economically, not just legally.

5.2 The Coase Theorem

At the center of property-economics lies the Coase Theorem:

> If property rights are well-defined and transaction

costs are zero, parties will negotiate to reach an
efficient allocation of resources, regardless of the
initial assignment of rights.

However, in the real world:

- bargaining is costly,

- information is imperfect,

- parties may be numerous,

- externalities are difficult to quantify,

- and strategic behaviour can distort outcomes.

Thus, the law's job is not simply to assign rights, but to assign
them in ways that minimize transaction costs and reduce
barriers to negotiation. Courts often prefer the allocation that
lowers long-term administrative and enforcement costs.

5.3 The Right to Exclude

The most economically significant aspect of property is the
right to exclude. This right prevents free-riding and preserves
incentives to invest. Without exclusion:

- private parties underinvest in maintenance and
  improvement,

- public goods become overused,

- and rivalrous resources become depleted.

Exclusion is what distinguishes private property from
commons or public regimes. It creates stable expectations and

mitigates the tragedy of the commons.

5.4 Tragedy of the Commons

When resources are held in common, individuals acting rationally in their self-interest impose external costs on one another. Because no one can exclude others, each user is incentivised to:

- harvest more than their share,

- invest less in maintenance,

- and ignore long-term sustainability.

Examples include:

- overfishing,

- overgrazing,

- congestion on public roads,

- pollution of air and waterways.

Property law responds by creating private rights, communal governance structures, regulatory controls, or hybrid systems that internalize costs and align individual incentives with social welfare.

5.5 Types of Property Regimes

Economically, property systems can be categorised as:

1. Private Property

Efficient when exclusion is inexpensive and resources are divisible.

2. Common Property

Efficient when communities can self-regulate through norms, monitoring, and shared governance.

3. Public Property

Efficient when resources serve collective needs or when exclusion is too costly (e.g., highways, national parks).

4. Open Access

The least efficient structure; no one has exclusion rights, leading to rapid depletion.

The law's role is to transition resources from inefficient regimes to more efficient ones as conditions evolve.

5.6 Property Rules vs. Liability Rules

Guido Calabresi and Douglas Melamed famously distinguished between:

Property Rules

Injurers must obtain consent before interfering with rights. **Economic effect:** encourages bargaining where transaction costs are low.

Liability Rules

Injurers may interfere but must pay court-determined damages. **Economic effect:** encourages efficient outcomes when bargaining is costly or impractical.

Courts alternate between these structures depending on whether the market or the judicial system is better positioned to determine efficient outcomes.

5.7   The Economics of Land Use and Zoning

Land is fixed in supply, making its use an inherently economic problem. Zoning and land-use regulations attempt to internalize spillover effects such as:

- noise,
- pollution,
- congestion,
- aesthetic harm,
- incompatible neighbouring uses.

These regulations aim to reduce negative externalities while preserving overall economic value. However, excessive regulation can create inefficiencies by:

- restricting supply,
- raising housing prices,

- impeding mobility,

- or distorting market incentives.

Economically optimal zoning balances regulation with flexibility.

5.8   Nuisance Law

Nuisance law addresses conflicts between neighbouring land uses. Courts often apply:

- **Reasonableness standards**,

- **Balancing tests**, or

- **Restoration vs. compensation remedies**

to minimize social costs. The remedies reflect Coasean thinking:

- Injunctions protect property rules where bargaining is feasible.

- Damages (temporary or permanent) use liability rules where bargaining is difficult.

The structure of the remedy affects incentives for future investment, mitigation, and negotiation.

5.9   First Possession

Economically, first possession rules (e.g., wild animals, oil and gas, groundwater) create incentives to invest in acquisition but risk:

- wasteful competition,

- resource depletion,

- excessive extraction speeds,

- and overinvestment in capture technology.

Modern systems temper these inefficiencies with regulatory regimes, unitisation, or proportional allocation schemes.

5.10   Intellectual Property

Intellectual property (IP) presents an economic paradox: ideas are non-rivalrous and can be copied at near-zero cost. IP rights:

- encourage innovation by granting exclusivity,

- but risk deadweight losses if protections are too strong or too long.

Economically optimal IP:

- provides incentives for creation,

- limits monopolistic distortion,

- and rewards genuine innovation rather than strategic behaviour.

5.11 Property Transfers and Transaction Costs

Property law facilitates transfer through:

- recording systems,
- title registries,
- notice statutes,
- adverse possession doctrines.

These mechanisms reduce information costs and increase market liquidity. The state's goal is to design a system where the cost of verifying and transferring rights does not overwhelm the value of the underlying asset.

5.12 Conclusion

The economics of property law demonstrates that ownership is not merely about possession—but about incentives, efficiency, and social welfare. Property rights reduce transaction costs, prevent waste, facilitate investment, and shape how societies manage scarce resources.

From exclusion and nuisance to zoning and intellectual property, the economic logic behind property law reveals a simple truth:

> The structure of property determines the structure of markets.

Chapter 6

Crime & Economics

Introduction

Criminal justice is often framed in moral or constitutional terms: harm, culpability, retribution, due process, proportionality. While these values remain indispensable, criminal law is also an economic institution. It structures incentives, allocates enforcement resources, deters harmful conduct, and balances the social costs of crime against the costs of preventing it.

Economic analysis does not replace moral judgment—it clarifies consequences, trade-offs, and institutional design. The fusion of law and economics in the criminal justice context allows us to understand why certain punishments deter while others do not, why policing strategies succeed or fail, and why procedural protections exist despite their cost.

This chapter examines how economic reasoning illuminates the purposes of punishment, the structure of criminal sanctions, and the design of enforcement and procedural systems.

6.1   The Economic Purpose of Criminal Law

Criminal law exists primarily to prevent conduct that produces significant negative externalities—harms that cannot be efficiently addressed through private bargaining, civil litigation, or market mechanisms.

Three core economic functions distinguish criminal law from civil law:

1. **Deterrence**: raising the expected cost of harmful acts.

2. **Incapacitation**: restricting the liberty of offenders to prevent future crimes.

3. **Expressive and Normative Enforcement**: reinforcing social norms when markets cannot.

Civil remedies are often inadequate because:

- perpetrators may be judgment-proof,

- victims may be unwilling or unable to sue,

- harms such as violence and fear cannot be monetized easily,

- the probability of detection is low, requiring sanctions that exceed mere compensation.

Criminal law steps in where private ordering and civil litigation fail.

6.2 Deterrence and the Expected Cost of Crime

In economic terms, individuals commit crimes when the expected benefit exceeds the expected cost. Criminal law alters this calculus by increasing the expected cost:

$$\text{Expected Cost of Crime} = P(\text{Detection}) \times P(\text{Conviction}) \times \text{Severity of Sanction}.$$

Each component carries economic implications:

1. Probability of Detection
Increasing detection generally enhances deterrence but requires greater investment in policing, surveillance, and investigative capacity. There are diminishing returns: beyond a certain level, each additional police officer yields smaller marginal reductions in crime.

2. Probability of Conviction
Higher conviction rates require procedural reform, prosecutorial resources, robust forensic systems, and improvements in evidence-gathering. But increasing conviction probability also raises the risk of Type I errors

(convicting the innocent), a costly failure the criminal justice
system must minimize.

3. Severity of Sanctions

Increasing punishment is cheaper than increasing detection,
but harsher sanctions may produce:

- diminishing marginal deterrence,

- reduced incentives for offenders to comply (e.g.,
  escalating violence to avoid capture),

- higher incarceration costs,

- long-term reductions in employability and social
  reintegration.

Economically efficient criminal law balances these dimensions
rather than maximizing any single one.

6.3   Incapacitation and the Allocation of Enforcement Resources

Not all offenders respond to deterrence equally. Some are
impulsive, addicted, mentally ill, or embedded in
environments that reduce sensitivity to expected costs. For
such offenders, incapacitation—physically preventing crime
through imprisonment—may be the most effective tool.

Economics asks:

- Which offenders pose high future-risk?

- What is the cost of imprisoning them?

- What are the diminishing returns of incarceration?

Selective incapacitation—focusing on high-risk, high-harm offenders—reduces social cost, while overly broad incarceration imposes large financial and human costs without proportional benefit.

6.4 The Economics of Punishment Types

Different sanctions produce different incentive structures. Economically, criminal punishment can be divided into:

1. Fines

Fines are efficient when offenders have the ability to pay. They impose minimal administrative cost and avoid the social cost of imprisonment. However, they are ineffective when:

- offenders are indigent,

- crimes yield high illicit gain,

- detection probability is low and fines cannot scale high enough to compensate.

2. Incarceration

Imprisonment provides incapacitation and deterrence but is economically costly. It also produces externalities:

- reduced future earnings,

- disrupted families,

- increased recidivism due to criminogenic environments,

- burden on taxpayers.

Optimal sentencing considers both immediate public safety and long-term social cost.

3. Probation and Community Sanctions

These sanctions reduce cost while maintaining supervision. They work best when monitoring technology is effective and offenders pose low risk of violence.

4. Restorative Justice

Restorative systems internalize harm directly by involving victims and communities. They can reduce recidivism and lower costs when properly implemented.

6.5   The Role of Enforcement: Policing, Prosecution, and Detection

Law enforcement agencies face their own incentive structures:

- budget constraints,

- political pressures,

- public expectations,

- technological capabilities,

- institutional culture.

Economics helps explain why some policing models succeed:

- **Hotspot policing** concentrates resources where crime clusters—efficient allocation.

- **Problem-oriented policing** targets the underlying economics of specific crime patterns.

- **Deterrence messaging** increases perceived detection probability with minimal cost.

Prosecutorial discretion is also an economic force. Prosecutors allocate scarce trial resources by:

- prioritizing high-harm cases,

- using plea bargains to conserve court capacity,

- pursuing charges with strong evidence.

6.6   The Economics of Plea Bargaining

Plea bargaining is the engine of modern criminal justice. Over 90 percent of criminal cases resolve by plea, not trial.

Economically, plea bargaining:

- conserves judicial resources,

- reduces administrative costs,

- increases certainty for both sides,

- allows differentiated sentencing based on evidence strength and cooperation.

But plea bargaining also creates risks:

- innocent defendants may plead to avoid the risk of trial,

- prosecutors may overcharge to induce pleas,

- inequality in bargaining power can distort outcomes.

A well-designed plea system must balance efficiency with fairness and transparency.

6.7   Error Costs in Criminal Justice

As with civil litigation—but more intensely—criminal adjudication is shaped by the economics of error. The system seeks to minimize:

- **Type I Errors**: convicting the innocent,

- **Type II Errors**: acquitting the guilty.

Because Type I errors impose greater moral and societal costs, criminal law raises the standard of proof to "beyond a reasonable doubt." But higher standards also increase Type II errors, reducing deterrence. The optimal balance reflects deep value judgments, constrained by economic reality.

6.8 Reentry, Recidivism, and Long-Term Incentives

Criminal justice policy must consider not only punishment but reintegration. High recidivism imposes enormous social cost. Economic analysis identifies several key leverage points:

- employment access,
- education and vocational programs,
- mental-health and addiction treatment,
- supervision quality,
- restoration of civil rights.

These interventions reduce crime by improving opportunity and lowering the expected benefit of reoffending.

6.9 Conclusion

Criminal justice is an inherently economic enterprise. It allocates resources, structures incentives, manages risks, and imposes sanctions designed to prevent harm. The economics of criminal justice does not weaken or cheapen the moral foundations of punishment; it sharpens our understanding of how rules actually function in the world.

An efficient criminal justice system:

- deters harmful conduct,

- protects the public,

- minimizes error,

- uses resources wisely,

- promotes rehabilitation where feasible,

- and reinforces the rule of law.

Understanding criminal law through an economic lens reveals a simple truth: the effectiveness of justice depends not only on moral principles, but on sound institutional design and rational incentive structures.

Chapter 7

A Law & Economics Synthesis of Asset Management

Introduction

Asset management is far more than the mechanical allocation of capital across securities. It is an intricate institutional enterprise shaped by markets, psychology, incentives, and legal constraints. The global world of institutional investing sits at the crossroads of financial economics, behavioral science, and regulatory design. Understanding how large pools of capital are managed requires an appreciation of both

the conceptual foundations of modern finance and the human
tendencies that cause markets to deviate from theoretical
ideals. It also requires a mature understanding of the legal
architecture—fiduciary duties, regulatory oversight, agency
relationships, and disclosure regimes—that establishes the
boundaries within which investment decisions are made.

This chapter blends these perspectives into a unified
framework. It begins with a global overview of institutional
investing, expands into the behavioral and psychological
dimensions of financial decision-making, and then examines
the law governing asset managers. It concludes with a full
law-and-economics treatment of asset management—analyzing
how incentives, governance structures, and market design
shape the performance and stability of the financial system.

7.1   The Evolution of Money and Markets Revisited: Rationality and Its Limits

Traditional finance describes the evolution of money and
markets as a story of increasingly efficient mechanisms for
storing and transferring value. Commodity money gave way
to fiat currency, capital markets developed for equity and debt
financing, and derivative markets emerged to manage risk.
Yet, while these developments increased liquidity and
broadened access to capital, they also revealed the limits of
human rationality.

Behavioral economics has shown that investors, including institutional decision-makers, do not always act as the rational agents envisioned by classical theory. Instead, they exhibit predictable cognitive biases: overconfidence, loss aversion, anchoring, present bias, and herd behavior. These biases help explain why asset bubbles occur, why markets sometimes overshoot fundamentals, and why long-term investment strategies are often abandoned during periods of volatility. Thus, the evolution of financial markets cannot be understood solely as a triumph of efficiency—it must be viewed through the lens of human psychology, institutional incentives, and periodic irrationality.

7.2 Institutional Investors and the Psychology of Large-Scale Capital

Institutional investors play a dominant role in global markets, yet they are not immune to behavioral tendencies. Pension boards may chase recent performance, endowment committees may exhibit groupthink, and sovereign wealth funds may succumb to political pressures that distort long-term objectives. Behavioral finance research reveals that even sophisticated investors rely on heuristics when evaluating risk and return, often underestimating tail risks or overreacting to narratives.

The psychology of committees is particularly relevant. Many institutional decisions emerge not from lone portfolio

managers but from governing bodies whose members possess
differing backgrounds, incentives, and time horizons. Social
dynamics—such as conformity pressure, authority bias, and
the desire to avoid embarrassment—shape allocation decisions,
manager selection, and responses to market crises.
Understanding institutional behavior thus requires examining
not only economic models but also the cognitive and social
factors that shape collective judgment.

7.3 Portfolio Management Through a Behavioral Lens

Portfolio theory traditionally frames investment decisions in
terms of expected return and volatility. While these concepts
remain fundamental, behavioral finance reveals that investors
do not experience gains and losses symmetrically. Prospect
theory demonstrates that losses loom larger than gains, and
that investors often prefer avoiding losses to maximizing
returns. This "loss aversion" contributes to suboptimal
behaviors: excessive risk aversion after downturns, reluctance
to sell losing positions, and overexposure to familiar or
domestic assets.

Behavioral research also challenges traditional notions of
diversification. Investors often construct portfolios that reflect
narratives or emotional comfort rather than optimal risk
spreading. They may overweight recently successful sectors,
avoid unfamiliar asset classes, or pursue complex strategies
without a clear understanding of risk. These tendencies shape
institutional portfolios and contribute to return dispersion

among institutions with similar mandates.

Risk management itself has a behavioral dimension. While
quantitative tools measure volatility and drawdowns,
institutional responses to risk are mediated by human
judgment—fear during crises, overconfidence during rallies,
and political or governance pressures during
underperformance. Thus, the practice of portfolio
management is as much psychological as it is mathematical.

7.4   The Legal Architecture of Asset Management

The asset-management industry operates within a
comprehensive legal and regulatory structure designed to
align incentives, protect beneficiaries, and reduce systemic
risk. Central to this framework is the law of fiduciary duty.
Asset managers, trustees, and investment committees owe
duties of loyalty and prudence to their clients or beneficiaries.
These duties require acting solely in the interest of the
beneficiary, avoiding conflicts of interest, and exercising the
care, skill, and diligence that a prudent professional would
employ under similar circumstances.

In the United States, the Employee Retirement Income
Security Act (ERISA) imposes rigorous standards for pension
fiduciaries. The Investment Advisers Act establishes
disclosure obligations and prohibits fraudulent practices, while
the Investment Company Act regulates mutual funds and
other pooled vehicles. Insurance companies face statutory

requirements governing reserves and permissible investments, and sovereign wealth funds must operate within the mandates created by national legislation.

Fiduciary law interacts deeply with behavioral tendencies. Because asset managers may be tempted to chase trends, overtrade, or select managers based on reputation rather than skill, legal duties operate as a corrective mechanism. They constrain excessive risk-taking, require justification for investment decisions, and provide a framework for accountability. The law thus serves as both a boundary and a stabilizing force within the asset-management ecosystem.

7.5   Agency Costs and the Economic Logic of Regulation

Asset management is fundamentally an agency relationship: one party (the agent) manages resources on behalf of another (the principal). Agency theory predicts that agents may act in their own interest rather than in the interest of clients unless legal and contractual mechanisms align incentives. Examples include excessive fee structures, closet indexing, window dressing, and risk shifting to maximize short-term performance metrics.

The law-and-economics approach analyzes how regulation mitigates these agency costs. Disclosure requirements reduce information asymmetry; prudence standards constrain reckless behavior; performance reporting enhances transparency; and governance structures—such as independent boards for

mutual funds—introduce oversight. Market mechanisms, such
as competition among asset managers and the ability of
institutions to redeem or reallocate funds, also help discipline
agents. Regulatory design thus reflects the economic need to
reduce agency costs and promote efficient capital allocation.

7.6 A Law & Economics Framework for Asset Management

A comprehensive law-and-economics framework for asset
management must account for the intricate interplay between
incentives, psychology, legal structure, and market design.
Asset management is not simply a technical discipline applied
to securities and portfolios; it is an institutional system
shaped by human behavior, governed by fiduciary norms,
constrained by regulatory oversight, and influenced by the
architecture of global markets. At the center of this system
lies the fundamental assumption of economics—that
individuals respond to incentives. Yet, in practice, those
responses are filtered through cognitive biases, organizational
pressures, and legal boundaries that influence whether
outcomes align with long-term welfare or deviate toward
instability. Understanding this ecosystem requires an
integrated view that blends economics, behavioral science,
and legal doctrine into a unified analytical lens.

Incentives form the spine of asset management.
Compensation structures, fee arrangements, performance
evaluations, and competitive dynamics motivate the decisions
of portfolio managers, analysts, risk officers, and investment

committees. Economic theory predicts that when incentives
align with client interests, capital is allocated efficiently, risk
is managed prudently, and investment strategies are selected
with a long-term perspective. However, if incentives
emphasize short-term performance, reward excessive
risk-taking, or encourage closet indexing, behavior begins to
shift. Short-term relative performance pressures, for example,
can induce herding, excessive trading, and abrupt
reallocations during volatile markets. Multi-manager
structures may foster internal competition that undermines
collaboration, while principal–agent tensions between
managers and beneficiaries can distort priorities. Incentives
determine whether institutions act with discipline or succumb
to the temptation to chase trends and narratives that lack
fundamental grounding.

Yet incentives alone cannot explain how asset-management
institutions behave. Human psychology exerts a profound
influence on market behavior, often amplifying or
counteracting economic forces. Portfolio managers may
intellectually endorse rational decision-making while still
experiencing fear during crises, euphoria during bull markets,
and aversion to realizing losses. Behavioral economics reveals
that overconfidence can lead managers to underestimate risk,
while anchoring causes them to rely too heavily on past
valuations or outdated assumptions. Herd behavior emerges
when institutions imitate peers rather than follow
independent analysis, especially under performance or career
pressure. Loss aversion may prompt committees to de-risk
portfolios prematurely, locking in losses and missing
recoveries. Narrative-driven investing—where emotionally

compelling stories overshadow empirical evidence—can shape
allocation decisions even among sophisticated practitioners.
The behavioral dimension introduces instability into an
otherwise rational system, and it is only by acknowledging
and understanding these tendencies that institutions can
develop safeguards against them.

The legal structure governing asset management introduces a
stabilizing force into this psychologically complex
environment. Fiduciary duties anchor the actions of trustees,
investment advisers, board members, and portfolio managers.
These duties—loyalty, prudence, care, and adherence to
governing instruments—require decision-makers to prioritize
the interests of beneficiaries above personal or institutional
gain. Regulatory regimes, such as the Investment Advisers
Act and ERISA in the United States, further shape conduct
by mandating disclosure, limiting conflicts of interest,
requiring documentation of investment decisions, and
enforcing standards of care through oversight bodies. The law
creates a disciplined framework within which incentives must
operate, counterbalancing impulses toward excessive
risk-taking or speculation. It also imposes accountability by
enabling beneficiaries, regulators, and courts to evaluate
whether actions were consistent with prudent professional
judgment. Legal constraints therefore function as both
boundaries and incentives: boundaries that prevent harmful
conduct, and incentives that encourage thoughtful,
evidence-based, and well-justified decision-making.

Market architecture completes this institutional equilibrium.
The structure of financial markets—their liquidity,
transparency, available instruments, cross-border accessibility,

and regulatory harmonization—shapes the environment in
which asset managers deploy capital. Deep, liquid markets
support efficient price discovery and allow institutions to
transact without undue cost or impact. Transparent markets
reduce the informational advantages of insiders and moderate
the behavioral biases that flourish under uncertainty.
Fragmented or opaque markets, by contrast, heighten the role
of heuristics and narratives, making decision-making more
vulnerable to psychological distortions. The increasing
globalization of capital flows adds another layer of complexity:
shifts in monetary policy, geopolitical tensions, and currency
fluctuations influence both risks and opportunities, often
introducing volatility that tests the resilience of institutional
processes and governance structures.

Seen through this integrated lens, asset management operates
as a delicate equilibrium shaped by the tension and
interaction among incentives, psychology, law, and market
design. When incentives are well-aligned, behavioral
tendencies are understood and mitigated, legal constraints are
respected, and market architecture supports transparency and
liquidity, institutions tend to promote efficient allocation,
long-term investment horizons, and systemic stability.
Investment committees behave deliberately; strategies remain
grounded in economic fundamentals; and market cycles, while
inevitable, do not threaten institutional integrity.

When these forces fall out of alignment, however, the
consequences can be dramatic. Incentive structures that
reward short-term gains can magnify psychological biases,
encouraging managers to chase momentum or conceal risk
exposures. Weak legal oversight or lax fiduciary enforcement

can allow conflicts of interest to proliferate, undermining
beneficiary trust and distorting capital flows. Market
structures that lack transparency or that amplify volatility
can trigger behavioral contagion, leading to coordinated
selling, liquidity spirals, or asset-price bubbles detached from
fundamentals. Historical episodes—from the dot-com bubble
to the global financial crisis—illustrate how misaligned
incentives, unchecked behavioral tendencies, insufficient legal
safeguards, and fragile market mechanisms can combine to
generate instability across the financial system.

A law-and-economics approach therefore views asset
management not as a static set of principles, but as a
dynamic institutional system requiring continuous calibration.
It emphasizes that legal rules should be designed to align
incentives with long-term welfare, mitigate predictable
behavioral distortions, and foster transparency and
accountability. It argues that market architecture must
support robust price discovery, minimize hidden risks, and
ensure that liquidity does not evaporate under stress. It
recognizes that psychology cannot be eliminated from
decision-making, but it can be anticipated, measured, and
moderated through governance structures, audit processes,
documentation requirements, and cultural norms. And it
acknowledges that incentives, when properly structured, can
transform behavioral complexity into disciplined action rather
than allowing it to become a source of fragility.

This expanded framework highlights the profound
interconnectedness of law, economics, and psychology within
the asset-management ecosystem. Institutions succeed not
because any single force dominates, but because the system as

a whole balances those forces in a way that promotes stability, efficiency, and fairness. When well-calibrated, this equilibrium ensures that the management of capital contributes to long-term growth, financial resilience, and the prosperity of the beneficiaries whose futures depend on prudent stewardship. When misaligned, it becomes a source of systemic vulnerability—a reminder that discipline, transparency, and legal integrity are essential not only to the practice of asset management but to the health of global markets themselves.

7.7   Conclusion

Asset management is a profoundly interdisciplinary field. It reflects centuries of financial evolution, the cognitive architecture of human decision-making, and a complex legal framework designed to align incentives and protect beneficiaries. The behavioral and psychological dimensions of investing complicate the neat elegance of classical portfolio theory, while the law introduces necessary discipline into a system prone to excess. A full law-and-economics approach reveals asset management as a dynamic ecosystem where rational models, human tendencies, and legal institutions interact to shape the deployment of global capital.

Understanding this fusion is essential not only for investors and policymakers but for anyone seeking to grasp how financial markets function—and occasionally fail—in the real world.

Chapter 8

Forensic Economics

8.1   History

Forensic economics is the application of economic theories,
methods, and data to issues of fact in a legal forum. At its
core, it is an investigative and evidentiary discipline: one that
seeks to objectively assess and quantify economic harm within
the framework of judicial proceedings. Whether evaluating
lost earnings, life care costs, or damages from wrongful
termination, forensic economists are tasked with translating
complex human experiences into measurable financial values.

The term *forensic* derives from the Latin *forensis*, meaning
"of or before the forum," referring to the public courts of
ancient Rome. In modern parlance, anything "forensic"
implies the use of specialized knowledge for purposes of legal

investigation or testimony. Forensic economics, then, is the intersection of economic science and legal adjudication. It is where the abstract becomes evidentiary, and where data meet deliberation.

8.2   Origins & Evolution

The formal practice of forensic economics began to crystallize as a distinct professional and academic discipline in the United States during the mid-20th century, emerging alongside broader societal shifts in tort litigation, industrial development, actuarial science, and legal procedural reforms. While economists had offered opinions in commercial and regulatory contexts for decades, the structured application of economics to quantify individual damages, especially in personal injury and employment litigation, did not coalesce into a recognized subfield until the post-World War II era.

Pre-Modern Foundations

Long before the term "forensic economics" entered legal or academic discourse, economists played advisory roles in valuation-related legal matters such as antitrust damages, railroad rate cases, and public utility regulation. As early as the 1920s and 1930s, economists provided expert testimony in breach of contract and trade disputes. However, these early engagements lacked formal structure, peer-reviewed literature, or a professional identity distinct from general economic consulting.

The legal landscape also played a formative role. The

industrialization of the U.S. economy and the rise of statutory protections in labor and employment (e.g., workers' compensation laws, the Fair Labor Standards Act) created new avenues for litigation. Courts began recognizing the need for expert assistance to quantify complex economic losses—particularly those involving future earnings, benefits, and business valuation.

Postwar Emergence

It was in the aftermath of World War II that the necessary ingredients for a specialized forensic economic discipline came together:

- **Expansion of Tort Law:** American courts broadened access to recovery for personal injury and wrongful death. The development of comparative negligence and strict liability doctrines led to increased demand for damage valuation.

- **Economic Prosperity and Data Availability:** The 1950s and 1960s saw the emergence of richer, more granular labor market data from sources such as the U.S. Census, the Bureau of Labor Statistics (BLS), and Social Security Administration (SSA). These databases enabled economists to project earnings and life expectancy with far greater precision.

- **Actuarial Science Integration:** Life tables, worklife expectancy models, and discounting techniques began to be systematically incorporated into damage models.

- **Computational Advances:** The advent of mainframe

computing and, later, personal computers allowed for
more sophisticated simulations, statistical analysis, and
customized projections.

Institutionalization of the Field

By the 1970s and 1980s, forensic economics was becoming
formalized as both a scholarly discipline and a courtroom
profession:

- **Formation of Professional Associations:** The
  National Association of Forensic Economics (NAFE)
  was established in the early 1980s, providing a
  professional home, ethical guidelines, and opportunities
  for networking and continuing education.

- **Peer-Reviewed Scholarship:** The launch of *The
  Journal of Forensic Economics* in 1987 created a forum
  for academic rigor, methodological development, and
  case study analysis. This elevated the intellectual
  credibility of forensic economics and encouraged more
  standardized practices.

- **Courtroom Precedents:** Judicial decisions during this
  period, including early *Daubert*-like challenges, began to
  define the parameters of admissibility, requiring
  economists to articulate not only their conclusions but
  also the empirical basis and reliability of their methods.

Economists began to publish widely cited papers on topics
such as personal consumption deduction rates, worklife
expectancy, real versus nominal discounting, and the
valuation of fringe benefits. These foundational works remain

heavily cited in litigation and expert reports today.

Methodological Growth

Throughout the 1990s and 2000s, forensic economics
expanded its theoretical and technical toolkit by drawing on
adjacent academic fields:

- **Labor Economics:** Models of earnings capacity, wage
  growth, and occupational transitions.

- **Health Economics:** Used to estimate long-term
  medical costs, life care plans, and the economic impact
  of chronic disability.

- **Corporate Finance and Valuation:** Especially
  relevant in commercial litigation and partnership
  dissolution cases.

- **Statistics and Econometrics:** The use of regression
  analysis, time series forecasting, and stochastic
  modeling has become increasingly common in large-scale
  or class action cases.

- **Behavioral Economics:** Newer applications explore
  the economic impact of trauma, the willingness to pay
  to avoid injury (hedonics), and the cost of emotional
  distress.

Training programs, academic symposia, and interdisciplinary
publications helped forensic economics solidify its identity not
only in law but also within the broader economics profession.
University departments began offering courses and even
concentrations in forensic economics as part of applied
economics or public policy programs.

Modern Diversification

Once primarily concerned with wage loss in personal injury
and wrongful death cases, forensic economics has evolved into
a broad-ranging field relevant to:

- **Employment Discrimination:** Estimating back pay,
  front pay, and opportunity loss in cases involving Title
  VII or ADA violations.

- **Intellectual Property and Business Tort
  Valuation:** Assessing the economic value of lost
  licensing revenue, goodwill, or brand equity.

- **Pension and Retirement Disputes:** Quantifying
  defined benefit and defined contribution plan losses in
  divorce or employment-related claims.

- **Class Action and Mass Tort Claims:** Performing
  statistical extrapolation and loss modeling across large
  plaintiff pools.

- **Wrongful Incarceration and Civil Rights Cases:**
  Calculating lost life opportunity, employment loss, and
  reputational damage for exonerated individuals.

Additionally, forensic economists are increasingly being asked
to consult on policy-related matters, such as victim
compensation fund design, insurance rate litigation, and
governmental regulatory impact analysis. As alternative
dispute resolution mechanisms such as arbitration and
mediation have become more common, the demand for
neutral economic valuation continues to grow.

Global Influence

Although initially U.S.-centric, the field has begun to influence practices in Canada, the United Kingdom, Australia, and the European Union. Many international courts and arbitration panels now accept forensic economic testimony using U.S.-derived methods, particularly in cases involving multinational corporations or human rights litigation.

Meanwhile, the integration of technology has further expanded the discipline:

- **Big Data and Cloud Analytics:** Economists now use large labor force datasets to build predictive models tailored to individual plaintiffs.

- **Machine Learning**: Emerging tools allow for the detection of wage discrimination, forecasting of career outcomes, and simulation of large-scale tort exposure scenarios.

- **Digital Visualization Tools:** Graphs, interactive dashboards, and courtroom-ready demonstratives enhance the communication of findings to juries and judges.

With these developments, the modern forensic economist is expected to be both a rigorous analyst and a compelling communicator—capable of translating complex financial models into accessible narratives for use in the adversarial system.

Conclusion

What began as a loosely defined consulting function has
evolved into a robust, multidisciplinary, and global profession.
Forensic economics now encompasses a wide array of
substantive domains, from tort and labor to finance and
intellectual property, and requires practitioners to be both
methodologically rigorous and legally literate.

Its evolution has been driven not only by legal demand but by
a commitment to intellectual integrity, professional standards,
and the belief that economic measurement, when applied
responsibly, can play a critical role in promoting justice,
compensating harm, and restoring lost value. The next
generation of forensic economists will inherit a tradition rich
in analytical tools, academic respectability, and ethical
responsibility, ready to meet the growing complexity of
twenty-first-century litigation.

8.3   Function of Experts

The primary role of a forensic economist is to serve as an
expert witness who provides structured economic analysis and
opinion testimony in civil or administrative proceedings. This
role sits at the intersection of empirical economic modeling,
legal reasoning, and effective communication. It requires not
only mastery of technical tools but also an appreciation of the
legal forum in which the analysis will be contested.

Forensic economists are typically retained by one party in
litigation but must adhere to strict professional norms of
impartiality and transparency. Their ultimate duty is to the

truth—not to advocacy. Courts rely on expert economists to clarify complex financial matters, bridge technical gaps between attorneys and juries, and provide a reasoned basis for assessing compensatory damages.

The function of a forensic economist typically involves four key domains of engagement, which are described in depth below:

1. Valuation of Damages

This is the cornerstone function of forensic economics: converting the effects of a tort, breach, or employment violation into quantifiable economic losses. The valuation process must be tailored to the type of harm, the identity of the plaintiff, and the nature of the litigation.

- **Earnings Loss**: Estimating lost income due to personal injury, wrongful termination, or death involves modeling expected career trajectory "but for" the harmful event. This includes analysis of historical earnings, projected future wages, career growth rates, and retirement age.

- **Fringe Benefits**: Lost employer-paid contributions (e.g., to health insurance, retirement, bonuses) are valued based on actual records or labor statistics.

- **Household Services**: Valued using market replacement cost or time-use surveys, particularly relevant in wrongful death and caregiving cases.

- **Business Losses**: For self-employed plaintiffs or business owners, the economist may assess profit streams, goodwill loss, or partnership interest valuation.

- **Discounting to Present Value**: Losses that occur in

the future must be discounted using appropriate real or nominal rates based on current economic conditions and accepted actuarial practice.

All valuations must distinguish between gross and net-of-tax income (depending on jurisdiction), account for worklife expectancy, and reflect proper adjustments for inflation, productivity growth, and risk.

2. Consultation

Before trial, forensic economists serve as consultants who help attorneys evaluate the economic merit of a case. This includes an early-stage review of available records, identification of missing data, and preliminary quantification of damages.

Key consultation tasks include:

- **Data Discovery Guidance**: Advising attorneys on which documents are essential (e.g., tax returns, employment records, life care plans, business ledgers) to support or challenge economic claims.

- **Interrogatory and Deposition Support**: Preparing questions for opposing experts or plaintiffs to clarify assumptions, highlight inconsistencies, or uncover mitigation behavior.

- **Settlement Valuation**: Offering economic insights into possible settlement ranges, incorporating time value, legal costs, and likelihood of trial outcomes.

- **Evaluation of Opposing Reports**: Critically reviewing opposing expert analyses for methodological flaws, misapplied data, unreasonable assumptions, or logical errors.

- **Strategy Development**: Helping attorneys understand the strengths and vulnerabilities of economic claims to craft a more informed legal strategy.

This early involvement is essential for ensuring that the economic narrative aligns with the legal theory of the case and that expert testimony will ultimately survive admissibility challenges.

3. Report Preparation

A written expert report serves as the foundational document for all expert testimony. It is both a scientific analysis and a legal exhibit, often introduced in court under Federal Rule of Evidence 702 or equivalent state rules. The strength of a forensic economist's written report can greatly influence whether the case settles, proceeds to trial, or is dismissed.

A well-structured expert report includes:

- **Statement of Assignment**: A clear description of what the expert was retained to analyze.

- **Assumptions and Limitations**: An honest accounting of what the analysis relies upon and the scope of the available data.

- **Economic Methodology**: A detailed, transparent explanation of the models, formulas, tables, or statistical methods used.

- **Findings and Results**: All numerical outcomes, properly labeled and supported with backup calculations.

- **Documentation of Sources**: Citing labor statistics, actuarial tables, CPI indices, Bureau of Labor Statistics (BLS) datasets, tax codes, and academic references.

- **Appendices**: Supporting spreadsheets, data tables, calculation logic, and summary exhibits.

Reports must be written in language understandable to both attorneys and laypeople while still reflecting rigorous economic modeling. Clarity is not optional—it is essential for credibility, especially in the face of opposing expert critiques.

4. Testimony and Expert Defense

The economist's testimony is where expert analysis meets persuasion. During deposition or trial, the expert must present their conclusions with clarity and withstand aggressive cross-examination.

The testimony phase includes:

- **Direct Examination**: The retained attorney guides the expert through qualifications, methodology, and key findings. The goal is to educate and persuade the trier of fact without appearing biased or defensive.

- **Cross-Examination**: The opposing attorney will test the expert's assumptions, challenge credibility, and attempt to find gaps or inconsistencies. Preparation is critical.

- **Rebuttal Testimony**: The economist may respond to the opposing expert's conclusions by highlighting flawed assumptions, omitted variables, or inconsistent application of principles.

- **Demonstratives**: Visual aids such as tables, graphs, and PowerPoint presentations are often used to simplify key calculations for the court or jury.

- **Voir Dire and Daubert Hearings**: The economist may be subjected to preliminary questioning on qualifications and methodology before being certified as an expert witness.

Successful testimony requires not only technical mastery but also poise, concision, and the ability to explain complex models in plain language. Many economists engage in mock trials or consult with presentation coaches to refine their courtroom presence.

Professional Standards

Forensic economists occupy a unique position of public trust. Unlike attorneys, whose role is to advocate zealously for one side, the expert's responsibility is to assist the court in understanding facts that require specialized knowledge. Therefore, ethical objectivity is not just a moral ideal—it is a legal requirement.

Professional associations such as the National Association of Forensic Economics (NAFE), the American Academy of Economic and Financial Experts (AAEFE), and the American Economic Association (AEA) provide ethical codes and best practices to which practitioners are expected to adhere. Core principles include:

- **Independence**: Opinions must be rendered without regard to the outcome desired by the retaining party.

- **Transparency**: All assumptions must be clearly stated and all methods explained in sufficient detail to allow replication.

- **Competence**: Experts must accept assignments only within their field of training and experience.

- **Integrity**: Willfully ignoring contradictory evidence, cherry-picking data, or applying double standards constitutes ethical violations and may result in exclusion of testimony or professional sanction.

This commitment to ethical objectivity distinguishes the forensic economist from hired advocates and enhances the credibility of economic testimony across courts, arbitration panels, and tribunals.

Conclusion

In sum, the role of the forensic economist encompasses far more than number-crunching. It involves damage quantification, litigation strategy, scientific communication, and courtroom performance, all rooted in an unwavering commitment to objectivity and transparency. From the first consultation to the final verdict, the forensic economist must walk the fine line between technical precision and accessible explanation, helping courts bridge the gap between legal liability and financial consequence.

8.4 Key Domains

In the context of litigation, forensic economic analysis commonly arises in a variety of specialized domains, each of which presents its own theoretical challenges, data constraints, and legal considerations. The forensic economist must adapt their methods to the nature of the harm, the jurisdiction in which the claim is filed, and the role the plaintiff played in the economic ecosystem prior to the injury or loss. The domains outlined below represent the principal categories of civil litigation where forensic economics plays a central evidentiary role.

1. Personal Injury and Wrongful Death

Personal injury cases involve the quantification of economic losses sustained by individuals who have suffered harm due to negligence, medical malpractice, defective products, or other tortious acts. The objective is to determine the "but for" economic condition—what the individual would have earned or contributed had the injury not occurred—versus their actual post-injury status.

Key components include:

- **Loss of Earnings Capacity**: Projected future income trajectories, accounting for education, occupation, career path, and expected retirement.

- **Fringe Benefits**: Employer-provided benefits such as healthcare, pensions, bonuses, and profit-sharing.

- **Household Services**: The value of unpaid labor,

especially in caregiving, cooking, cleaning, and home maintenance.

- **Discounting**: Present value adjustments based on appropriate discount rates and inflation expectations.

- **Residual Capacity**: Post-injury employment potential, retraining options, or permanent disability ratings.

In **wrongful death** cases, economists model losses to survivors, including dependent support, loss of inheritance, and funeral expenses. The analysis may require joint life expectancy tables, survivor dependency ratios, and personal consumption deductions.

2. Employment Litigation

In employment-related lawsuits, the forensic economist plays a pivotal role in valuing lost earnings due to wrongful termination, discrimination (based on race, sex, age, religion, or disability), harassment, breach of employment contract, or failure to accommodate.

These valuations often include:

- **Back Pay**: Compensation lost from the date of termination to the date of trial or reinstatement.

- **Front Pay**: Projected future losses after the trial, where reinstatement is not possible or practical.

- **Fringe Benefits**: Lost employer contributions to health insurance, pensions, or matching retirement accounts.

- **Mitigation Analysis**: The plaintiff's duty to seek comparable employment; earnings from substitute employment must be subtracted from damages.

- **Promotion and Career Trajectory**: Evaluation of foregone promotions, merit increases, or career advancement due to discriminatory or retaliatory practices.

The economist may also be asked to respond to statistical analyses of hiring or firing patterns, such as those based on regression models used in class-based employment claims.

3. Medical Costs and Life Care Planning

In catastrophic injury cases, especially those involving traumatic brain injuries, spinal cord injuries, or chronic diseases, the forensic economist is tasked with calculating the present value of future medical and non-medical costs required for the plaintiff's lifetime.

A full analysis may involve:

- **Life Care Plans**: Developed by medical professionals, these outline anticipated therapies, surgeries, medications, equipment, and caregiving needs.

- **Non-Medical Needs**: Housing modifications, transportation, assistive technology, and personal assistance services.

- **Cost Sources**: Unit cost data may come from commercial vendors, Medicare reimbursement rates, or regional pricing databases.

- **Duration of Care**: Requires mortality and morbidity tables, and sometimes co-morbidity adjustments.

- **Inflation Adjustments**: Health care costs often rise faster than general inflation; economists must consider medical-specific inflation indices.

Valuing future care is often contentious due to assumptions regarding longevity, the availability of public health care, and future medical innovation. The Affordable Care Act (ACA) and similar reforms in other countries may also affect whether certain costs are compensable by the defendant or assumed to be covered by third-party payers.

4. Commercial Damages

Forensic economists are frequently retained in business litigation to assess economic loss arising from contract breaches, business interruption, fraud, defamation, tortious interference, or intellectual property infringement.

Analysis may include:

- **Lost Profits**: Evaluating what the business would have earned but for the disruption. Requires forecasting revenue and cost streams using historical data, market analysis, and industry comparables.

- **Diminution in Value**: Especially in partnership disputes or commercial torts, assessing the decrease in fair market value of a business interest.

- **Goodwill Valuation**: Quantifying reputational damage or loss of customer loyalty.

- **Startup and Early-Stage Businesses**: These present special difficulties due to limited historical data and higher uncertainty in forecasting.

- **Causation**: Establishing a direct link between the
  alleged action and the economic harm, a key hurdle in
  business damages claims.

Economists must also be prepared to reconcile damages
models with accounting reports, tax returns, and
industry-specific benchmarks, and to respond to Daubert
challenges regarding forecasting assumptions or profit
margins.

5. Class Actions and Mass Tort Claims

In cases involving multiple plaintiffs—such as defective
products, pharmaceutical injuries, environmental disasters, or
wage and hour violations—economic damages must be
aggregated, often under intense scrutiny for methodological
consistency.

This typically includes:

- **Statistical Sampling and Extrapolation**: Drawing
  from representative data to infer losses for the larger
  population of claimants.

- **Damage Schedules**: Predefined tables of
  compensation amounts based on severity or injury
  categories, sometimes used in settlement negotiations or
  administered through victim compensation funds.

- **Econometric Models**: Regression analysis, propensity
  score matching, or Monte Carlo simulations to control
  for confounding variables.

- **Commonality Standards**: Meeting Rule 23(b)(3)
  requirements for predominance and common damages

methodology in U.S. federal court.

- **Aggregate versus Individual Damages**: Weighing
  the trade-offs between efficiency and precision in
  quantifying harm.

These cases often require extensive coordination with
statisticians, actuaries, and legal teams to ensure that the
damages methodology is both scientifically valid and legally
acceptable. Economists must prepare for vigorous
cross-examination on model selection, data reliability, and
causality.

Cross-Cutting Factors in All Domains

While each domain has its own analytical emphasis, all
require careful attention to individualized plaintiff
characteristics and the legal doctrines of the relevant
jurisdiction. Key cross-cutting considerations include:

- **Demographics**: Age, education, gender, race, and
  location can all affect projected earnings and life
  expectancy.

- **Labor Market Trends**: Regional employment shifts,
  industry-specific downturns, and macroeconomic cycles
  influence mitigation assumptions.

- **Tax Implications**: State and federal tax treatment of
  damage awards, net-of-tax adjustments, and gross-up
  calculations are especially relevant in employment and
  wrongful death cases.

- **Jurisdictional Rules**: Some states limit damages for
  pain and suffering or impose caps on medical damages,

affecting the overall valuation framework.

Table 8.1: Summary of Key Domains in Forensic Economic Analysis

Domain	Typical Plaintiff	Common Damages Valued	Key Analytical Challenges
Personal Injury & Wrongful Death	Injured individuals or family of deceased	Lost income, fringe benefits, household services	Life expectancy, consumption, residual capacity
Employment Litigation	Fired or discriminated employees	Back pay, front pay, lost benefits, promotions	Mitigation, speculative career paths, inflation
Medical Costs & Life Care	Severely injured individuals	Medical care, assistive devices, home services	Life care plans, ACA impact, pricing volatility
Commercial Damages	Business owners, partners	Lost profits, business value, goodwill	Forecasting, causation, limited historical data
Class Actions & Mass Torts	Groups of similarly affected plaintiffs	Aggregate wage loss, property harm, tiered models	Sampling, regression, model consistency

Conclusion

The practice of forensic economics spans a wide and growing array of litigation domains. Each type of case presents its own analytical framework, evidentiary demands, and ethical challenges. A skilled forensic economist must therefore be part modeler, part legal interpreter, and part communicator—translating complex numerical findings into persuasive, admissible testimony that serves the court's pursuit of just compensation.

8.5   Legal Admissibility

The role of the forensic economist exists within a legal architecture that demands both *relevance* and *reliability*. Expert economic testimony, whether addressing loss of earnings, fringe benefits, or present value discounting, must adhere not only to rigorous analytical standards but also to established legal thresholds for admissibility. These thresholds serve to ensure that juries and judges are not misled by speculative, biased, or scientifically invalid evidence, particularly in high-stakes civil litigation where monetary judgments can reach into the millions.

In the United States federal court system, the cornerstone of admissibility analysis for expert testimony is the *Daubert* standard, stemming from the Supreme Court's decision in *Daubert v. Merrell Dow Pharmaceuticals, Inc.*, 509 U.S. 579 (1993). In *Daubert*, the Court held that trial judges must act as "gatekeepers" to ensure that any and all scientific testimony or evidence admitted is not only relevant but also methodologically sound. This replaced the older and more rigid *Frye* standard, which admitted scientific evidence only if it had gained "general acceptance" in its respective field. While some state jurisdictions still use *Frye*, most have now adopted or adapted *Daubert* to varying degrees.

Under *Daubert*, four principal factors guide the court's

determination of reliability:

- Whether the methodology or technique has been empirically tested,

- Whether it has been subjected to peer review and publication,

- Whether it has a known or potential rate of error,

- Whether it has attained general acceptance within the relevant scientific community.

These are not rigid criteria but flexible guidelines intended to ensure methodological integrity. A forensic economist offering an expert opinion must therefore demonstrate that their models, projections, and valuation strategies are derived from recognized principles of economic science and are applied consistently with those principles.

This responsibility was further clarified in subsequent landmark decisions, including *General Electric Co. v. Joiner*, 522 U.S. 136 (1997), which emphasized that courts may exclude expert testimony if there is an analytical gap between the data and the conclusions drawn, and *Kumho Tire Co. v. Carmichael*, 526 U.S. 137 (1999), which extended *Daubert's* gatekeeping obligation to all expert testimony, not only scientific but also technical and other specialized knowledge, including economic analysis.

In the forensic economics context, this means that the expert must:

- Clearly document all data sources and justify the selection of those data,

- Provide logical explanations for assumptions, such as expected retirement age or income growth rates,

- Describe any statistical models or actuarial tools used and explain their relevance,

- Show how methods align with accepted practice within the forensic economics community,

- Avoid arbitrary adjustments or speculative forecasts unsupported by empirical evidence.

Failure to meet these standards can result in exclusion of testimony through a motion in limine or a pretrial *Daubert* hearing. Such exclusions are not merely procedural inconveniences, they can be case-defining. Courts have dismissed entire claims or significantly reduced damage awards when an expert's testimony was found inadmissible. As such, the forensic economist must operate with a high degree of precision and transparency, aware that their work may be dissected in open court and challenged by opposing counsel, other experts, and ultimately the judge.

Cross-Examination

The adversarial nature of litigation ensures that expert testimony does not go unchallenged. During deposition and trial, the opposing party may attempt to impeach the economist's credibility by attacking their assumptions, exposing bias, or highlighting deviations from standard methodologies. A skilled cross-examination can illuminate overgeneralizations, omissions, or inconsistent application of data—especially in high-profile cases with complex damages

Table 8.2: Comparison of the Daubert and Frye Standards for Expert Testimony

Criteria	Daubert Standard	Frye Standard
Legal Origin	Daubert v. Merrell Dow Pharmaceuticals, 509 U.S. 579 (1993)	Frye v. United States, 293 F. 1013 (D.C. Cir. 1923)
Applicability	Applies to all expert testimony (scientific, technical, or specialized knowledge) in most U.S. courts	Applies mostly to scientific evidence; used in a few state courts
Judicial Role	Judge acts as gatekeeper assessing both relevance and reliability	Judge determines whether methodology is generally accepted
Admissibility Criteria	Reliability evaluated using testing, peer review, error rates, and general acceptance	Sole focus is on general acceptance in the scientific community
Flexibility	Allows novel or emerging methods; non-exhaustive checklist	Conservative; may exclude valid but less established methods
Burden of Proof	Proponent must show evidence is both reliable and relevant (Rule 702)	Proponent must show method is widely accepted by experts
Trend in Courts	Adopted by the U.S. Supreme Court and most states	Still used in some states, but declining in favor of Daubert

claims.

In light of this, forensic economists must be fluent not only in the substance of their models but also in their legal presentation. Testimony should be crafted to withstand both

technical scrutiny and lay comprehension. Jurors, in
particular, often have limited familiarity with economic
modeling; thus, effective expert witnesses distill complexity
into clarity without sacrificing accuracy.

The Interplay

Legal admissibility is not purely a technical matter, it is also
deeply ethical. The forensic economist occupies a
quasi-judicial role: not an advocate for one side, but a neutral
interpreter of data and economic consequence. While experts
are typically retained by one party in an adversarial
proceeding, their ultimate duty lies with the court, not with
counsel. This fiduciary responsibility to objectivity is central
to the legitimacy of forensic economics as a discipline.

To that end, many professional bodies have articulated ethical
codes that reinforce the expectation of impartiality and
academic rigor. For instance:

- The **National Association of Forensic Economics
  (NAFE)** emphasizes adherence to scientific principles,
  accurate communication of findings, and avoidance of
  misrepresentation.

- The **American Academy of Economic and
  Financial Experts (AAEFE)** outlines responsibilities
  including truthfulness, independence, and the obligation
  to revise or retract erroneous conclusions.

- The **American Economic Association (AEA)**
  provides a general ethical framework applicable to all
  economists, stressing the importance of transparency,

reproducibility, and avoidance of conflicts of interest.

Practicing within these boundaries strengthens the admissibility and weight of an economist's testimony. Courts are more likely to credit an expert who not only meets technical criteria but also displays intellectual honesty, balance, and credibility under cross-examination.

Emerging Trends

While *Daubert* is the dominant standard in federal court and in a majority of U.S. states, important variations remain. For example, states such as New York and California historically followed the *Frye* standard, though both have seen judicial and legislative movement toward more rigorous evidentiary scrutiny in recent years. Understanding the prevailing standard in a given venue is therefore essential for forensic economists who practice across multiple jurisdictions.

Moreover, emerging trends in admissibility practice warrant continued attention:

- Courts are increasingly scrutinizing the *fit* between methodology and facts—requiring contextual relevance in addition to methodological soundness.

- Novel forms of evidence, including big data analytics and AI-based projections, are testing the boundaries of traditional admissibility frameworks.

- The post-pandemic era has raised new challenges for projecting future earnings and economic conditions, requiring experts to document how they incorporate economic uncertainty into damage models.

These developments underscore that admissibility is not static but evolving. Forensic economists must remain current with both legal precedent and methodological innovation if they wish to maintain credibility and influence in the courtroom.

Conclusion

In sum, legal admissibility is the threshold through which all expert economic testimony must pass. It is not enough to be numerically accurate; one must be methodologically transparent, contextually relevant, and ethically grounded. Forensic economists must not only meet the technical requirements set forth in *Daubert, Joiner*, and *Kumho Tire*, but also prepare to justify their conclusions before opposing experts, attorneys, and the bench. By doing so, they uphold the integrity of the discipline and help courts arrive at just, well-informed outcomes.

8.6   Global Contexts

Although this book focuses on litigation in the United States, the principles and practices of forensic economics have gained increasing relevance in international legal systems. As civil litigation becomes more globalized, and as nations wrestle with common challenges in assessing economic harm, the methodologies used by forensic economists are being scrutinized, adopted, and adapted across multiple jurisdictions. This global diffusion brings with it both opportunity and complexity—requiring forensic experts to navigate differing legal standards, cultural assumptions, data sources, and valuation norms.

Forensic Economic Practice

In common law countries such as Canada, the United
Kingdom, and Australia, the role of economic experts in civil
litigation bears strong resemblance to that in the United
States. These countries permit economic testimony in cases
involving personal injury, wrongful death, employment
discrimination, and business valuation. However, the
procedural frameworks and evidentiary standards may differ
significantly.

Canada.   Canadian courts allow the use of economic expert
testimony to assess damages in tort claims, particularly in
personal injury and family law matters. Canadian forensic
economists often rely on Statistics Canada data for modeling
worklife expectancy, income trajectories, and consumption
rates. Canadian courts, while influenced by *Daubert*-like
reasoning, generally provide judges with greater discretion
over admissibility. In provinces such as British Columbia and
Ontario, there is a growing emphasis on the clear presentation
of economic assumptions and the communication of
uncertainty ranges rather than point estimates.

United Kingdom.   In England and Wales, the Civil
Procedure Rules govern expert evidence. Unlike the
adversarial model of the U.S., the UK courts may appoint a
single joint expert to serve both parties. Forensic economists,
often referred to as "economic loss experts," participate in
personal injury, medical negligence, and employment claims.
The UK tends to emphasize a "heads of claim" structure for
damages, and courts frequently apply multipliers drawn from
the *Ogden Tables*, which are actuarially developed discount

factors based on mortality and employment data.

Germany. Germany, as a civil law country, follows a different model. Judges have far greater control over expert selection, often appointing neutral court experts from official registries. German legal tradition places significant weight on written expert reports, and oral testimony is less emphasized. Forensic economics in Germany is well-developed in commercial and contractual disputes, though less so in personal injury claims, where statutory compensation schemes sometimes prevail.

Australia. Australia bridges common and civil law practices. Expert testimony in economic damages is routinely used in negligence, medical malpractice, and employment law. Australian courts emphasize procedural fairness and transparency in expert communication, and recent reforms have sought to reduce the adversarial nature of expert participation through "hot-tubbing"—a process where opposing experts testify and are questioned together in court to clarify areas of agreement and disagreement.

Cross-Border Litigation

The expansion of international commercial arbitration has significantly elevated the importance of forensic economics beyond national courts. Forums such as the International Centre for Settlement of Investment Disputes (ICSID), the International Chamber of Commerce (ICC), and the London Court of International Arbitration (LCIA) routinely involve disputes where valuation of damages—often in the hundreds of millions or even billions of dollars—is essential.

In such cases, forensic economists are called upon to perform complex valuations involving:

- Expropriation of assets by foreign governments,

- Breach of investment treaties,

- Business interruption due to geopolitical conflict or regulatory change,

- Transfer pricing and international tax disputes.

The challenge in international arbitration is heightened by divergent expectations across legal cultures, differences in data availability, and the need to account for currency risk, sovereign risk, and differing discounting norms. Experts must also be mindful of the tribunal's composition—often consisting of arbitrators with diverse legal and economic backgrounds.

Valuation Methodologies

Beyond legal rules, forensic economic valuation is shaped by deep-rooted cultural, economic, and policy norms. What constitutes "fair compensation" in one country may be viewed as excessive or inadequate in another. For example:

- In the U.S., lost earnings are often based on projected lifetime earnings capacity with explicit tax treatment.

- In France, moral damages (for *préjudice moral*) are routinely awarded alongside material damages.

- In South Africa, actuarial calculations are used for road accident claims under a partially state-managed fund.

- In Japan, compensation values for wrongful death are

significantly lower than in U.S. jurisdictions, reflecting different societal expectations around loss.

Forensic economists working in or advising on international cases must be sensitive not only to legal differences but to the cultural context of valuation—particularly where the societal role of the individual (e.g., worker, caregiver, business owner) is conceived differently.

Toward Harmonization

The proliferation of cross-border torts, multinational corporations, and global data infrastructures raises the question: will forensic economics move toward global standards of practice? The answer is nuanced. While there is no immediate prospect of universal harmonization, there are several indicators of convergence:

- International actuarial societies and economic expert groups are beginning to collaborate on methodological frameworks for life expectancy, discounting, and risk adjustment.

- The United Nations and World Bank have produced frameworks for valuing human capital in developing economies, which sometimes inform damage modeling in global contexts.

- Multinational corporations increasingly seek consistency in the valuation of economic losses across jurisdictions to reduce litigation uncertainty and manage global risk.

Still, the inherent diversity in legal systems, levels of economic development, and cultural attitudes toward litigation make a fully unified framework unlikely in the near term. Nonetheless, the trend toward methodological transparency, replicability, and interdisciplinary integration continues to reshape how damages are argued and adjudicated globally.

Global Forces

Looking ahead, several transformative trends are poised to influence the global practice of forensic economics:

- **Big Data and Machine Learning:** Access to large-scale, real-time labor market data and predictive analytics tools allows for increasingly granular earnings models, but raises questions about algorithmic fairness and interpretability across legal systems.

- **Global Labor Mobility:** As individuals work across borders, damage assessments must consider multinational earnings trajectories, cross-border pension rights, and tax residency issues.

- **Health Policy Shifts:** In jurisdictions with universal health care, the cost of future care may be borne by the state, impacting individual damage awards and requiring new approaches to life care valuation.

- **Pandemic and Climate Risk:** Long-term modeling must now consider large-scale disruptions, both public health and environmental, adding new dimensions to risk discounting and scenario analysis.

- **Equity, Diversity, and Inclusion (EDI):** Jurisdictions are re-evaluating traditional wage data that may reflect structural inequality. Forensic economists are increasingly asked to provide counterfactual models that account for discriminatory labor market barriers.

Across Borders

In sum, forensic economics is both a technical discipline and a moral endeavor, one that must operate in legal systems with divergent goals and standards, but united in their search for just and rational compensation. As the discipline continues to evolve, it provides a unique vantage point into how societies around the world quantify the value of time, labor, caregiving, health, and opportunity. Practicing forensic economists who engage with international issues must cultivate not only statistical skill but also cultural competence, legal literacy, and ethical vision. In doing so, they help bring clarity to the complex human stories that lie at the heart of every economic damages claim, whether heard in a courtroom in Chicago, an arbitration panel in Geneva, or a tribunal in Johannesburg.

8.7   Conclusion

Forensic economics is the application of economic reasoning, data analysis, and valuation techniques to questions of fact and loss in legal disputes. Rooted in civil litigation and increasingly relevant across a wide array of legal domains, the field requires the economist to function as both analyst and communicator, translating complex models into persuasive and admissible testimony. From estimating damages in personal injury and employment cases to scrutinizing business valuations and market behavior, the forensic economist

operates within a structured but adversarial environment that
demands precision, credibility, and methodological rigor.

This introductory chapter has surveyed the origins, scope, and
evolving applications of forensic economics, including its
integration into tort, contract, and regulatory disputes. It has
also outlined the foundational role of expert testimony, the
importance of standards of admissibility, and the intersection
between economic theory and legal norms.

To deepen our understanding of how forensic economics
became an established discipline, we now turn to its
theoretical foundations, where ideas from law and economics,
pioneered by Coase, Posner, Calabresi, and others, laid the
groundwork for a functional and incentive-based view of legal
systems.

Chapter 9

Theoretical Foundations

9.1 Introduction

Law and Economics is the interdisciplinary field that applies
economic principles to the analysis of legal rules and
institutions. It seeks to evaluate how legal outcomes can be
optimized to produce efficient, predictable, and socially
beneficial results. This field emerged formally in the United
States during the mid-20th century and gained prominence
with the intellectual leadership of the University of Chicago.

9.2 Intellectual Origins

The intersection of legal reasoning and economic
analysis—today known as the field of *law and economics*—has

reshaped both academic legal theory and judicial decision-making in profound ways. Once a marginal and speculative endeavor, the discipline matured into a dominant framework by the end of the twentieth century, influencing tort law, antitrust policy, contract enforcement, regulatory design, and constitutional interpretation. The development of this interdisciplinary field was neither spontaneous nor inevitable. Rather, it was driven by the intellectual labor of key pioneers, institutional support from elite law schools and foundations, and a shifting sociopolitical landscape that demanded more empirical and functional tools for understanding legal systems.

From Formalism to Functionalism

The roots of law and economics trace back to a historical transformation in the philosophy of law. In the early twentieth century, American legal thought was largely dominated by *legal formalism*, which conceived law as a closed logical system in which judges deduced decisions from abstract principles. But the economic upheaval of the Great Depression and the expansive reforms of the New Deal challenged this paradigm. Legal scholars and policymakers began to view law less as a self-contained system and more as a dynamic tool for social engineering.

This shift dovetailed with broader intellectual trends, including the rise of *institutional economics* led by thinkers like Thorstein Veblen and John R. Commons. However, it was not until the mid-twentieth century that a rigorous economic approach to legal problems took hold, fueled by developments in microeconomics and a rising interest in market-based reasoning.

The Chicago School and the Intellectual Founders

At the heart of the modern law and economics movement was the University of Chicago. It was there that **Aaron Director**, a libertarian economist with a deep skepticism of state intervention, laid the foundation for a new way of thinking about law. Director's course on antitrust and economic regulation, and his role as founding editor of the *Journal of Law and Economics*, provided a platform for interdisciplinary scholarship that sought to evaluate legal rules in terms of efficiency, incentives, and market impact.

Among his most influential collaborators was **Ronald Coase**, whose 1960 paper *The Problem of Social Cost* became a seminal text in both economics and legal studies. Coase introduced the now-famous *Coase Theorem*, arguing that under conditions of zero transaction costs, legal rules governing externalities would not affect the ultimate allocation of resources—private bargaining would lead to efficient outcomes regardless of legal entitlements. This radical proposition forced legal scholars to rethink the importance of liability rules, property rights, and institutional costs.

Another pivotal figure was **Richard A. Posner**, who became the movement's most prolific and polemical voice. As both a professor at the University of Chicago Law School and later as a judge on the U.S. Court of Appeals for the Seventh Circuit, Posner advocated for a utilitarian conception of law grounded in economic efficiency. His book *Economic Analysis of Law*

(1973) systematized the field and served as a blueprint for applying cost-benefit analysis to nearly every branch of law—from torts to family law.

Yale and the Expanding Canon

While the University of Chicago was the crucible of the movement, other institutions played crucial roles in its diffusion and diversification. At Yale Law School, **Guido Calabresi**, a scholar trained in both law and economics, helped pioneer the economic analysis of torts in his landmark work *The Costs of Accidents* (1970). Calabresi's emphasis on minimizing the social costs of harm, rather than merely assigning blame, reshaped the understanding of liability and the role of insurance.

Yale was also home to **Robert H. Bork**, a constitutional theorist and antitrust scholar whose writings on consumer welfare and market competition helped redefine U.S. antitrust policy during the Reagan era. His influence, alongside Director and Posner, brought a more conservative and market-oriented ethos to the field.

Meanwhile, **Henry Manne**, an institutional entrepreneur, worked tirelessly to integrate economics into legal education more broadly. Through programs like the Law and Economics Center at George Mason University, Manne trained generations of judges and legal scholars in economic reasoning, thereby embedding the field within the judiciary itself.

Institutionalization and the American Law and Economics Association

The formalization of law and economics as a distinct discipline culminated with the founding of the **American Law and Economics Association (ALEA)** in 1991. The association provided a platform for scholarly exchange, peer-reviewed publication, and interdisciplinary collaboration between economists, legal scholars, and public policy experts. ALEA's annual meetings and its flagship *American Law and Economics Review* accelerated the field's growth and legitimacy.

The emergence of university-based centers, such as the **John M. Olin Center for Law, Economics, and Public Policy** at Yale (co-directed by George L. Priest), further institutionalized the discipline. These centers funded research, hosted conferences, and supported students interested in applying economic tools to legal questions.

A New Lens for Legal Analysis

Today, law and economics is not merely a subfield—it is a lens through which many legal questions are initially framed. Its emphasis on incentives, market structures, transaction costs, and efficiency has made it a preferred methodology in areas ranging from environmental regulation to corporate governance. However, the field has also faced critiques, particularly from scholars who argue that it can obscure issues of justice, equity, and power.

Nonetheless, the intellectual legacy of the movement's

founders—Director, Coase, Posner, Calabresi, Bork, and
Manne—remains central. As George L. Priest articulates in
The Rise of Law and Economics, the field represents a
synthesis of empirical rigor and normative ambition, striving
to make the law not just logical or just, but functionally
optimal for a complex and evolving society.

9.3 Key Contributions

Ronald Coase

Ronald Coase's landmark 1960 article, *The Problem of Social
Cost*, is widely regarded as one of the foundational texts in
the field of Law and Economics. In this seminal work, Coase
challenged the prevailing assumptions of legal scholarship by
introducing the idea that private bargaining can, under the
right conditions, resolve externalities without the need for
government intervention.

Historical Context and Core Insight: Prior to Coase,
economic externalities—such as pollution or noise—were seen
as problems requiring legal remedies or regulatory action.
Coase argued that if transaction costs are negligible and
property rights are clearly defined, parties will negotiate to an
efficient allocation of resources regardless of who initially holds
the rights. This principle, later dubbed the **Coase Theorem**
by George Stigler, suggests that the law's primary role should
be to minimize transaction costs and clarify entitlements.

Example: Consider a rancher whose cattle wander onto a
neighboring farmer's land, damaging crops. If the rancher has
the right to let cattle roam, the farmer may pay for fencing. If

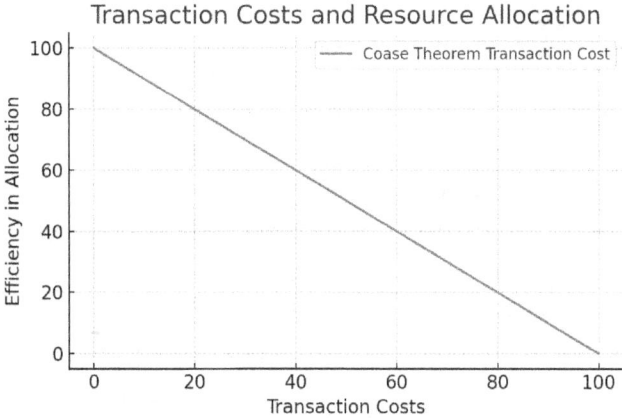

Figure 9.1: Coase Theorem: Marginal Cost vs. Marginal Benefit

the farmer has the right to be free from damage, the rancher may pay to fence in the cattle. According to Coase, the outcome will be efficient either way—*provided the parties can negotiate without cost.*

Application in Case Law: Coase's ideas gradually penetrated American jurisprudence, influencing judicial opinions and legal doctrine. Notably, his principles underlie the economic analysis in:

- *Boomer v. Atlantic Cement Co.*, 26 N.Y.2d 219 (1970), where the New York Court of Appeals considered whether to enjoin a cement plant causing pollution or require payment of damages instead. The court favored damages, reflecting an implicit Coasean logic that economic efficiency may be better served through compensation than cessation.

- *Spur Industries, Inc. v. Del E. Webb Development Co.*, 494 P.2d 700 (Ariz. 1972), where the Arizona Supreme Court balanced the interests of a developer and an existing cattle feedlot, ultimately ordering relocation of the feedlot with developer-paid compensation.

Policy Implications: Coase's work revolutionized the understanding of legal entitlements in nuisance law, environmental law, and torts. Rather than viewing harms as binary (right vs. wrong), the Coase Theorem encourages courts and policymakers to assess *efficiency* and consider whether private ordering can yield better results than litigation or regulation.

Critiques and Limitations: Despite its influence, the Coase Theorem has notable limitations:

- **Transaction Costs:** In reality, transaction costs are rarely negligible—especially in cases with many affected parties (e.g., air pollution).

- **Information Asymmetry:** Parties may not possess the necessary information to value harm accurately or negotiate effectively.

- **Power Imbalances:** Negotiations may not reflect true efficiency if one party holds disproportionate bargaining power.

Nonetheless, these critiques have spurred further economic modeling of legal rules, encouraging scholars to examine when and how law can lower transaction costs or incentivize optimal behavior.

Extensions and Interdisciplinary Reach: Coase's
insight gave rise to a broader analytical framework:

- **Property Law:** Demsetz (1967) built on Coase's work
  to argue that property rights emerge to internalize
  externalities as societies grow.

- **Contract Law:** Calabresi and Melamed's seminal 1972
  article, "Property Rules, Liability Rules, and
  Inalienability," operationalized Coase's insight into legal
  remedies.

- **Environmental Law:** Tradable emissions permits and
  pollution markets are modern policy instruments built
  on Coasean foundations.

Negotiation Outcomes Under the Coase Theorem

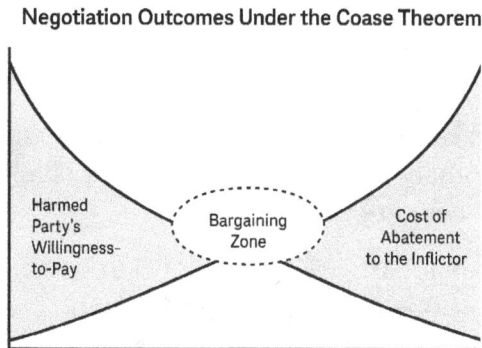

Figure 9.2: Negotiation Outcomes Under the Coase Theorem

Visualizing Coase's World: In the diagram, the overlap
between the willingness-to-pay of the harmed party and the

cost of abatement by the inflictor represents the bargaining zone. If transaction costs are low, parties will agree to a mutually beneficial solution within this range.

Conclusion

Ronald Coase's contributions reshaped the way economists and legal scholars understand the role of law in a market economy. His insights into externalities, transaction costs, and property rights remain central to legal theory, policy design, and case law interpretation. The Coase Theorem is not merely a theoretical proposition—it is a lens through which entire legal doctrines can be reassessed in pursuit of economic efficiency.

End-of-Section Problems

1. Define the Coase Theorem and explain its assumptions. Why are those assumptions often unrealistic in practice?

2. Suppose a nightclub emits noise that disturbs a nearby condo. Who should bear the cost of abatement under a Coasean analysis? Would your answer change if 50 condo owners are involved?

3. In *Boomer v. Atlantic Cement Co.*, the court awarded damages instead of granting an injunction. Analyze this choice through the lens of the Coase Theorem.

4. Identify a real-world legal dispute (environmental, tort, or nuisance) that could benefit from Coasean bargaining. What would efficient bargaining look like in that case?

5. Use a diagram to illustrate how transaction costs shrink or eliminate the bargaining zone between two parties.

Aaron Director and the Chicago School

Often regarded as the intellectual godfather of the law and economics movement, **Aaron Director** played a pivotal role in shaping the foundations of the Chicago School's interdisciplinary approach to law. A trained economist and deeply principled libertarian, Director joined the University of Chicago Law School in the 1940s and later became the founding editor of the *Journal of Law and Economics*, which he co-edited with Ronald Coase. Though he published little himself, Director's influence stemmed from his ability to mentor, provoke, and inspire an entire generation of legal scholars and economists.

Director's central philosophical commitment was to limited government and free market principles. He viewed the legal system as a framework that should support and preserve the spontaneous order of markets, rather than intervene to correct every perceived inefficiency. This view manifested in his early teachings on antitrust law, where he challenged prevailing assumptions that big businesses were inherently harmful to competition. Instead, he promoted a theory that antitrust policy should focus narrowly on consumer welfare and economic efficiency, rather than political concerns about size or corporate power.

Director's classroom influence was legendary. He taught courses in economic reasoning to law students, instilling in them the habit of scrutinizing legal doctrines for their incentive structures and economic consequences. Among his most prominent students were Robert Bork and Richard Posner, both of whom expanded on Director's ideas and carried them into the judiciary and public policy.

Through his leadership at the *Journal of Law and Economics*, Director institutionalized a space for scholarship that blurred the lines between legal analysis and economic modeling. The journal became a crucible for pathbreaking articles on topics ranging from property rights to regulatory capture. Director's legacy lies not in a prolific body of written work, but in his role as an architect of a paradigm shift—one that recentered legal analysis around individual choice, market signals, and institutional constraints.

Robert Bork and Antitrust Reform

Robert H. Bork, a Yale Law professor and later a judge on the U.S. Court of Appeals for the D.C. Circuit, was one of the most forceful and influential advocates of applying economic reasoning to legal doctrine, particularly in the realm of antitrust law. A student of Aaron Director and a leading figure of the Chicago School, Bork argued that the primary aim of antitrust policy should be the promotion of *consumer welfare*, not the protection of competitors or the maintenance of market decentralization.

Bork's 1978 book, *The Antitrust Paradox*, stands as a foundational text in both legal and economic circles. In it, Bork criticized decades of Supreme Court decisions that, in his view, overreached in breaking up firms or blocking mergers without clear evidence of consumer harm. He argued that such actions often reduced economic efficiency and raised prices, thus undermining the very purpose of antitrust law. By reframing antitrust as a tool for maximizing allocative efficiency, Bork aligned the law with neoclassical economic principles and redirected enforcement priorities for generations of regulators and judges.

Bork's influence extended beyond the academy. His ideas significantly shaped U.S. Department of Justice and Federal Trade Commission policies in the 1980s, leading to a more lenient approach toward mergers and monopolistic behavior so long as consumer prices were unaffected. This shift, often termed the "Borkian revolution," marked a departure from structuralist views of antitrust and emphasized market performance over market structure.

Although Bork is perhaps best known for the controversy surrounding his failed Supreme Court nomination in 1987, his academic and policy legacy within law and economics remains profound. His application of rigorous economic logic to legal interpretation helped shift antitrust law from a politically driven field to one grounded in analytical precision. Whether celebrated or criticized, Bork's work epitomizes the power of interdisciplinary scholarship to reshape core legal doctrines.

George L. Priest and the Institutional Foundations of Law and Economics

George L. Priest, the Edward J. Phelps Professor of Law and Economics at Yale Law School, has been a central figure in the development and institutionalization of the law and economics movement. Distinguished for his rigorous scholarship, historical sensitivity, and commitment to integrating empirical and theoretical approaches, Priest has shaped key debates in tort law, liability theory, and the

economic role of legal institutions. His contributions lie not
only in original theory-building, but also in narrating and
interpreting the intellectual evolution of the field itself.

Priest's most direct impact has been in the area of *tort law
and liability systems.* In a series of influential articles, he
challenged conventional assumptions about the efficiency and
purpose of the tort system. Notably, his article *The Common
Law Process and the Selection of Efficient Rules* (1977)
argued that the common law exhibits a natural tendency to
evolve toward economically efficient outcomes. Drawing from
evolutionary models and economic analysis, Priest suggested
that inefficient rules tend to generate higher litigation rates
and are therefore more likely to be challenged and reformed
through judicial decisions. This "selection mechanism" thesis
positioned the judiciary not merely as an interpreter of
precedent, but as a market-like engine for institutional
adaptation.

Priest's tort theory also emphasized the broader social
function of liability rules. He explored how legal doctrines,
such as strict liability, negligence, and comparative fault,
shape the behavior of firms, individuals, and insurers. His
work frequently examined the interface between law and
insurance markets, shedding light on how legal standards
affect risk distribution and moral hazard. This systems-level
view aligns with the broader law and economics agenda:
understanding law as a set of incentives embedded within
institutional arrangements.

In addition to his doctrinal work, Priest has been a major
institutional architect. As the co-director of the **John M.**

Olin Center for Law, Economics, and Public Policy at Yale, he has helped to support a new generation of scholars working at the intersection of economics, law, and policy. The Center provides research funding, facilitates interdisciplinary seminars, and coordinates scholarly exchanges that have deepened the intellectual infrastructure of the field. Under Priest's leadership, the Olin Center has become a flagship institution for law and economics research in the United States.

Priest's role as an historian of the movement is equally significant. In his recent book, *The Rise of Law and Economics*, he provides a comprehensive account of the intellectual origins and development of the field from the early 20th century to the present. Priest traces the lineage of key figures such as Aaron Director, Ronald Coase, Richard Posner, Guido Calabresi, and Henry Manne, weaving their contributions into a broader narrative about how legal scholarship came to embrace economic analysis as both a normative and descriptive framework. Importantly, he situates this rise within broader political and institutional contexts, including the influence of the New Deal, the growth of administrative governance, and the transformation of legal education.

Unlike some of the more ideologically rigid members of the Chicago School, Priest's work often displays a pragmatic and context-sensitive approach to economic analysis. While he supports the use of efficiency as a benchmark, he is attentive to the limitations of economic models in capturing legal complexity, judicial behavior, and public policy trade-offs. His work incorporates insights from political economy, legal realism, and comparative institutional analysis, making him a bridge between the first-generation theorists and more empirically grounded modern scholars.

Priest's legacy also includes his influence on the pedagogy of law. Through his teaching and mentorship at Yale, he has shaped how law students and scholars approach private law with an economic lens. His classes on torts, insurance law, and law and economics are noted for their intellectual rigor and their integration of theory with practical application. Many of his students have gone on to hold academic, judicial, and policy-making roles, perpetuating the interdisciplinary ethos he champions.

In sum, George L. Priest stands out not merely as a contributor to law and economics, but as a steward of its growth and institutional integrity. His scholarship on tort law, judicial evolution, and institutional design, along with his historical work chronicling the movement, reflects a deep commitment to understanding law as both a normative system and a mechanism of social coordination. His career represents the maturation of law and economics into a discipline that is at once rigorous, reflective, and responsive to the complexities of legal life.

Henry Manne and Legal Education

Henry G. Manne was one of the great institutional entrepreneurs of the law and economics movement. Whereas Aaron Director and Robert Bork focused on theory and doctrine, Manne's legacy lies in transforming the educational landscape of legal scholarship. Through his pioneering

programs, Manne introduced economic analysis into
mainstream legal education, shaping generations of lawyers,
judges, and academics.

Trained in both law and economics, Manne was deeply
concerned with the gap between legal education and economic
literacy. In response, he founded the **Law and Economics
Center** at the University of Miami in the 1970s, which later
moved to Emory University and eventually George Mason
University. These centers became hubs for interdisciplinary
teaching, scholarship, and judicial training. Manne's most
impactful innovation was his *Law and Economics Institute for
Judges*, a program that brought sitting judges into week-long
seminars where they studied economic theory, game theory,
and price mechanisms as applied to tort, contract, and
regulatory law.

Manne was also instrumental in expanding the scope of law
and economics to include corporate governance. His writings
on insider trading, corporate takeovers, and market
mechanisms challenged conventional views on fiduciary duty
and securities regulation. In works such as *Insider Trading
and the Stock Market* (1966), he provocatively argued that
insider trading could serve a valuable economic function by
promoting market efficiency. Though controversial, these
arguments sparked robust academic and regulatory debates
that continue to this day.

Perhaps most importantly, Manne was committed to
democratizing access to economic ideas in the legal world. He
believed that every legal professional, not just economists,
should be equipped to reason about efficiency, incentives, and

systemic consequences. Through his educational leadership, publishing initiatives, and institution-building, Manne helped embed economic reasoning into the fabric of American legal culture.

His work remains a testament to the idea that ideas matter, but so too does infrastructure. By creating the educational and institutional architecture for law and economics to flourish, Henry Manne ensured that the movement would persist and evolve across generations and disciplines.

Richard Posner and the Economic Analysis of Law

Judge Richard A. Posner, building on Coase's work, popularized economic reasoning in legal decision-making through his seminal book *Economic Analysis of Law* (1972). Posner argued that common law tends toward efficiency over time and advocated for a utilitarian view of legal adjudication.

His writings introduced concepts such as:

- The law of contracts promoting reliance and optimal breach

- Tort law as a system for minimizing accident and administrative costs

- Criminal law as a deterrent mechanism based on rational behavior models

Guido Calabresi and Accident Law

Among the most influential figures in the development of law
and economics, particularly in the realm of tort law, is Yale
Law School's **Guido Calabresi**. A scholar uniquely trained
in both economics and law, Calabresi helped establish a
rigorous framework for understanding accident law not as a
moralistic system of blame, but as an economic institution
designed to minimize social costs. His landmark work, *The
Costs of Accidents* (1970), fundamentally altered the way legal
scholars and judges conceptualize liability, deterrence, and the
distribution of accident-related losses.

In contrast to the traditional corrective justice model—which
focuses on fault and fairness between individual
parties—Calabresi introduced a utilitarian and systems-based
perspective. He argued that the purpose of accident law
should be to reduce the total costs associated with accidents,
which he broke down into three main categories: (1) the cost
of accidents themselves (including bodily injury, property
damage, and loss of life), (2) the cost of precautions taken to
prevent accidents, and (3) the administrative costs of running
the legal and insurance systems that adjudicate and
compensate such harms. Legal rules, in his view, should be
assessed according to their effectiveness in minimizing this
total sum.

One of Calabresi's most enduring contributions to this
economic approach is the concept of the *least-cost avoider*.
This principle suggests that liability should be assigned to the
party who can prevent the harm at the lowest overall cost to
society. This does not always align with moral intuitions

about blameworthiness, but it serves the broader function of encouraging actors to internalize the costs of their decisions and take economically efficient levels of precaution. For instance, in a car-pedestrian accident, the driver may be the least-cost avoider due to access to technology and training, even if the pedestrian was partially at fault. This subtle shift from "who caused the harm" to "who could have avoided it most efficiently" introduced a fundamentally different rationale for assigning legal responsibility.

Calabresi's model also addresses the problem of uncertainty and asymmetrical information in tort law. In many real-world contexts, it is unclear how much precaution is appropriate or feasible, or what level of risk society is willing to tolerate. By introducing probabilistic thinking into legal reasoning, Calabresi encouraged courts and policymakers to think in terms of expected value and marginal cost-benefit calculations. The ideal policy is not one that eliminates all accidents (an impossible task), but one that optimally balances precautionary behavior against residual risk.

Beyond judicial doctrines, Calabresi explored the allocation of accident costs through mechanisms such as private insurance markets, employer liability systems, and public compensation schemes. He understood that law does not operate in a vacuum: the presence of first-party insurance, workers' compensation, social security, or government-backed health programs dramatically alters the incentive structure created by tort rules. For this reason, he insisted on a holistic view of the "accident cost system," urging lawmakers to consider how each legal rule fits into a larger network of institutional incentives and behavioral responses.

A distinct dimension of Calabresi's contribution lies in his interdisciplinary method. Drawing upon welfare economics, systems theory, and moral philosophy, he offered a robust framework for integrating economic rationality with legal realism. His work is characterized not by crude cost-cutting, but by a deep engagement with the normative purposes of law: to structure incentives, protect human welfare, and do so in a way that is administratively feasible and morally defensible. His economic lens did not ignore distributive concerns, and he frequently acknowledged that efficiency must be balanced against considerations of justice and dignity.

Moreover, Calabresi's influence extended beyond the academy into the judiciary. Appointed as a judge to the U.S. Court of Appeals for the Second Circuit in 1994, he brought his theoretical insights into practical application, interpreting statutory and common law questions through an economic and institutional lens. His judicial writings reflect the same intellectual clarity and commitment to functional reasoning found in his scholarship. As a jurist, he embodied the rare synthesis of legal theorist and practitioner, enriching both domains with reciprocal insight.

Calabresi's intellectual trajectory also reflects a continual evolution. In his later works, such as *Ideals, Beliefs, Attitudes, and the Law* (1985) and *A Common Law for the Age of Statutes* (1982), he tackled problems of legal change, democratic legitimacy, and judicial review. These writings, while less strictly economic, still reveal his concern for the unintended consequences of legal rules and the institutional mechanisms necessary for adaptive governance. His judicial philosophy became a touchstone for debates on constitutional interpretation, administrative law, and legislative supremacy.

Critics of Calabresi's model have raised concerns that economic efficiency, while valuable, cannot be the sole metric for legal responsibility. They argue that cost-minimization frameworks risk obscuring fundamental issues of fairness, autonomy, and corrective justice. Furthermore, the identification of the least-cost avoider is often fraught with epistemic challenges, including imperfect information, strategic behavior, and disparities in bargaining power. Calabresi himself acknowledged these limitations and often stressed that his framework was a tool—not a substitute—for legal judgment.

Despite these critiques, Calabresi's contributions have stood the test of time. His ideas have been integrated into tort law syllabi across law schools, influenced model legislation and restatement doctrines, and shaped how courts assess causation, foreseeability, and proximate harm. In the broader context of law and economics, he served as a vital counterweight to the Chicago School's emphasis on free markets and deregulatory ideology. Whereas figures like Posner and Director often leaned toward laissez-faire presumptions, Calabresi advocated a more nuanced and institutionally sensitive form of economic analysis, one that accounted for real-world constraints and the limits of market mechanisms.

Finally, Calabresi's impact is also pedagogical and institutional. As Dean of Yale Law School from 1985 to 1994, he fostered a culture of interdisciplinary inquiry and mentorship, encouraging generations of legal scholars to engage with economics, philosophy, and policy analysis. He was instrumental in supporting the development of law and economics centers, student research programs, and judicial training workshops, many of which disseminated economic insights into broader legal practice.

In sum, Guido Calabresi stands not merely as a contributor, but as an architect of modern tort theory. His work exemplifies the best of law and economics: intellectually rigorous, institutionally grounded, and normatively ambitious. His legacy endures in the structure of contemporary tort doctrine, the curriculum of legal education, and the design of accident compensation systems throughout the world. By reframing accident law as a domain of strategic incentives and institutional design, Calabresi expanded both the reach and the sophistication of legal analysis in the modern era.

Gary Becker and the Economics of Crime

Gary S. Becker, awarded the Nobel Prize in Economic Sciences in 1992, revolutionized multiple disciplines by applying economic reasoning to domains traditionally considered beyond the scope of economics. Among his most influential contributions was his extension of microeconomic theory to the study of criminal behavior. In his seminal 1968 paper, *Crime and Punishment: An Economic Approach*, Becker developed a model in which potential offenders are treated as rational decision-makers who weigh the expected utility of committing a crime against the potential costs, namely the probability of being apprehended and the severity of punishment.

Becker's work departed radically from earlier criminological theories, which emphasized psychological, sociological, or environmental causes of criminality. Instead of focusing on the pathology or moral defects of the individual, Becker framed crime as a utility-maximizing activity, not unlike labor market participation or consumer choice. He assumed that individuals decide whether to engage in illegal activity in the same way they decide whether to accept a job: by comparing expected benefits with expected costs.

In Becker's model, the *expected cost* of crime is a function of two variables: the probability of apprehension and conviction (p), and the monetary or psychological disutility of the imposed punishment (F). The product pF represents the expected penalty. The potential criminal compares this value against the expected gains from the crime, such as stolen money, avoided labor, or illicit status. If the expected utility of crime exceeds that of lawful alternatives, the individual commits the offense. The model predicts, therefore, that increases in either the likelihood of detection or the harshness of punishment should deter criminal behavior, assuming rationality.

Becker's framework led to several important implications. First, it offered a systematic method for policymakers to analyze the deterrent effects of law enforcement policies. For instance, holding the severity of punishment constant, a higher probability of detection (such as through increased policing or surveillance) should reduce crime more effectively than merely increasing prison sentences. Second, it illuminated trade-offs between enforcement costs and social harm. If detection is expensive, the model might support the use of harsh penalties as a cost-effective way to deter crime—a principle echoed in the design of some criminal justice systems that rely on lengthy sentences for high-risk offenders.

Furthermore, Becker's model introduced the possibility of *optimal crime rates*. Unlike earlier conceptions that treated any crime as a societal failure, Becker acknowledged that the complete elimination of crime would be prohibitively expensive. From a social welfare perspective, the objective is not zero crime, but rather a minimization of the combined costs of crime, punishment, and prevention. This insight allowed for more nuanced policy analysis, emphasizing marginal deterrence and the efficient allocation of law enforcement resources.

Beyond theoretical elegance, Becker's economic model of crime spurred empirical studies attempting to measure the elasticity of criminal behavior with respect to changes in punishment and detection. Subsequent research by economists and criminologists has tested these predictions in a variety of contexts—including violent crime, white-collar crime, and drug offenses. Some studies found support for the hypothesis that certainty of punishment (i.e., arrest rates) has a stronger deterrent effect than severity (i.e., sentence length), consistent with Becker's predictions. Other scholars have explored heterogeneity in offender rationality, extending the model to account for risk aversion, time preferences, and behavioral biases.

Importantly, Becker's work was not limited to street-level crime. His model applies equally well to corporate malfeasance, regulatory violations, tax evasion, and environmental crimes. These "crimes of calculation," as they are sometimes called, involve agents who are often highly informed and responsive to marginal changes in legal rules and penalties. Thus, the Beckerian framework has had profound implications for the design of civil fines, corporate compliance regimes, and regulatory enforcement strategies.

Critics of Becker's model argue that it overstates the rationality of offenders. Not all criminal behavior appears to be based on careful cost-benefit analysis. Crimes of passion, impulsivity, addiction, and structural deprivation may defy the assumptions of forward-looking utility maximization. Behavioral economists have responded by introducing bounded rationality, present bias, and prospect theory into extensions of Becker's model, creating more psychologically realistic variants. For example, an offender might underestimate the probability of being caught due to optimism bias or might heavily discount future punishment due to hyperbolic time preferences.

Additionally, critics point out that Becker's model, if implemented without ethical constraints, could justify draconian penalties in the name of efficiency. If one simply seeks deterrence, then punishments can be made arbitrarily severe to reduce enforcement costs. This logic leads to morally troubling conclusions, especially when it disregards issues of proportionality, due process, or rehabilitative justice. Becker himself acknowledged these critiques, noting that economic models must be embedded within broader normative frameworks that account for fairness, legitimacy, and human dignity.

Nonetheless, the power of Becker's approach lies in its generalizability and its insistence that human behavior—even when illicit or deviant—can be analyzed through the same tools used to study markets and consumers. His methodology paved the way for an entire field now known as the *economics of crime*, which blends econometric techniques, game theory, and institutional analysis to explore issues ranging from policing and incarceration to bail systems and sentencing reform.

Becker's broader intellectual project, often called "economic imperialism," extended rational choice theory to a wide array of domains, including education, marriage, discrimination, fertility, and addiction. His central message was that individuals respond to incentives, and that understanding those incentives is key to crafting effective policies. Nowhere was this more controversial—and more influential—than in his analysis of crime and punishment.

In the realm of forensic economics, Becker's model provides essential theoretical tools for evaluating liability, deterrence strategies, and the design of sanctions. It informs expert testimony on expected behavior under different legal regimes and underlies models for projecting criminal justice expenditures or estimating the marginal deterrent effect of specific laws. In torts, it can help assess punitive damages and their behavioral effects. In regulatory enforcement, it provides a rational framework for calibrating fines to deter corporate wrongdoing.

In sum, Gary Becker's contribution to the economics of crime represents a paradigm shift in both criminal law theory and public policy. By transforming crime from a moral failing into a rational choice, he opened new avenues for understanding, predicting, and ultimately reducing criminal behavior. While his assumptions may be debated, the analytical clarity and empirical relevance of his work have left an indelible mark on legal scholarship, economic theory, and the practice of justice itself.

9.4   Judicial Adoption

Coasean Logic in Federal Courts

Federal courts have referenced Coasean bargaining in cases involving externalities and land use disputes. For example:

> "In a world of zero transaction costs, parties will bargain to efficient outcomes regardless of the initial allocation of rights."
> *Spur Industries, Inc. v. Del E. Webb Development Co.*, 494 P.2d 700 (Ariz. 1972)

Posner's Influence from Bench to Textbook

As a judge on the U.S. Court of Appeals for the Seventh Circuit, Posner authored opinions that directly applied economic analysis. In *Indiana Harbor Belt R.R. Co. v. American Cyanamid Co.*, 916 F.2d 1174 (7th Cir. 1990), he applied cost-benefit reasoning to evaluate strict liability claims.

The Hand Formula and Negligence Law

Judge Learned Hand's famous negligence formula became formalized through Law and Economics:

$$B < P \times L \qquad (9.1)$$

Where:

- B = burden of precautions
- P = probability of harm
- L = magnitude of loss

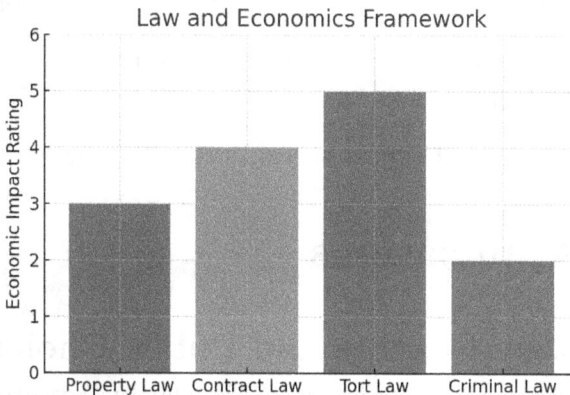

Figure 9.3: Hand Formula: Economic Test for Negligence

This formula is often cited in tort law as an objective test of due care.

Economic Rationales in Antitrust and Contract Law

Economics is foundational in antitrust cases, particularly under the Sherman and Clayton Acts. In contract law, the "efficient breach" theory has allowed courts to uphold breaches when damages fully compensate the non-breaching party.

9.5   Critiques

While Law and Economics is highly influential, it is not without critics. Detractors argue that:

- Economic efficiency may conflict with justice or equity

- Human behavior is not always rational or utility-maximizing

- Distributional effects of legal rules may be ignored

9.6   Applications

Regulatory Capture and Public Choice

Law and Economics also warns of "regulatory capture," where industries influence the very agencies meant to regulate them.

Economic Modeling in Legislative Forecasting

Congressional Budget Office (CBO) scoring, tax policy modeling, and health care law design often rely on econometric simulations rooted in this discipline.

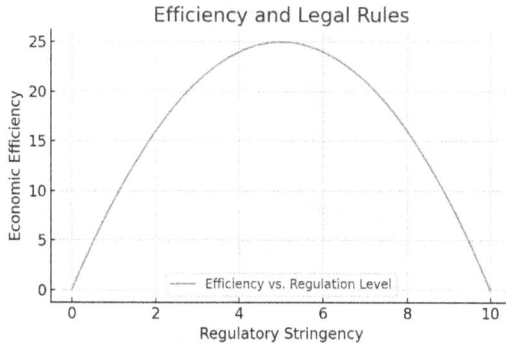

Figure 9.4: Regulatory Capture: Disparity in Influence

9.7   Key References

- Becker, G. S. (1968). *Crime and Punishment: An Economic Approach. Journal of Political Economy*, 76(2), 169–217.

- Bork, R. H. (1978). *The Antitrust Paradox: A Policy at War with Itself.* Basic Books.

- Calabresi, G. (1970). *The Costs of Accidents: A Legal and Economic Analysis.* Yale University Press.

- Calabresi, G., & Melamed, A. D. (1972). Property Rules, Liability Rules, and Inalienability: One View of the Cathedral. *Harvard Law Review*, 85(6), 1089–1128.

- Coase, R. H. (1960). *The Problem of Social Cost. Journal of Law and Economics*, 3, 1–44.

- Demsetz, H. (1967). Toward a Theory of Property

Rights. *American Economic Review*, 57(2), 347–359.

- Director, A. (1951). The Parity of the Economic Market Place. *Journal of Law and Economics*, 1(1), 1–6.

- Kitch, E. W. (Ed.). (1983). *The Fire of Truth: A Remembrance of Law and Economics at Chicago, 1932–1970. Journal of Law and Economics*, 26(1), 163–234.

- Landes, W. M., & Posner, R. A. (1987). *The Economic Structure of Tort Law*. Harvard University Press.

- Manne, H. G. (1966). *Insider Trading and the Stock Market*. Free Press.

- Manne, H. G. (1974). The Case for Insider Trading. *The Wall Street Journal*, March 7.

- Posner, R. A. (1972). *Economic Analysis of Law*. Little, Brown.

- Posner, R. A. (1981). *The Economics of Justice*. Harvard University Press.

- Priest, G. L. (1977). The Common Law Process and the Selection of Efficient Rules. *Journal of Legal Studies*, 6(1), 65–82.

- Priest, G. L. (2024). *The Rise of Law and Economics*. Yale University Press.

- Stigler, G. J. (1966). The Theory of Economic Regulation. *Bell Journal of Economics and Management Science*, 2(1), 3–21.

9.8   Conclusion

The field of Law and Economics has emerged as one of the most influential methodologies for analyzing legal systems, doctrines, and institutional behavior. As this chapter has shown, its development was shaped by a confluence of economic theory, legal realism, and intellectual entrepreneurship. From Ronald Coase's insight into transaction costs and externalities to Gary Becker's application of rational choice theory to crime, the pioneers of this movement demonstrated that legal rules are not just normative expressions but mechanisms that influence and respond to incentives.

Their collective contributions have reframed how we evaluate torts, contracts, antitrust enforcement, corporate governance, and criminal law. Through interdisciplinary rigor and a commitment to functional analysis, Law and Economics offers a powerful lens for predicting behavior, designing policy, and evaluating institutional performance. Yet the approach is not without its limits and critics, and its continued vitality depends on acknowledging the importance of distributional justice, institutional context, and human complexity alongside economic efficiency.

As we move from theory to legal procedure, we must now consider one of the most consequential frameworks in any legal system: the allocation of the burden of proof. While economic reasoning has reshaped how we understand legal rules, it is the structure of evidentiary burdens that determines how those rules are invoked, contested, and enforced. In the next chapter, we turn our attention to this crucial procedural foundation.

9.9 Problems

1. Suppose a product defect imposes an expected loss of $40 on each consumer. If a manufacturer can fix the defect at $5 per unit, should they be liable under the Hand Formula? Explain.

2. In a Coasean world with zero transaction costs, a rancher and farmer are in dispute over stray cattle damaging crops. Analyze how the final outcome would be efficient regardless of legal entitlements.

3. Identify one real-world federal case (not discussed in this chapter) that relies on economic principles in its reasoning. Brief it using Law and Economics logic.

4. Assume a merger between two firms in a concentrated industry. Use Herfindahl-Hirschman Index (HHI) thresholds and price elasticity assumptions to determine if the merger would raise antitrust concerns.

5. Reflect on whether economic efficiency should be the sole criterion in evaluating criminal justice policy. Include ethical, social, and legal perspectives.

Chapter 10

Burden of Proof

10.1 Introduction

Forensic economics does not operate in a vacuum, it functions within the legal architecture of civil litigation. Understanding this context is essential for any economist offering expert opinion in court. The legal framework governs not only how damages are claimed, but also how they must be proven, evaluated, and defended. Each jurisdiction applies specific standards of proof, definitions of causation, and statutory or common law doctrines that shape how economic loss is quantified and compensated.

This chapter examines the legal landscape that forensic economists must navigate, including tort law and contract disputes, the concept of legal causation, evidentiary

thresholds, and cross-jurisdictional variations in damage
recovery. It also explores the economist's role in satisfying the
plaintiff's burden of proof—a foundational requirement in all
civil claims.

10.2   Legal Foundations

Civil litigation typically arises when one party claims that
another party caused harm through either a violation of a
duty (tort) or failure to perform a contractual obligation
(contract). In both contexts, the injured party (plaintiff) must
not only show that the harm occurred and was caused by the
defendant's actions, but also demonstrate the extent of
economic loss.

Tort Law

Tort law addresses civil wrongs that result in injury, loss, or
damage, and is the primary area of law where forensic
economists operate. Common tort claims include:

- **Personal Injury:** Injuries caused by negligence, such
  as in auto accidents, medical malpractice, or premises
  liability.

- **Wrongful Death:** Lawsuits brought by survivors of a
  deceased individual, often involving loss of support,
  services, and companionship.

- **Product Liability:** Harm caused by defective or
  dangerous products.

- **Professional Negligence:** Breaches of duty by

professionals, including accountants, doctors, and
financial advisors.

In each case, the plaintiff must prove the elements of duty,
breach, causation, and damages. The forensic economist's role
lies chiefly in establishing the monetary value of
damages—both past and future economic losses—but this
valuation is contingent on legal determinations of liability and
causation.

Contract Law

Contractual claims arise when one party fails to perform as
agreed under a binding contract. Economic damages in
contract cases are usually governed by the principle of
"expectation interest"—the amount necessary to put the
plaintiff in the position they would have been in had the
contract been fully performed.

Common categories include:

- **Lost Profits:** Revenue not realized due to breach.

- **Reliance Damages:** Costs incurred in preparation or
  performance.

- **Consequential Damages:** Secondary losses traceable
  to the breach (e.g., reputational harm, collateral
  business disruption).

Unlike tort claims, punitive damages are rarely available in
contract disputes. The economist must work within these
limitations, often relying on market comparables, historical
records, and profit margin projections to quantify harm.

10.3   Law vs. Economics

A fundamental concept in both tort and contract litigation is
causation—the requirement that the defendant's conduct
must have caused the plaintiff's loss. However, legal causation
and economic causation are not always the same.

Legal Causation

Legal systems distinguish between:

- **Cause-in-fact ("but for" causation):** Would the
  harm have occurred but for the defendant's conduct?

- **Proximate cause:** Is the connection between the
  conduct and harm legally sufficient and not too remote?

Forensic economists generally assume causation has been
established by the court or jury, but they may be asked to
opine on whether a loss would have occurred regardless of the
defendant's actions. This is especially true in employment
cases (e.g., mitigation of damages) or when multiple causes of
harm exist.

Legal Causation and the Concept of Nexus

In legal and forensic contexts, *causation* is not merely a
philosophical inquiry into what brought about a harm, but a
critical threshold that plaintiffs must meet to establish
liability and recover damages. At the core of the causation
inquiry is the concept of nexus—the legal and factual link
between a defendant's conduct and the plaintiff's injury.
Courts distinguish between two primary forms of causation:

cause-in-fact and *proximate cause*, both of which must be
satisfied to prove a legally actionable harm. Understanding
this nexus is essential for forensic economists when assessing
whether, and to what extent, an economic loss is compensable.

**Statistical Nexus and the Distinction from
Correlation**   In statistics, causation signifies a direct,
influence-based relationship in which a change in one variable
(the cause) directly produces a change in another variable (the
effect). This stands in contrast to correlation, which merely
observes that two variables move together—without asserting
that one causes the other. While correlation can suggest
patterns worthy of investigation, it lacks the evidentiary force
to establish responsibility in legal proceedings. Courts and
forensic experts must avoid the logical fallacy post hoc ergo
propter hoc ("after this, therefore because of this") by
subjecting relationships to rigorous scrutiny.

Establishing causation statistically requires the use of
advanced techniques—such as regression analysis,
instrumental variable estimation, propensity score matching,
and Granger causality testing—which aim to isolate the effect
of a single variable while controlling for confounders. In
litigation, these methods help assess whether the defendant's
conduct materially contributed to the plaintiff's economic
harm, as distinct from background noise or unrelated life
events.

Cause-in-Fact (Actual or "But For" Causation)   The
first prong in any legal causation analysis is cause-in-fact, also
known as "but for" causation. This test asks: But for the
defendant's conduct, would the plaintiff have suffered the

harm? It focuses on factual necessity. For example, if an employee alleges wrongful termination resulted in financial loss, the question is whether they would have sustained the same loss even absent the termination—for instance, due to industry-wide layoffs or unrelated health issues.

Courts often use the "but for" test as a gatekeeper, and forensic economists rely on it to build counterfactual scenarios—economic models of what would have happened in the absence of the wrongful act. These models may use baseline earnings, career trajectories, and market forecasts to project expected losses, contingent upon proving that the defendant's act was the factual catalyst.

Proximate Cause (Legal Sufficiency of the Nexus)
Beyond factual cause, the law imposes a constraint on the scope of liability through proximate cause. This doctrine ensures that liability does not extend infinitely to every consequence of a defendant's action. Instead, it asks whether the harm is the type of result that was reasonably foreseeable and not too attenuated or speculative.

For instance, in a personal injury case, proximate cause may limit recovery for speculative future earnings if the injured party's career path was inherently uncertain. Courts often use analogies, policy considerations, and precedents to define the contours of proximate cause. Forensic economists must remain aware that even if a loss is mathematically demonstrable, it may not be legally recoverable if the nexus is too remote.

Multiple Causes and Complex Causality   In many real-world scenarios, harm arises from a confluence of factors, rather than a single proximate event. This presents significant analytical challenges. If multiple actors or events contributed to the plaintiff's condition, courts must determine whether the defendant's actions were a substantial factor in bringing about the harm. Even when not the sole cause, liability can attach if the defendant's conduct materially increased the risk of injury.

Forensic economists navigating such cases must build scenarios that account for joint causation. For example, in occupational illness cases, a worker may have been exposed to multiple toxic agents. An expert might quantify the incremental risk or marginal contribution of each exposure using epidemiological data and economic modeling, thereby clarifying the role of the defendant's conduct within the causal web.

Foreseeability and the Chain of Events   Foreseeability is a crucial element of proximate cause and directly impacts the establishment of a legal nexus. Courts ask whether a reasonable person in the defendant's position could have anticipated the general type of harm. In economic damages, this may pertain to whether lost profits, emotional distress, or downstream business impacts were reasonably predictable.

For example, if a vendor breaches a supply contract, the foreseeability test helps determine whether resulting customer losses or reputational harm were within the realm of contemplation at the time of agreement. In such cases, forensic economists may be asked to opine on whether the damages claimed represent an unexpected windfall or a foreseeable consequence consistent with standard industry expectations.

**Expert Testimony: The Bridge Between Data and
Causation**   The testimony of expert witnesses is often
pivotal in proving or disputing nexus. In complex
litigation—such as medical malpractice, employment
discrimination, or environmental damage—expert opinions
translate statistical findings into legally relevant narratives.

Forensic economists use tools like life tables, earnings
projections, and actuarial discounting to establish the
monetary impact of harms, but these tools only carry
evidentiary weight when causation is firmly grounded.
Experts may also be asked to evaluate mitigation,
determining whether a plaintiff failed to take reasonable steps
to reduce their losses, which can affect both causation and the
damages calculation.

Superseding and Intervening Acts   Even when a
defendant's conduct is a factual and proximate cause, the
presence of a superseding or intervening act may break the
chain of causation. A superseding act is a later event that is
unforeseeable and sufficiently independent to sever the legal
connection. For example, if a plaintiff is injured due to
negligence but suffers greater harm due to an unrelated third
party's criminal act, the latter may be deemed the
superseding cause.

In such scenarios, forensic economists must often reevaluate
damages based on alternative timelines or revised causality
assumptions. Courts scrutinize the timing, foreseeability, and
independence of such acts when determining whether liability
continues to flow from the original defendant.

Causation in Contract vs. Tort Contexts While causation in tort law focuses on injury due to breach of a duty, contract law emphasizes expectation damages resulting from breach of contractual terms. Nevertheless, nexus remains central in both. Plaintiffs must demonstrate that the breach directly caused quantifiable harm and that such harm was within the scope of foreseeable damages under *Hadley v. Baxendale* principles.

In breach of contract cases, forensic economists may assess lost profits, business interruption, or diminished business value, but must carefully delineate between damages caused by the breach versus losses due to market forces, mismanagement, or unrelated events.

Judicial Assumptions vs. Expert Inquiry In many trials, courts or juries establish causation as a threshold question before economic experts are permitted to testify. Forensic economists generally assume that causation has been judicially determined. However, they may be called upon to test the strength of the assumed nexus—i.e., would the loss have occurred regardless of the defendant's actions?

This is especially relevant in cases involving alleged wrongful termination, defamation, or loss of business opportunity. In these instances, forensic economists construct models of the "but-for world," examining how a person's life or business would likely have unfolded absent the alleged harm, based on historical data and comparable benchmarks.

Economic Causation

Economists rely on counterfactual reasoning—comparing the plaintiff's actual condition to a "but for" world where the harm did not occur. This might involve:

- Projecting earnings had a termination not occurred.

- Estimating lost profits if a contract had been honored.

- Comparing pre- and post-incident business valuation.

However, economic models must be sensitive to issues of speculation. Courts may exclude testimony that lacks a firm factual basis or appears to assume causation without sufficient analysis.

10.4   Burden of Proof

In civil cases, the burden of proof falls on the plaintiff to establish their claim by a preponderance of the evidence—meaning it is more likely than not that the claim is true. For economic damages, this means:

- Demonstrating that a loss occurred,

- Showing the loss was caused by the defendant,

- Quantifying the amount of the loss with reasonable certainty.

The "reasonable certainty" standard is less stringent than "beyond a reasonable doubt," but it still prohibits speculative or conjectural estimates. Courts recognize that future losses cannot be proven with absolute precision but require evidence that is more than hypothetical. Forensic economists must therefore support projections with reliable data, conservative assumptions, and transparent methodologies.

10.5 Jurisdictional Variants

Although forensic economic methods rely on objective data and modeling principles, the application of those methods varies across jurisdictions. Courts in different states—and in different countries—apply distinct rules governing the types and limits of recoverable damages. Understanding these legal nuances is essential for tailoring expert reports and testimony to the specific venue.

Types of Recoverable Damages

Most jurisdictions recognize several categories of economic damages, though their definitions and limits may differ:

- **Past Economic Loss:** Income and benefits lost between the date of injury or breach and the date of trial.

- **Future Economic Loss:** Projected earnings, benefits, or business profits lost after the date of trial, discounted to present value.

- **Household or Replacement Services:** The value of unpaid domestic labor lost due to injury or death.

- **Medical and Life Care Costs:** Future treatment, caregiving, assistive devices, and home modifications.

- **Mitigation-Offset Adjustments:** Earnings or income from alternative employment or investments that reduce total damages.

Some jurisdictions allow for more expansive or restricted categories of economic harm. For example, California allows for hedonic damages in limited circumstances, while Texas caps certain types of noneconomic awards in medical malpractice cases. Federal courts may also differ in how they calculate or limit damages, especially in employment or constitutional torts.

Caps and Limitations on Recovery

Several U.S. states impose statutory caps on damages, which may affect the relevance or admissibility of forensic economic evidence:

- **Noneconomic Damage Caps:** While not directly related to economic testimony, these caps may influence settlement value or trial strategy.

- **Medical Malpractice Limits:** States such as Florida and Missouri have historically capped certain categories of damages, affecting future medical cost modeling.

- **Wrongful Death Beneficiary Restrictions:** Some jurisdictions restrict recovery to specific classes of survivors or limit damages based on the plaintiff's age, earning potential, or dependency status.

These caps may not affect the methodology of damage computation but do influence how economists structure their reports and how attorneys frame damages at trial.

Collateral Source Rules

A key jurisdictional distinction is whether courts allow the offset of damages by amounts received from third-party sources (e.g., insurance payments, government benefits). Known as the "collateral source rule," its application varies:

- **Traditional Rule (e.g., New York):** Benefits received by the plaintiff from independent sources do not reduce the defendant's liability.

- **Modified or Abolished Rule (e.g., Indiana, Colorado):** Courts may permit offsets, thereby reducing the plaintiff's economic recovery.

Forensic economists must be aware of the rule's application in the relevant jurisdiction. Whether to include or exclude certain reimbursements can materially affect the damage calculation and the admissibility of the expert's assumptions.

10.6 From *Frye* to *Kelly*

The Evolution of Scientific Evidence Standards

While *Frye v. United States*, 293 F. 1013 (D.C. Cir. 1923), established the foundational standard for the admissibility of scientific evidence in American courts, it was further refined and clarified in California through the decision in *People v. Kelly*, 17 Cal. 3d 24 (1976). This landmark ruling in the Supreme Court of California reaffirmed the general acceptance requirement but introduced additional procedural protections and clarified the role of expert testimony in laying the foundation for novel scientific techniques. Together, these cases form what is commonly known in California and other jurisdictions as the **Kelly-Frye Rule.**

IRAC Analysis: *Frye v. United States* (1923)

Issue: Whether expert testimony based on a novel scientific technique—the systolic blood pressure deception test (a precursor to the polygraph)—should be admitted in evidence.

Rule: The *Frye* standard held that a scientific technique must be "sufficiently established to have gained general acceptance in the particular field in which it belongs."

Application: The D.C. Circuit excluded the lie detector evidence, reasoning that the technique had not yet attained general acceptance among scientists.

Conclusion: The court ruled that the scientific principle upon which the testimony was based was not sufficiently established to warrant admission.

The *Frye* rule thus imposed a relatively narrow and conservative gatekeeping role, emphasizing consensus within the scientific community over judicial evaluation of methodology or reasoning.

IRAC Analysis: *People v. Kelly* (1976)

Issue: Whether voiceprint analysis—used to match the defendant's voice to a recording—was admissible under California law, and whether the foundation laid for this technique met the threshold required for novel scientific evidence.

Rule: The California Supreme Court reaffirmed the *Frye* principle of general acceptance but added a tripartite test that is now referred to as the **Kelly-Frye standard**:

1. The reliability of the scientific technique must be established—i.e., the technique must have gained general acceptance in the relevant scientific community.

2. The witness testifying about the technique must be a qualified expert on the subject.

3. The proponent must show that correct scientific procedures were followed in the particular case.

Application: The Court found that the voiceprint technique had not achieved sufficient scientific acceptance and thus failed the first prong of the test. It also expressed concern that the expert testimony did not adequately explain the methodology, and the procedures employed in the case were not shown to be reliable or repeatable.

Conclusion: The Court excluded the voiceprint evidence and reversed the conviction, holding that all three prongs of the *Kelly-Frye* standard must be satisfied before a novel scientific technique is admissible.

Case Brief: *People v. Kelly*, 17 Cal. 3d 24 (1976)

Facts: Robert Emmett Kelly was convicted of robbery, with key evidence including a voiceprint analysis purportedly matching his voice to a recording of the perpetrator. The

defense challenged the admissibility of this technique as
unreliable.

Procedural History: The trial court admitted the
voiceprint evidence. Kelly appealed.

Issue: Whether the admission of voiceprint analysis violated
California evidentiary standards regarding novel scientific
evidence.

Holding: No. The Supreme Court of California reversed the
conviction.

Reasoning: The Court articulated a three-part test for novel
scientific evidence: general acceptance in the scientific
community, expert qualification, and proper application of the
method. The Court found the voiceprint evidence deficient in
all three areas.

Outcome: Conviction reversed; new trial ordered.

Doctrinal Impact: The *Kelly-Frye* Rule

The decision in *People v. Kelly* did not abandon the *Frye*
standard but rather expanded it into a more robust
procedural safeguard, especially in California and other states
that adopted the reasoning. The *Kelly-Frye* rule can be
summarized as follows:

- **Preserves the General Acceptance Requirement:**
  Like *Frye*, *Kelly* requires that the underlying scientific
  theory must be generally accepted in its field.

- **Adds Procedural Safeguards:** Kelly requires proof of
  the expert's qualifications and verification that the

technique was properly applied in the particular instance.

- **Focuses on Foundation:** The rule emphasizes the need for a proper evidentiary foundation through expert testimony and documentary evidence to support the reliability of the technique.

- **Limits Jury Exposure to Unreliable Science:** By empowering trial courts to act as gatekeepers, *Kelly* helps protect jurors from being misled by impressive but methodologically flawed expert presentations.

Thus, while *Frye* focused narrowly on community acceptance, *Kelly* introduced judicial oversight over expert qualifications and methodological integrity, laying the groundwork for later developments under the *Daubert* framework at the federal level. Together, *Frye* and *Kelly* form the doctrinal foundation for evaluating scientific evidence in many state courts that have not adopted the federal rules.

10.7 *Daubert*

Daubert v. Merrell Dow Pharmaceuticals, Inc.
Supreme Court of the United States
509 U.S. 579 (1993)

Justice Blackmun delivered the opinion of the Court.

Petitioners Daubert and Schuller are minor children born with serious birth defects. They and their parents sued Merrell Dow Pharmaceuticals, Inc. (Merrell Dow) in a California state court, alleging that the children's mothers' ingestion of

Bendectin, a prescription anti-nausea drug marketed by Merrell Dow, had caused the birth defects. Merrell Dow removed the suits to federal court on diversity grounds and moved for summary judgment, contending that Bendectin does not cause birth defects. In support of its motion, Merrell Dow submitted the affidavit of a well-credentialed expert epidemiologist who concluded, based on published studies involving over 130,000 patients, that maternal use of Bendectin during the first trimester of pregnancy had not been shown to be a risk factor for human birth defects.

Petitioners responded with the testimony of eight experts of their own, each of whom had concluded that Bendectin can cause birth defects. Their conclusions were based on animal studies, chemical structure analyses, and the "reanalysis" of previously published human statistical studies. The District Court granted Merrell Dow's motion for summary judgment, essentially excluding petitioners' evidence as inadmissible under the "general acceptance" standard announced in *Frye v. United States*, 293 F. 1013 (D.C. Cir. 1923). The Court of Appeals affirmed.

We granted certiorari to determine the standard for admitting expert scientific testimony in a federal trial.

I. The Role of Rule 702

The Federal Rules of Evidence govern the admissibility of expert testimony in federal courts. Rule 702 provides:

> If scientific, technical, or other specialized knowledge will assist the trier of fact to understand the evidence or to determine a fact in

issue, a witness qualified as an expert by
knowledge, skill, experience, training, or
education, may testify thereto in the form of an
opinion or otherwise.

Nothing in the text of this Rule establishes "general
acceptance" as an absolute prerequisite to admissibility. Nor
does the Rule incorporate the *Frye* test.

II. Scientific Validity and Relevance

The primary criterion for admissibility is whether the
testimony is both relevant and reliable. This requires a
preliminary assessment of whether the reasoning or
methodology underlying the testimony is scientifically valid
and whether that reasoning or methodology properly can be
applied to the facts in issue.

The inquiry envisioned by Rule 702 is a flexible one. Its
overarching subject is the scientific validity—and thus the
evidentiary relevance and reliability—of the principles that
underlie a proposed submission. Many factors may bear on
the inquiry, including:

1. Whether the theory or technique can be (and has been)
   tested;

2. Whether it has been subjected to peer review and
   publication;

3. The known or potential error rate;

4. The existence and maintenance of standards controlling
   the technique's operation;

5. Whether the theory or technique enjoys general
   acceptance within a relevant scientific community.

These factors are not a "definitive checklist or test." The
gatekeeping function of the trial judge is to ensure that expert
testimony is both reliable and relevant.

III. Judicial Discretion and Scientific Expertise

It is not the role of the trial judge to determine which of
several competing scientific theories has the best provenance.
The judge's task is to ensure that the expert's testimony rests
on a reliable foundation and is relevant to the task at hand.

Vigorous cross-examination, presentation of contrary evidence,
and careful instruction on the burden of proof are the
traditional and appropriate means of attacking shaky but
admissible evidence.

IV. Conclusion

We conclude that the *Frye* test was superseded by the
adoption of the Federal Rules of Evidence. The trial judge
must ensure that any and all scientific testimony or evidence
admitted is not only relevant, but reliable.

The judgment of the Court of Appeals is vacated, and the
case is remanded for further proceedings consistent with this
opinion.

It is so ordered.

Rehnquist, C.J., with whom Stevens, J., joins, concurring in part and dissenting in part

While I agree that the *Frye* test should no longer be applied in federal courts, I am concerned that the majority gives insufficient guidance to trial judges. Determining what is "scientific knowledge" is no simple task, and judges lack the scientific training to make such assessments.

I therefore dissent from Part III of the Court's opinion, and would retain more deference to existing standards of professional consensus.

End of Opinion.

10.8   Standards for Admissibility

An economist's conclusions are only as valuable as the court's willingness to admit them into evidence. The admissibility of forensic economic testimony hinges on both the economist's qualifications and the reliability of their methods, especially in establishing causation and valuation.

Daubert, *Frye*, and Hybrid Standards

In the realm of forensic economics, the admissibility of expert testimony is not solely a matter of professional qualifications or intuitive logic—it is governed by judicially recognized evidentiary standards. These standards ensure that expert opinions presented to judges and juries are grounded in reliable methods, relevant reasoning, and rigorous analysis. Across jurisdictions, three principal approaches shape the landscape: the *Daubert* standard, the *Frye* standard, and a range of hybrid or modified rules that borrow from both.

Historical and Legal Context   The development of evidentiary standards for expert testimony evolved from growing judicial concerns about the proliferation of unreliable science in courtrooms. Historically, courts relied on the *Frye* standard, which emerged from the 1923 case *Frye v. United States*, 293 F. 1013 (D.C. Cir. 1923). This standard focused on general acceptance—whether the methodology used by an expert was widely recognized and endorsed within the relevant scientific field.

In 1993, the U.S. Supreme Court significantly reshaped this landscape with its decision in *Daubert v. Merrell Dow Pharmaceuticals, Inc.*, 509 U.S. 579 (1993). There, the Court ruled that under Federal Rule of Evidence 702, trial judges must serve as "gatekeepers," independently assessing the scientific validity and applicability of expert methods before allowing them to be presented to the jury. This decision ushered in a more flexible, multi-factor analysis that placed emphasis on scientific reliability over general acceptance.

The Daubert Standard (Federal and Majority of States)   The *Daubert* standard, as articulated by the Supreme Court and expanded in subsequent decisions such as *General Electric Co. v. Joiner*, 522 U.S. 136 (1997), and *Kumho Tire Co. v. Carmichael*, 526 U.S. 137 (1999), provides a comprehensive framework for evaluating expert testimony. The court evaluates whether:

- The theory or technique can be—and has been—tested.

- The methodology has been subjected to peer review and publication.

- The known or potential error rate has been identified.

- Standards and controls exist and are maintained.

- The technique enjoys widespread acceptance within a relevant scientific community.

The trial judge's role is to assess the fit between the expert's methodology and the facts of the case, ensuring that the opinion offered is not only based on sound science but also logically supports the conclusions reached. In practice, this means that forensic economists testifying under the *Daubert* framework must fully document their methods, disclose data sources, and explain all assumptions used in their models. Any failure to provide a transparent chain of reasoning may result in exclusion of their testimony.

The *Frye* Standard (Minority of States)   Under the *Frye* standard, the admissibility of expert testimony depends on whether the technique or principle upon which the testimony is based is "generally accepted" by a meaningful segment of the associated scientific community. While less flexible than *Daubert*, this approach emphasizes scientific consensus and defers heavily to the standards of the relevant profession.

Although often criticized for being overly conservative or slow to adapt to novel scientific advancements, some jurisdictions—such as California (until its more recent adoption of *Daubert*-like standards)—continued to apply *Frye* or variations thereof. In these states, forensic economists must carefully document that their techniques (e.g., present value modeling, wage projections, discounting methodologies) are consistent with those routinely employed and accepted by their professional peers.

The key to meeting *Frye*'s threshold is demonstrating that the economist's approach reflects not personal theory or innovation, but the mainstream, established practice in forensic economics. Expert reports should include references to professional standards published by bodies such as the National Association of Forensic Economics (NAFE) or widely cited academic texts in labor economics and valuation.

Hybrid or Modified Standards Some states have adopted hybrid approaches or developed unique procedural rules that integrate elements of both *Daubert* and *Frye*, or that impose additional criteria altogether. For example:

- **New York:** Although historically a *Frye* state, New York has increasingly required greater articulation of methodological reliability, particularly in complex litigation involving economics or statistical inference.

- **Florida:** Transitioned from *Frye* to the *Daubert* standard as codified in Fla. Stat. § 90.702, aligning with federal evidentiary rules. Courts in Florida now require explicit demonstrations of methodological reliability, peer review, and logical relevance.

- **Illinois and Pennsylvania:** These states have adopted modified approaches where courts may consider both general acceptance and reliability, creating ambiguity that requires forensic economists to exceed the baseline standards of either test.

Forensic experts practicing in hybrid jurisdictions must be especially cautious. Reports should anticipate both scientific scrutiny (reliability and error rate) and professional consensus (general acceptance). Experts should be prepared to defend their conclusions with both empirical evidence and reference to prevailing economic practices.

Best Practices for Forensic Economists Across Jurisdictions   Given the variation among jurisdictions, forensic economists must tailor their methods and reporting style to meet the specific evidentiary burdens of the court in which they testify. This involves several key strategies:

- **Full Transparency:** Every data source, model assumption, and computational step should be explained and, where possible, cited to peer-reviewed literature or public databases.

- **Consistency with Established Practice:** Experts should avoid novel or untested techniques unless clearly warranted and well-defended. Use of standard models such as present value calculations, discounting formulas, and regression analyses increases the likelihood of admissibility.

- **Jurisdictional Familiarity:** Economists must know the evidentiary standard applicable in their case's venue and adapt their report accordingly. A federal court may require greater detail than a state court relying on a relaxed interpretation of *Frye*.

- **Documentation for Cross-Examination:**

Anticipating Daubert or similar challenges, economists
should prepare to explain their method's error rates,
calibration processes, and points of departure from
alternative approaches. This may include retaining
underlying spreadsheets or coding used to generate
calculations.

Case Law Trends   Over the past decade, appellate and
trial courts have increasingly scrutinized expert testimony in
economic damages cases. Exclusions have been upheld for
experts who:

- Relied on anecdotal or speculative assumptions.

- Failed to conduct a differential analysis in employment
  discrimination claims.

- Ignored mitigation or used arbitrary discount rates.

- Provided conclusory statements unsupported by
  underlying data.

In contrast, well-prepared economists whose models closely
align with accepted economic methods and who document
their reasoning are consistently admitted. Judicial
commentary from such cases often praises clarity,
reproducibility, and rigor—underscoring the continuing
importance of compliance with both *Daubert* and *Frye*
principles.

Conclusion   The admissibility of expert economic testimony
is ultimately a function of methodological integrity and legal
awareness. Whether governed by the rigor of *Daubert*, the
consensus-based approach of *Frye*, or a hybrid model, courts

expect forensic economists to present opinions that are reliable, relevant, and firmly rooted in sound science and accepted practice. Expert witnesses who take the time to understand their jurisdiction's evidentiary standard, clearly articulate their reasoning, and defend their models under cross-examination serve as invaluable guides for the court, and dramatically improve the odds that their opinions will be admitted and credited.

Admissibility of Causation Assumptions

Economists are typically not permitted to opine on legal causation, but they may make factual assumptions about causation when modeling damages. Courts distinguish between:

- **Assuming Liability:** The economist may assume that the defendant is liable, provided the assumption is clearly stated.

- **Assuming Causation:** The economist may assume that the defendant's conduct caused the loss, but may not independently testify that causation has been established.

- **Modeling Alternative Scenarios:** In some cases, courts may allow "if-then" models—e.g., "If the jury finds that X caused Y, then the estimated loss is $Z."

Economists must be careful to avoid offering legal conclusions and should clearly delineate the scope of their analysis to remain within admissible bounds.

Valuation Methodologies

In forensic economics, the credibility and admissibility of an expert's damage valuation often hinge on the soundness of the methods employed. Courts are not merely interested in the final numbers, but in the logical, transparent, and replicable process by which those numbers were derived. A well-executed valuation must balance economic theory, empirical data, and legal sufficiency. To withstand admissibility challenges, particularly under Rule 702 of the Federal Rules of Evidence and corresponding state evidentiary standards, the expert's methodology must be demonstrably reliable, relevant to the issues at hand, and applied with professional integrity.

Foundations of Admissibility: Rule 702 and Daubert Standards   Rule 702 requires that expert testimony be based on "sufficient facts or data," be the "product of reliable principles and methods," and that the expert has "reliably applied the principles and methods to the facts of the case." In practice, this means that forensic economists must not only employ generally accepted valuation techniques, but also must articulate the rationale behind their inputs, assumptions, and interpretations. Courts often conduct a *Daubert* hearing to test the methodological reliability of expert evidence, and forensic economists must be prepared to defend every facet of their report.

1. Rely on Reliable Data   The cornerstone of any credible damages valuation is the use of dependable, up-to-date data sources. Forensic economists commonly draw on:

- U.S. Bureau of Labor Statistics (BLS) for wage and employment trends

- U.S. Census Bureau and Current Population Survey (CPS) data

- Internal Revenue Service (IRS) tax records

- Social Security Administration life and earnings tables

- Industry and occupational earnings databases such as the Occupational Employment and Wage Statistics (OEWS)

- Regional Consumer Price Index (CPI) measures for cost-of-living adjustments

- Court-admitted actuarial tables for mortality, disability, and work-life expectancy

Reliance on anecdotal evidence, self-reported earnings without corroboration, or outdated datasets can undermine the integrity of the analysis. In past cases, courts have excluded testimony where experts used obsolete wage data or failed to adjust for inflation. Forensic economists must update their data sources regularly and note their version or retrieval date within their reports.

2. Use Transparent Assumptions   Every valuation model rests on a series of assumptions—regarding future earnings growth, work-life duration, fringe benefit rates, inflation, discount rates, and tax effects. These assumptions must not only be disclosed but substantiated. A report that offers a conclusion without explaining the logic behind its parameters will almost certainly fail a Daubert challenge.

For example, if a valuation assumes a 3.5

3. Include Conservative Ranges   Courts prefer damage estimates that acknowledge uncertainty. Instead of asserting a single, speculative figure, it is generally advisable to provide a range of reasonable values based on high, medium, and low-case scenarios. These may incorporate sensitivity analyses that test the impact of changing key variables—such as employment duration, future career growth, or the time horizon for damages.

Providing a damages range reflects a cautious, evidence-based approach and mitigates the risk of appearing biased or outcome-driven. It also gives courts flexibility in determining awards without relying too heavily on a potentially disputed central estimate. Forensic economists should explain the rationale behind each scenario and avoid overly optimistic projections, which may be seen as advocating rather than analyzing.

4. Be Reproducible   A credible valuation should be reproducible by any qualified professional using the same inputs and methodology. This means:

- Clearly documenting all data sources and citing them properly.

- Explaining the formulas and computational logic used to arrive at conclusions.

- Avoiding proprietary models that cannot be replicated without specialized tools.

- Providing step-by-step calculations or appendices showing how values were derived.

Reproducibility supports the fundamental scientific value of peer review and increases the likelihood that testimony will survive evidentiary objections. Courts have excluded damages experts who failed to provide spreadsheets or source documentation, rendering their opinions unverifiable.

Common Pitfalls Leading to Exclusion Forensic economists must anticipate the types of errors or oversights that often lead to the exclusion of expert testimony:

- **Use of Outdated or Unverified Data:** Reliance on decade-old earnings data or failure to adjust for recent inflation can severely impair credibility.

- **Failure to Account for Mitigation:** Plaintiffs are typically expected to mitigate damages. If the expert fails to consider the plaintiff's earning capacity in alternate employment, their calculations may be deemed incomplete.

- **Application of Arbitrary Multipliers:** Use of unexplained or unsupported multipliers to inflate values (e.g., multiplying damages by a "pain factor") is viewed as speculative and inadmissible.

- **Ignoring Counterfactual Scenarios:** A robust valuation considers what the plaintiff's economic position would have been had the wrongful act not occurred.

Valuation Techniques in Practice Depending on the nature of the claim, wrongful termination, personal injury, wrongful death, business interruption, different valuation techniques may be used. Some commonly applied methods include:

- **Present Value of Lost Earnings:** Uses projected
  future income, adjusted for taxes, fringe benefits, and
  work-life expectancy, and discounted to present value.

- **Incremental Earnings Models:** Compares plaintiff's
  actual career trajectory with an estimated but-for
  scenario, often incorporating regression analysis based
  on labor market comparables.

- **Business Valuation:** Applies income-based,
  market-based, or asset-based valuation methods to
  determine losses in business interruption or breach of
  contract claims.

- **Hedonic Damages (in select jurisdictions):**
  Attempts to quantify loss of enjoyment of life using
  economic indicators—though controversial and not
  universally admissible.

Alignment with Legal and Procedural Standards

Economists must tailor their valuation reports to comply with
the legal standards of the forum. Beyond Rule 702, various
state court rules impose additional criteria:

- **Florida:** Applies the Daubert standard (as codified in
  Fla. Stat. § 90.702), which mirrors the federal approach.

- **California:** Historically more lenient under the
  Kelly/Frye standard, though moving toward stricter
  scrutiny.

- **Texas:** Requires a showing that methodology is not
  only generally accepted but directly applicable to the

facts of the case.

The forensic economist must not only understand these legal
distinctions but draft reports in a manner that anticipates
jurisdiction-specific scrutiny. Courts may strike entire reports
if they lack methodological clarity, fail to account for case law,
or include speculative damages.

The Role of Professional Judgment While forensic
economics is data-driven, it is not devoid of discretion. The
economist's professional judgment, when exercised
transparently, conservatively, and consistently with best
practices, is indispensable. Experts must navigate imperfect
data, conflicting records, and assumptions about future
behavior. The challenge is to present these elements with
intellectual honesty, clearly stating limitations and
uncertainties.

Conclusion Ultimately, a valuation is not just a number, it
is a narrative told with numbers. A properly constructed
valuation methodology tells a compelling, evidence-based
story of loss that integrates statistical precision with legal
admissibility. Forensic economists must embrace both the
rigor of economic modeling and the constraints of judicial
procedure, ensuring that their work can withstand adversarial
testing and serve as a reliable guide to the trier of fact.
Courts reward clarity, conservatism, and transparency.
Experts who deliver on these criteria are more likely to have
their testimony admitted, relied upon, and valued.

10.9   *Kelly–Frye* revisited

Modern   Application   of   the   *Kelly–Frye* Standard

While *People v. Kelly* (1976) originated in the context of voiceprint analysis, its principles have significantly influenced the admissibility of expert testimony across other fields, including forensic psychiatry and psychology. In jurisdictions that follow the **general acceptance** approach, the **Kelly–Frye** standard continues to provide a framework for evaluating whether psychological and psychiatric expert opinions meet admissibility thresholds.

In forensic psychology, for instance, testimony related to mental illness, personality assessments, malingering detection, and behavioral syndromes often hinges on the extent to which the methodology employed is both **generally accepted in the relevant scientific community** and applied correctly to the specific facts of the case.

Professional Practice Considerations

Key procedural expectations that align with the Kelly–Frye doctrine include the following:

- **Validated instruments:** Psychological tools such as the MMPI-2, WAIS-IV, or Structured Interview of Reported Symptoms (SIRS) must have demonstrated reliability and empirical support.

- **Appropriate application:** The expert must

demonstrate that the instrument or assessment was administered according to standard protocols and interpreted in a way consistent with established scientific literature.

- **Expert qualification:** Courts scrutinize whether the individual administering or interpreting the method possesses recognized credentials, training, and expertise in the domain.

- **Documented methodology:** Experts must articulate their reasoning clearly, support their conclusions with references, and acknowledge the limitations of their assessments.

Alignment with Ethical and Scientific Guidelines

Professional bodies such as the American Psychological Association and the American Academy of Psychiatry and the Law have issued practice guidelines that echo the foundational principles of Kelly–Frye. These include:

- Ensuring that opinions are based on data and methods consistent with the standards of the field;

- Disclosing potential sources of bias;

- Offering scientifically supportable alternative explanations when appropriate;

- Maintaining transparency in the reasoning that connects data to conclusions.

These ethical and procedural expectations reinforce the tripartite structure introduced in Kelly: **general acceptance of the scientific method, qualified expert testimony,** and **proper application of the technique to the case at hand.**

Impact on Expert Witness Testimony

The influence of Kelly–Frye in psychological and psychiatric expert testimony is particularly visible in cases involving:

- Competency evaluations;

- Criminal responsibility assessments;

- PTSD diagnoses and trauma syndromes;

- Risk assessments and future dangerousness predictions.

In each of these areas, courts may invoke Kelly–Frye to determine whether novel diagnostic frameworks or controversial syndromes (such as "battered woman syndrome" or "rape trauma syndrome") have sufficient acceptance and methodological support to be admissible.

10.10   SCOTUS Decisions

While the U.S. Supreme Court rarely mentions forensic economists by name, several pivotal decisions have hinged on the admissibility or quality of economic expert testimony. These rulings have established critical procedural and substantive thresholds for economic evidence in class actions, securities, and antitrust cases.

Wal-Mart Stores, Inc. v. Dukes (2011)

The U.S. Supreme Court's landmark decision in *Wal-Mart Stores, Inc. v. Dukes*, 564 U.S. 338 (2011), significantly altered the landscape of class certification, particularly in employment discrimination cases involving large, decentralized corporate defendants. In a 5–4 decision authored by Justice Scalia, the Court held that the proposed class of over 1.5 million female Wal-Mart employees failed to meet the commonality requirement under Rule 23(a)(2) of the Federal Rules of Civil Procedure. The plaintiffs alleged that Wal-Mart's policy of allowing store managers discretion in pay and promotion decisions had a disparate impact on women nationwide. However, the Court found that the plaintiffs failed to identify a specific corporate policy that uniformly affected all class members, and thus could not demonstrate that a common issue of law or fact tied their claims together in a manner justifying class treatment.

At the heart of the Court's reasoning was a demand for empirical rigor. Justice Scalia emphasized that the mere presence of discretion, even when exercised disproportionately, does not equate to a uniform employment practice unless supported by rigorous statistical proof. As a result, *Dukes* elevated the evidentiary burden for plaintiffs seeking class certification in discrimination claims, especially when the alleged discrimination stems from subjective decision-making rather than overtly discriminatory policies.

This decision marked a paradigm shift. Where once anecdotal accounts and centralized intent might suffice to demonstrate commonality, post-*Dukes* litigation requires granular statistical evidence to reveal patterns of systemic bias. Forensic economists and labor economists have become indispensable in this new era. Their role is to provide credible, peer-reviewed statistical methodologies capable of detecting class-wide discrimination patterns within corporate data systems.

Common methods employed include:

- **Hierarchical Linear Models (HLM):** These models account for nested data structures (e.g., employees within stores, stores within regions) and can isolate the impact of discriminatory trends at each level of the corporate hierarchy.

- **Propensity Score Matching (PSM):** This technique matches similarly situated employees across genders to estimate the treatment effect (e.g., salary, promotion rates) attributable to gender rather than other covariates.

- **Regression Analysis with Fixed Effects:** These models control for variables like job title, tenure, and store location to estimate the residual wage gap or promotion disparity attributable to discrimination.

- **Cluster Analysis:** Used to detect geographic or departmental concentrations of adverse treatment, enabling plaintiffs to argue that discrimination was not random or isolated, but concentrated and systemic.

- **Chow Tests and Oaxaca-Blinder Decompositions:** These methods statistically compare wage structures between demographic groups, identifying the portion of wage differentials unexplained by observable factors.

In practice, post-*Dukes* courts scrutinize these statistical submissions under a "rigorous analysis" standard. District judges, sometimes conducting mini-trials on certification, assess whether the expert's model is methodologically sound, based on representative data, and capable of answering the common question for all putative class members. A single regression across millions of employees may no longer suffice; forensic economists must demonstrate that the chosen methodology captures meaningful intergroup disparities and isolates them from confounding influences.

The economic implications of *Dukes* are profound. The ruling indirectly incentivizes corporations to decentralize employment decisions and document performance metrics in ways that obscure systemic trends. This places a greater burden on plaintiffs and their experts to extract statistical signals from highly noisy datasets. Consequently, the demand for advanced econometric techniques—and for economists who can explain them clearly in litigation contexts—has surged.

Moreover, *Dukes* fundamentally reshaped the procedural posture of employment discrimination suits. Plaintiffs must now frontload their cases with robust statistical analysis, often before discovery has yielded full access to the employer's personnel files. Forensic economists are called to build pre-certification models using limited data, drawing inferences with carefully qualified assumptions and ensuring that their conclusions survive Daubert scrutiny.

While the majority in *Dukes* focused on legal thresholds, the dissent (led by Justice Ginsburg) acknowledged the role of

empirical evidence in shaping class-wide inferences. She
argued that the plaintiffs had made a prima facie case of
commonality by combining statistical disparities with
sociological evidence showing that Wal-Mart's corporate
culture tolerated gender stereotyping. Forensic economists
play a crucial role in this hybrid evidentiary
model—quantifying the scope of harm while contextualizing it
within the firm's organizational structure.

In sum, *Wal-Mart v. Dukes* raised the bar for class
certification in systemic discrimination cases. It also
expanded the forensic economist's role from mere damages
quantifier to gatekeeper of commonality. Economic testimony
is no longer reserved for the merits stage; it is often the
decisive factor in whether a class sees the inside of a
courtroom. As such, the case has become a cornerstone in the
jurisprudence of class action economics, signaling that
precision, methodological integrity, and contextual nuance are
prerequisites for legal redress in the era of data-driven justice.

Comcast Corp. v. Behrend (2013)

The U.S. Supreme Court's decision in *Comcast Corp. v.
Behrend*, 569 U.S. 27 (2013), marked a pivotal shift in how
economic damages models are evaluated at the class
certification stage under Rule 23(b)(3). The case involved
subscribers to Comcast cable services in the Philadelphia
region who alleged antitrust violations stemming from
Comcast's strategy of acquiring competitors and
monopolizing regional cable markets. Plaintiffs advanced four
different theories of antitrust injury, but the district court
accepted only one: that Comcast's conduct deterred the entry

of "overbuilders"—rival cable providers that build competing infrastructure in the same geographic areas—resulting in inflated subscription prices.

However, the plaintiffs' expert economist presented a damages model that did not isolate the effect of this single, court-approved theory. Instead, the model measured aggregate damages resulting from all four original liability theories. The Supreme Court, in a 5–4 decision authored by Justice Scalia, reversed class certification. The majority held that Rule 23(b)(3)'s predominance requirement had not been satisfied because the damages model failed to "measure only those damages attributable to the theory of liability that survived."

Comcast effectively redefined the burden placed on plaintiffs and their economic experts at the class certification stage. Prior to this ruling, many lower courts had interpreted Rule 23 as primarily concerned with the existence of common questions, deferring questions of precise damages quantification until later stages of litigation. After *Comcast*, damages modeling and liability theory must be tightly aligned *ex ante*. The ruling elevates the certification stage to a quasi-merits phase, where rigorous scrutiny under standards akin to *Daubert v. Merrell Dow Pharmaceuticals* becomes common practice.

This jurisprudential pivot has profound implications for forensic economists:

- **Theory-Specific Damage Attribution:** Experts must disaggregate damages across competing liability theories and demonstrate that the model cleanly captures only the harm attributable to the specific legal theory certified by the court. Multi-theory aggregation without differentiation is now fatal to class certification.

- **Structural Consistency Between Law and Economics:** The economic model must be logically and empirically consistent with the legal claim. Courts now require that model specifications—functional forms, variables, assumptions—map directly onto elements of the legal cause of action.

- **Robustness and Confounder Control:** Plaintiffs' experts must control for all potential confounding factors, such as regional price differences, temporal effects, or unrelated market trends. Failure to do so may lead courts to view the model as speculative or overinclusive.

- **Microeconomic Precision:** Forensic economists are increasingly expected to utilize firm-level or consumer-level transaction data, rather than aggregate industry metrics, to validate the magnitude and distribution of damages. Courts now demand granularity and specificity, particularly in large and diverse classes.

- **Sensitivity Testing and Confidence Intervals:** In line with best practices in applied econometrics, modern damages models must incorporate robustness checks, error estimates, and sensitivity testing. These ensure that the model's conclusions remain stable across plausible assumptions or variable transformations.

In practice, *Comcast* has raised the cost, complexity, and
evidentiary burden of class certification in antitrust and
consumer protection litigation. Plaintiffs must now front-load
sophisticated expert analysis—often involving hundreds of
hours of data cleaning, model estimation, and statistical
review—prior to certification. Defendants, in turn, have
increasingly adopted a strategy of attacking expert models
under Rule 23 using both merits-based arguments and
Daubert-style challenges.

The ruling has also catalyzed doctrinal debates in the lower
courts about the role of economic modeling in defining
predominance. Some circuits have narrowly read *Comcast* as
requiring model alignment only when damages questions are
central to liability. Others have applied it broadly, treating
any mismatch between legal theory and economic
methodology as fatal to certification. In both camps, however,
the standard for economic admissibility at the class stage has
markedly increased.

Moreover, *Comcast* emphasizes that economic modeling is no
longer an auxiliary feature of complex litigation, it is often
the central hinge upon which certification turns. As a result,
forensic economists have been thrust into a new quasi-judicial
role: not only must their models be statistically valid, they
must be legally tailored, procedurally compliant, and
persuasively explained. This demands fluency not only in
econometrics, but in the legal philosophy underpinning Rule
23 jurisprudence.

For antitrust litigation especially, the implications of *Comcast*
are significant. Damage models must trace a direct line from

market power or collusion to price elevation, output reduction, or other distortions. Indirect purchaser classes, such as consumers in downstream markets, must demonstrate that alleged price effects traversed complex supply chains without dissipation, distortion, or attenuation. Without precise causal mechanisms validated by data, certification will likely be denied.

One of the practical effects of *Comcast* is the bifurcation of damages theories into "certifiable" and "non-certifiable" categories. Models that rely on average effects, national datasets, or top-down assumptions are now treated with skepticism. Courts increasingly prefer bottom-up models derived from transaction-level data, often customized per subclass or product category.

In summary, *Comcast Corp. v. Behrend* reinforced a fundamental principle at the intersection of law and economics: that precision matters, and that empirical models must be theory-driven, data-grounded, and legally faithful. It transformed the role of forensic economics from backend estimation to frontline gatekeeping, where success or failure at certification hinges on the clarity, integrity, and strategic fit of the damages model. For forensic economists, the lesson is clear, litigation in the post-*Comcast* era demands nothing less than a seamless fusion of econometric sophistication and doctrinal discipline.

Halliburton Co. v. Erica P. John Fund, Inc. (2014)

The Supreme Court's decision in *Halliburton Co. v. Erica P. John Fund, Inc.*, 573 U.S. 258 (2014), reaffirmed the "fraud-on-the-market" presumption established in *Basic Inc. v. Levinson*, 485 U.S. 224 (1988), while simultaneously reshaping its procedural application. This landmark ruling clarified that although plaintiffs in securities fraud cases may invoke a rebuttable presumption of reliance based on the Efficient Markets Hypothesis (EMH), defendants must be afforded the opportunity to rebut this presumption at the class certification stage by showing a lack of "price impact"—i.e., that the alleged misrepresentation did not actually affect the market price of the security.

This holding introduced a significant procedural and evidentiary shift, with broad implications for the use of forensic economics in securities litigation. Historically, the presumption of reliance allowed plaintiffs to bypass the individualized inquiry of whether each investor relied on a misrepresentation, thus facilitating class certification in securities fraud cases. However, by permitting defendants to rebut this presumption with econometric evidence *before* class certification, *Halliburton II* elevated the sophistication required in economic modeling at the threshold stage of litigation.

At the heart of this analysis is the concept of "price impact," which refers to the causal relationship between a public misstatement and the observable price movement of the affected security. Forensic economists now play a pivotal role

in assessing price impact through a variety of advanced tools
and models:

- **Event Studies:** Economists conduct statistically
  rigorous event studies to isolate the market reaction to
  company disclosures, regulatory actions, or corrective
  statements. These studies estimate abnormal returns by
  comparing the actual stock return to an expected return
  generated by a benchmark model, such as the Capital
  Asset Pricing Model (CAPM) or the Fama-French
  Three-Factor Model.

- **Regression Analysis with Control Variables:**
  Rebuttal analyses often include multivariate regressions
  that control for confounding variables such as
  industry-wide news, macroeconomic announcements, or
  contemporaneous disclosures unrelated to the alleged
  fraud.

- **Trading Volume and Volatility Tests:** Economists
  may analyze whether alleged misstatements coincide
  with spikes in trading volume or unusual return
  volatility, which may corroborate or undermine claims of
  market significance.

- **Market Efficiency Diagnostics:** To assess whether
  the fraud-on-the-market doctrine applies, economists
  evaluate market efficiency by examining bid-ask spreads,
  analyst coverage, trading frequency, and autocorrelation
  in returns.

- **Corrective Disclosure Testing:** In addition to
  examining initial misstatements, economists are often

tasked with analyzing whether subsequent corrective
disclosures led to statistically significant negative
returns, thereby establishing the causal link between the
fraud and the loss.

Halliburton II thus deepened the role of empirical economics
in securities law by demanding rigorous, data-driven proof not
merely of misstatements and scienter, but of their actual
influence on security prices. The ruling reemphasized that
Rule 23's predominance requirement cannot be satisfied by
legal theory alone—it must be substantiated with quantitative
evidence capable of surviving adversarial scrutiny.

In practical terms, the decision has had several transformative
effects on securities litigation strategy:

1. **Early Battle of Experts:** Plaintiffs and defendants
   now routinely submit dueling expert reports during
   certification briefing. Courts must resolve complex
   disputes over statistical methods, confidence intervals,
   and empirical validity at an earlier stage than ever
   before.

2. **Strategic Use of Public Disclosures:** Defense
   counsel increasingly scrutinize public disclosure histories
   to argue that other news—not the
   misrepresentation—caused the price movement.
   Plaintiffs, conversely, must carefully frame corrective
   disclosures to show a direct causal impact.

3. **Increased Costs at Certification Stage:** The need
   for detailed econometric modeling, data acquisition, and
   expert deposition has elevated the cost of class action

litigation even before discovery on the merits begins.

4. **Disparate Circuit Interpretations:** Post-*Halliburton II*, lower courts have developed differing standards for evaluating price impact. Some circuits allow modest price movement as sufficient, while others demand statistically significant shifts or corroborating economic logic.

5. **Impact on Settlement Dynamics:** Because successful rebuttal of price impact can torpedo certification, defendants now have greater leverage in early settlement negotiations. Plaintiffs must balance the risk of pre-certification dismissal with the high cost of statistical proof.

Moreover, *Halliburton II* reopens broader philosophical debates about the assumptions underlying market efficiency. While the fraud-on-the-market doctrine is grounded in the notion that securities markets rapidly absorb all material information, critics note that not all stocks trade in perfectly efficient markets. Thinly traded or illiquid securities, penny stocks, or securities on foreign exchanges may not exhibit price responsiveness sufficient to support the presumption of reliance. As a result, courts may apply different standards of scrutiny depending on market context, further complicating the forensic economist's role.

The ruling also reveals a tension between legal pragmatism and economic theory. While the Supreme Court reaffirmed the doctrinal utility of Basic's presumption, it simultaneously constrained its application with heightened evidentiary rigor. In doing so, it elevated the importance of expert economic testimony from a supporting actor to a lead protagonist in the class certification drama.

In the years since the decision, courts have expanded their use of Bayesian modeling, Monte Carlo simulations, and high-frequency trading data to evaluate price impact claims. New litigation technologies, such as AI-driven sentiment analysis of disclosures and real-time news impact modeling, are beginning to supplement traditional methods. As the landscape evolves, forensic economists must continue to adapt, blending classical finance theory with emerging empirical tools to meet the ever-increasing demands of judicial scrutiny.

Ultimately, *Halliburton Co. v. Erica P. John Fund, Inc.* illustrates the fusion of doctrinal evolution with economic sophistication. It demands that courts, attorneys, and economists speak a common empirical language when adjudicating securities fraud. In this way, it exemplifies the modern convergence of law and econometrics—where the fate of class actions increasingly hinges on statistical rigor, economic logic, and market realism.

Kumho Tire Co. v. Carmichael (1999)

In *Kumho Tire Co. v. Carmichael*, 526 U.S. 137 (1999), the United States Supreme Court extended the principles established in *Daubert v. Merrell Dow Pharmaceuticals, Inc.*, 509 U.S. 579 (1993), to all forms of expert testimony—not just scientific experts, but also those whose expertise is grounded in technical skill, experience, or other specialized knowledge. The case arose from a tire blowout that allegedly caused a fatal automobile accident. The plaintiffs' expert, a tire failure analyst, based his opinion on visual inspection and comparative observations. The district court excluded the testimony under *Daubert*, concluding it lacked methodological rigor, and the Eleventh Circuit reversed. The Supreme Court, however, reinstated the district court's decision, emphasizing that the gatekeeping function of the trial judge under Rule 702 of the Federal Rules of Evidence applies universally to all expert testimony, regardless of discipline.

This clarification had a seismic effect on the admissibility of expert economic testimony in civil litigation. Although *Kumho* did not involve forensic economists per se, its holding unmistakably applies to economic experts who rely on applied statistics, econometric modeling, or financial theory to estimate damages or causation. The Court underscored that the trial judge must assess not only the qualifications of the expert but also the reliability and relevance of the methodology as applied to the facts of the case. This expanded the trial court's role from a procedural referee to an empirical gatekeeper.

The decision affirmed that no distinction exists between "scientific knowledge" and "technical or other specialized knowledge" when it comes to evidentiary scrutiny. As Justice Breyer wrote, "the objective of the gatekeeping requirement is to ensure the reliability and relevance of expert testimony." Thus, economists offering testimony in areas such as lost profits, antitrust damages, class certification, or labor economics must now meet a rigorous burden of demonstrating methodological soundness.

Key implications of *Kumho* for forensic economists include:

- **Empirical Validation:** Economists must show that the models and methods they use have been subjected to peer review, exhibit known error rates, and are generally accepted in the relevant professional community. This includes common tools such as regression analysis, Monte Carlo simulations, time-series forecasting, or hedonic pricing models.

- **Fit to the Facts:** Courts will scrutinize whether the method is appropriately applied to the specific data and facts of the case. An economic model that is theoretically sound but ill-matched to the evidentiary record may be excluded under *Kumho*.

- **Disclosure of Assumptions:** Experts must clearly articulate all assumptions, identify data limitations, and demonstrate that their conclusions do not rest on speculative or untestable premises. This transparency requirement aims to prevent the overreach of expert authority cloaked in technical jargon.

- **Cross-Disciplinary Challenges:** Economists often rely on data generated by engineers, medical professionals, or social scientists. Under *Kumho*, they must critically evaluate the provenance and reliability of such inputs, lest their own analysis be tainted by upstream methodological flaws.

- **Judicial Empowerment:** Trial judges are now explicitly authorized—and in fact required—to engage with technical economic issues, often leading to pretrial *Daubert* hearings where the validity of regression coefficients, sensitivity analysis, or control variable selection is debated in detail.

Since *Kumho*, lower courts have developed increasingly nuanced frameworks for evaluating economic evidence. For instance, in antitrust class actions, expert opinions involving common impact analysis and market structure modeling are now routinely challenged under *Daubert/Kumho* principles. In employment discrimination cases, economists' use of statistical disparities must be accompanied by methodologically rigorous explanations that account for sample size, standard deviation thresholds, and explanatory variables.

Moreover, the decision incentivized lawyers to adopt greater sophistication when presenting or challenging economic experts. It is no longer sufficient to claim that a method is "commonly used" or "generally accepted." Litigants must articulate how that method was implemented, why it is suitable to the facts, and how its limitations were addressed.

Judicial decisions post-*Kumho* have built upon its reasoning. Courts now commonly ask:

- Were alternative economic methods considered and reasonably rejected?

- Is the data used in the model representative, reliable, and complete?

- Are the results robust across sensitivity tests and assumptions?

- Has the expert conducted diagnostic checks (e.g., R-squared, multicollinearity tests, residual plots) to assess model validity?

- Would the expert's conclusions hold under adversarial
  replication?

The broader legacy of *Kumho Tire* is a judicial culture
increasingly attuned to empirical nuance. Forensic economists,
as experts situated at the intersection of law, markets, and
quantitative reasoning, must embrace not only technical
excellence but also procedural transparency. They must be
able to teach, defend, and refine their models under
adversarial conditions—just as they would in peer-reviewed
academic settings.

Ultimately, *Kumho Tire* reaffirmed that expertise must be
earned, tested, and demonstrated—not assumed. It elevated
the role of the trial judge as curator of truth and gave
economic testimony a higher evidentiary hurdle to clear. In
doing so, it protected the integrity of litigation against the
risk of what Justice Breyer termed "conjecture masquerading
as science."

Broader Impacts on Litigation

The evolving landscape of Supreme Court
jurisprudence—particularly through landmark decisions such
as *Wal-Mart v. Dukes, Comcast v. Behrend, Halliburton v.
Erica P. John Fund*, and *Kumho Tire v. Carmichael*—has
dramatically reshaped the expectations placed on forensic
economic experts. Their role has evolved from back-end
quantifiers of damages to front-line architects of legal strategy,
responsible for constructing models that drive core questions
of liability, certification, and admissibility.

1. Enhanced Credibility Standards and the Rise of Empirical Rigor

Federal courts now demand a level of analytical precision from economic experts that rivals academic publishing standards. It is no longer sufficient to offer conclusions that appear reasonable on their face. Courts require that:

- All assumptions be articulated and grounded in the factual record;

- Sensitivity analysis demonstrate the robustness of conclusions to changes in model structure or variable inclusion;

- Methodologies conform with peer-reviewed economic literature and industry standards;

- Confounding factors be identified and either controlled for or acknowledged with transparency;

- Models exhibit replicability, which allows opposing experts and courts to reconstruct and evaluate the results.

This shift has encouraged the emergence of what might be called "litigation econometrics"—an applied subfield where academic rigor intersects with legal plausibility.

2. Legal-Theory Alignment and Evidentiary Fit

Post-*Comcast*, courts scrutinize whether an economic expert's model aligns tightly with the surviving legal theory of the case. In antitrust litigation, for instance, plaintiffs may advance multiple theories (e.g., price-fixing, exclusionary conduct, bundling), but only one may withstand summary judgment. If the economist's model calculates aggregate damages without isolating those attributable solely to the viable claim, the court may decertify the class or exclude the model entirely.

The "fit" requirement also impacts causation modeling in employment discrimination cases, wage-and-hour class actions, and product liability suits. Forensic economists must:

- Build econometric models with explanatory variables that directly relate to legal causation;

- Avoid attributing damages to conduct no longer part of the case;

- Maintain clear variable definitions and causal pathways;

- Link economic results to specific legal standards (e.g., market definition in antitrust, willfulness in FLSA).

This evolution has pushed legal teams to work more closely with experts during early motion practice to ensure evidentiary compatibility.

3. Early Engagement of Experts in Case Strategy

The procedural sequence of litigation has been altered. Whereas experts once entered the fray at the damages stage, they are now engaged much earlier—sometimes during pre-suit investigation or initial complaint drafting. Their early contributions include:

- Evaluating class-wide impact or reliance in consumer fraud and securities cases;

- Assessing commonality under Rule 23(a)(2) and

predominance under Rule 23(b)(3);

- Identifying data availability and gaps in corporate record-keeping;

- Advising on the scope and format of discovery requests, especially regarding transactional data.

In some jurisdictions, economists assist with class certification declarations as early as the motion for preliminary injunction, helping shape the narrative about how alleged harms manifest across a putative class.

4. Greater Defensibility and the Culture of Rebuttal

The adversarial environment surrounding economic testimony has intensified. Rebuttal experts are not only commonplace—they are often decisive. Courts increasingly favor side-by-side methodological comparisons, weighing:

- Competing damage estimates derived from alternative assumptions;

- Strength of model diagnostics and sensitivity checks;

- Transparency of computational steps;

- Use of proprietary versus public data;

- Mathematical robustness and logical consistency.

Furthermore, litigants are increasingly filing detailed *Daubert* motions that critique expert testimony on grounds such as omitted variable bias, statistical insignificance, improper extrapolation, or flawed proxy variable selection. As a result, economic experts must be both substantively skilled and rhetorically effective, capable of defending their model in live testimony and written declaration alike.

5. Broader Cultural and Strategic Shifts in Litigation

These doctrinal and procedural changes have contributed to broader shifts in the culture of litigation:

- **Strategic bifurcation of damages and liability:** Litigants increasingly bifurcate liability and damages phases, especially in complex antitrust and securities fraud cases, to isolate economic testimony and increase control over evidentiary scope.

- **Judicial comfort with technical material:** Courts have developed a growing tolerance—if not fluency—for technical economic evidence. Judges regularly engage with regression outputs, p-values, R-squared metrics, and confidence intervals in their written opinions.

- **Cost escalation:** The need for high-caliber economic experts—especially those who publish, teach, or testify frequently—has driven up litigation costs and led to a growing premium on "big-name" academic experts from elite institutions.

- **Technology integration:** Advanced statistical tools such as Python-based modeling, machine learning classification algorithms, and AI-driven document clustering are increasingly used in forensic economic practice, raising novel questions about admissibility and explainability.

6. Future-Proofing Expert Testimony: Challenges and Opportunities

As courts continue to push for greater evidentiary rigor and transparency, forensic economists face both challenges and opportunities. Future trends may include:

- **Greater use of open-source modeling:** Courts and litigants may prefer statistical models built on transparent, reproducible platforms like R or Python over black-box proprietary software.

- **Standardization of methodologies:** Particularly in class action contexts, judges may seek greater uniformity in how loss causation or common impact is demonstrated.

- **Evidentiary audits:** In high-stakes litigation, courts may appoint special masters or third-party auditors to review and validate expert computations.

- **Ethical scrutiny:** As litigation becomes more data-driven, economists may face ethical questions about selection bias, confirmatory modeling, and the manipulation of assumptions to serve adversarial goals.

The forensic economist of the modern era must be more than a statistician. They are expected to be a legal theorist, a data scientist, a policy analyst, and a compelling communicator. Supreme Court precedent has made clear: the path to admissibility and influence is paved with transparency, rigor, and evidentiary humility.

Conclusion

The *Kelly–Frye* standard remains a cornerstone of admissibility analysis in jurisdictions that prioritize consensus and professional rigor. In forensic psychiatry and psychology, its emphasis on scientific validity, expert qualification, and procedural integrity continues to shape how courts evaluate and gatekeep expert testimony. This enduring framework ensures that complex and potentially persuasive psychological testimony is only admitted when it meets well-defined standards of reliability and scientific legitimacy.

10.11   Conclusion

Causation is not merely a threshold to be crossed; it is the bridge between injury and redress, between the chaos of misfortune and the order of legal remedy. This chapter has traversed the nuanced terrain where law and economics converge, where burdens of proof are borne not only by plaintiffs and attorneys, but also by the silent scaffolding of data, logic, and expert analysis. In this realm, truth must be distilled from probability, and justice must be expressed in the language of numbers. The forensic economist stands here as both cartographer and witness, mapping out the contours of loss while respecting the boundary stones of admissibility, foreseeability, and causation.

Yet even the most precise models of loss are incomplete without a reckoning with time. The law does not merely ask what was lost, but when. For in every valuation lies a quiet question: how much is a dollar tomorrow worth today? It is

to this temporal alchemy, to the art and science of
discounting future harm to present value, that we now turn.
In the next chapter, we shall pass through the veil of
causation and into the fourth dimension of damages: the
inexorable, invisible weight of time.

Table 10.1: Comparison of Tort and Contract Law in Forensic
Economic Context

Legal Element	Tort Law	Contract Law
Nature of Wrong	Civil wrong arising from breach of duty (e.g., negligence, intentional harm)	Breach of a legally binding agreement between parties
Purpose of Damages	Compensate for injury or loss and restore to pre-injury status	Place injured party in position as if contract had been performed
Common Economic Damages	Lost earnings, fringe benefits, medical expenses, household services, life care costs	Lost profits, reliance damages, consequential losses, business interruption
Causation Standard	Must establish duty, breach, cause-in-fact, and proximate cause	Must show breach caused foreseeable financial harm
Mitigation Requirement	Plaintiff must attempt to return to work or reduce losses where possible	Plaintiff must avoid incurring unnecessary or avoidable losses
Punitive Damages	May be awarded in cases of gross negligence or intentional misconduct (varies by state)	Rarely available; generally limited to compensatory recovery
Common Forensic Roles	Valuation of injury-related economic losses, future care, wrongful death support	Calculation of lost business value, contract price vs. market value, economic expectancy
Admissibility Challenges	Emphasis on causation, future loss projections, pre-existing conditions	Emphasis on certainty of loss, historical earnings, and foreseeability

Chapter 11

Time Value of Money

11.1   The Time Value of Money

Conceptual Foundation

The **time value of money** (TVM) is a cornerstone concept in finance, economics, and forensic valuation. It encapsulates the principle that a sum of money has more value today than it does in the future, even if the numerical amount remains unchanged. This foundational idea arises from the recognition that money available in the present can be invested or utilized to generate additional value—through interest accumulation, capital gains, reinvestment in productive assets, or the mitigation of liabilities. Therefore, money today carries a potential utility beyond its face value, giving rise to the core logic of TVM.

To understand this principle deeply, consider three interlocking factors that justify why a dollar today is worth more than a dollar tomorrow:

1. **Opportunity Cost:** Money held today can be invested to earn returns. The foregone return from not having access to money is the opportunity cost, which forms the analytical basis for discounting future cash flows.

2. **Inflation and Purchasing Power:** Over time, inflation erodes the purchasing power of money. A dollar today will likely buy more goods and services than a dollar received years later. This devaluation must be factored into any serious economic projection or damage model.

3. **Risk and Uncertainty:** The future is inherently uncertain. Even contractual obligations carry enforcement risk, default probabilities, or delay potential. Present money is free of that future risk.

The TVM concept is typically formalized through two dual mathematical operations: *compounding* and *discounting*.

- **Compounding** calculates the future value (FV) of a present amount using a defined interest rate over a specific time period. For example:

$$FV = PV \times (1 + r)^n$$

  where PV is the present value, r is the interest rate, and n is the number of compounding periods.

- **Discounting** is the inverse—calculating the present value (PV) of a future amount. This operation is

essential in forensic economics, where future lost
earnings, medical expenses, or annuities must be valued
today. The general formula is:

$$PV = \frac{FV}{(1+r)^n}$$

In the legal context—particularly in tort, contract, and
employment litigation—the time value of money informs a
wide range of forensic calculations, such as:

- Valuation of lost wages or earnings over time.

- Calculation of the present value of pension streams or
  annuities.

- Discounting future medical expenses or life care costs to
  the present.

- Adjusting damage awards to reflect inflation or real
  interest rates.

Courts, especially in cases involving structured settlements or
long-term damage horizons, require forensic economists to
perform TVM-based modeling to present reliable, actuarially
sound estimates. Failure to account for TVM can lead to
either overcompensation (by awarding future values as if they
were present) or undercompensation (by failing to incorporate
appropriate growth or inflation assumptions).

Another important application involves distinguishing
between *nominal* and *real* rates of return. Nominal rates
reflect actual dollars, while real rates remove the effect of
inflation, providing a truer measure of purchasing power over

time. Forensic economists must clearly disclose which rate is being used, particularly when working in jurisdictions or cases where inflation is volatile or uncertain.

Example: Suppose an individual is awarded $1,000,000 in damages for future medical care to be used over the next 25 years. A forensic economist might model these costs annually, apply an appropriate inflation index to forecast nominal costs, and then discount each year's projected cost back to present value using a suitable real discount rate. The resulting sum represents the fair award today that reflects both economic loss and the principles of efficient compensation.

In summary, the time value of money serves as the analytical backbone of financial reasoning in litigation. It is a lens through which fairness, accuracy, and economic rationality are brought into the valuation of legal damages. Without it, damage estimates risk being either speculative or economically unsound. Properly applied, TVM ensures that damage awards neither overcompensate nor undercompensate claimants, but rather anchor the legal remedy in rigorous economic reasoning.

Why Money Loses Value Over Time

Understanding why money becomes less valuable over time is fundamental to the concept of the time value of money. Four key drivers—**inflation, interest rates, risk and uncertainty**, and **consumption preference**—collectively shape the declining real worth of currency held over long periods. These dynamics are interwoven into economic theory, legal compensation models, and individual decision-making processes.

1. **Inflation: The Erosion of Purchasing Power**

   Inflation is the most immediate and visible reason
   money loses value. Defined as a general increase in
   prices across an economy, inflation reduces the amount
   of goods and services that a unit of currency can
   purchase. For example, if the annual inflation rate is
   3%, a product that costs $100 today will cost $103 a
   year from now. Thus, $100 saved today would only buy
   97% of what it could previously afford.

   Inflation is tracked using indices such as the Consumer
   Price Index (CPI) or the Producer Price Index (PPI),
   which measure average changes in price levels across
   broad baskets of goods and services. Persistent inflation
   forces both consumers and investors to recalibrate
   expectations. Forensic economists frequently use
   historical CPI data or projected inflation curves when
   modeling future damages in litigation.

   In long-term legal settlements—such as structured
   payments for medical care, pensions, or
   annuities—ignoring inflation can result in substantial
   undercompensation. Conversely, overestimating inflation
   in discounting future values can lead to unjust
   enrichment.

2. **Interest Rates: The Opportunity to Grow
   Wealth**

   Money today can be invested to yield returns, which
   reflects its opportunity cost. This is the central insight

behind the time value of money. If a person deposits
$1,000 in a savings account earning 5% interest, after
one year they will have $1,050. This ability to earn a
return means that money held today is more valuable
than the same amount in the future.

Interest rates serve as the economy's price of time. They
reflect both the reward for saving and the cost of
borrowing. Central banks like the Federal Reserve
adjust benchmark rates to influence borrowing,
spending, and investment. Higher interest rates increase
the incentive to receive money sooner, while lower rates
reduce the opportunity cost of delay.

Forensic economists must carefully select appropriate
discount rates that reflect the prevailing risk-free rate or
relevant investment alternatives. These rates often come
from government bond yields, corporate borrowing rates,
or expert consensus benchmarks.

3. **Risk and Uncertainty: The Volatility of Future
   Payment**

The future is inherently uncertain. Any promise of
future payment involves counterparty risk: the chance
that the payer defaults, delays, or fails to fulfill their
obligation. Even a seemingly safe contract is subject to
externalities such as bankruptcy, inflation shocks,
recession, legal disputes, or macroeconomic crises.

This risk premium must be factored into present value
calculations. The more uncertain a future payment, the
less valuable it becomes today. Courts often weigh the

reliability of promised future earnings when calculating damages, especially in wrongful death cases, long-term disability awards, or projected business income loss.

Additionally, litigation itself introduces uncertainty. Future cash flows tied to the outcome of an appeal, settlement, or collection procedure are discounted heavily. A forensic economist adjusts for this by embedding a risk premium in the discount rate or by using probabilistic weighting across various legal outcomes.

4. **Consumption Preference: Behavioral Time Bias**

Human behavior also plays a significant role in why money is valued more in the present. This is known in behavioral economics as "present bias"—a tendency to favor immediate gratification over delayed rewards. Given the choice, most individuals will prefer to spend money now rather than wait for a larger payoff later.

This preference is rooted in evolutionary psychology, scarcity avoidance, and subjective utility. It is also influenced by factors such as liquidity needs, health, age, and cultural values. For example, a retiree may value $10,000 today more than $15,000 spread over the next ten years due to immediate consumption needs or reduced life expectancy.

Legal systems recognize this phenomenon when compensating victims. Lump-sum settlements are often preferred over long-term installment payments because they align more closely with consumption preferences

and allow claimants to address pressing medical,
housing, or educational expenses.

Forensic economists sometimes use utility-adjusted
discounting to account for consumption bias in damage
valuation. This ensures that the present value figure
truly reflects the subjective value to the claimant.

Together, these four factors explain why the same nominal
sum holds less real-world power as time progresses. Whether
evaluating long-term contractual obligations, future wage
losses, or recurring medical expenses, the legal system relies
on these economic truths to ensure that compensation is fair,
proportional, and economically grounded. Accurate
application of these principles by forensic experts ensures the
integrity of financial testimony and the equitable dispensation
of justice.

Legal and Economic Relevance

The **time value of money (TVM)** is not a theoretical
abstraction—it is a powerful, practical framework embedded
in the architecture of modern legal and economic systems.
TVM governs how courts, lawyers, economists, businesses,
and governments evaluate the value of cash flows that occur
across time. It is central to nearly every domain in forensic
economics and legal damages analysis, particularly in the
pursuit of fair, proportional, and economically sound remedies.

- **Litigation and Damages: Valuing Losses in
  Today's Terms**

  In nearly all civil litigation involving future monetary

harm, courts rely on TVM to discount projected damages to their *present value*. This is especially critical in:

- *Wrongful death or injury* cases, where lifetime lost wages and future medical costs must be valued today.

- *Employment discrimination* claims involving back pay or front pay.

- *Breach of contract* cases, where promised payments were expected years into the future.

The failure to apply proper discounting can lead to either overcompensation or undercompensation, both of which raise concerns about equity and proportionality. Courts expect forensic economists to select appropriate discount rates that reflect market interest rates, inflation expectations, risk profiles, and the unique context of the case.

In some jurisdictions, statutory guidance provides rules on how future damages must be discounted. For example, the Florida Standard Jury Instructions specify how jurors should treat discounting in personal injury cases, while federal courts often look to expert economic evidence in diversity and class action litigation.

- **Settlement Structuring: Comparing Periodic and Lump-Sum Awards**

  Structured settlements offer periodic future payments instead of a one-time lump sum. Common in tort litigation, especially in cases involving minors, medical malpractice, and long-term disability, these arrangements aim to ensure ongoing financial support.

However, determining whether a structured settlement is *equivalent* or *superior* to a lump-sum payout requires TVM analysis. The lump sum represents the *present value* of all future payments, discounted at an appropriate rate to reflect inflation, investment opportunity, and risk. Forensic economists and settlement consultants often use present value calculators or annuity modeling software to compare options.

Plaintiffs' attorneys must understand these concepts to advocate effectively for fair deals, and defense counsel must evaluate the long-term financial exposure. Judges may also scrutinize structured settlement offers under fairness reviews, particularly when minors or incapacitated parties are involved.

- **Contract Negotiations: Interpreting Cash Flow Timing in Law**

  Legal contracts frequently involve obligations that span years or decades. Examples include:

  - Commercial leases with escalating rent schedules.

  - Equipment purchase agreements with deferred payment terms.

  - Long-term loan agreements and bond indentures.

  - Royalties in licensing agreements or publishing

deals.

TVM allows lawyers to determine the *real economic value* of future cash flows. For instance, an attorney negotiating a software licensing contract may use TVM to assess the net present value (NPV) of three-year payment terms, comparing them to competing proposals.

In litigation over contract breaches, TVM is used to measure the value of lost profits, liquidated damages, or rescission alternatives. Courts often admit expert testimony to interpret the monetary impact of delayed performance or early termination.

- **Business Valuation and Corporate Finance: The DCF Method**

  In the realm of mergers and acquisitions (M&A), shareholder litigation, bankruptcy, and estate disputes, business valuation becomes essential. The dominant methodology for valuing a company or project is the *Discounted Cash Flow* (DCF) model, which is grounded in TVM.

  DCF valuation involves forecasting a company's future cash flows and discounting them back to present value using a discount rate that reflects the firm's cost of capital or risk profile. Key TVM concepts in DCF include:

  - The *Weighted Average Cost of Capital (WACC)* as a discount rate.

- Forecasting free cash flow to the firm (FCFF) or to equity (FCFE).

- Terminal value estimation based on Gordon Growth Model or exit multiples.

Attorneys representing buyers, sellers, or shareholders must understand these calculations to challenge or defend valuation reports. Delaware Chancery Court opinions in appraisal actions—such as *Dell, Inc. v. Magnetar Global Event Driven Master Fund Ltd.*—have shaped national standards for acceptable discounting and forecasting practices.

- **Tort Reform and Legislative Policy: Discounting in Statutes**

In legislative policy, TVM is reflected in statutes that require or prohibit the discounting of damages. Some jurisdictions mandate that damages be discounted using a specified statutory rate, while others leave the decision to judicial discretion. For example, the Federal Tort Claims Act (FTCA) and many state laws instruct courts on how to treat inflation and discount rates when determining economic damages.

Legislators and legal reform advocates often debate the selection of discount rates. Using a high discount rate favors defendants by lowering the present value of future liabilities. A low rate, in contrast, increases plaintiff recovery. Forensic economists sometimes testify in legislative hearings or draft policy briefs concerning the real-world effects of different discounting rules.

- **Class Action Settlements and Claims
  Distribution: Present Value Calculations at Scale**

  In class action litigation—especially cases involving
  antitrust violations, wage-and-hour claims, or mass
  torts—TVM is used to allocate funds from settlement
  pools. Courts, claims administrators, and special
  masters must:

    - Discount delayed distributions to reflect their
      reduced present value.

    - Adjust for inflation in long-term injury or pension
      claims.

    - Ensure equitable compensation across claimants
      with different timing profiles.

  In such cases, forensic economists are often asked to
  simulate different payout schedules or test the
  sensitivity of present value assumptions under
  alternative interest rate scenarios. These simulations
  form the basis of judicial findings about fairness,
  adequacy, and reasonableness under Rule 23(e).

In sum, the legal system consistently relies on the time value
of money to deliver economic justice. It ensures that awards
reflect both the reality of financial markets and the principles
of proportionality and equity. Whether in individual tort
claims, large-scale corporate transactions, or courtroom
damage models, TVM functions as a critical bridge between
economics and law—a shared language for understanding
value across time.

Core Principles

The concept of the time value of money (TVM) is
foundational to both economic theory and financial
jurisprudence. It stems from the intuitive and empirically
validated notion that a sum of money available in the present
is worth more than the same amount in the future, due to its
potential earning capacity and the inherent risks of time delay.
This principle supports modern economic planning,
investment analysis, and judicial damage valuation.

Several interrelated concepts constitute the core machinery of
TVM:

- **Future Value (FV):** Future value refers to the amount
  a current investment will grow to over a specified period
  at a given interest rate. The FV concept is central to
  forward-looking decision-making and strategic financial
  planning. It captures the cumulative growth resulting
  from reinvested interest or returns and is pivotal in
  modeling retirement funds, annuities, and expected
  returns in court-mandated settlements.

  Mathematically, future value is calculated as:

  $$FV = PV \times (1 + r)^n$$

  where PV is the present value, r is the rate of return,
  and n is the number of periods. This formula underpins
  everything from structured settlement growth to delayed
  compensation assessments in wrongful death cases.

- **Present Value (PV):** Present value reflects how much
  a future amount of money is worth today, adjusted for a

discount rate. Courts use PV to reduce future damage estimates to a single compensable sum, ensuring that awards today are economically equivalent to future harms. This technique prevents overcompensation or undercompensation in long-term harm or benefit cases.

The basic PV formula is:

$$PV = \frac{FV}{(1+r)^n}$$

This function is indispensable in civil litigation, particularly in personal injury, employment law, and class action settlements involving long-term payout structures.

- **Discounting:** Discounting is the process of translating future cash flows into present value equivalents. Legal professionals rely on discounting to assess the economic cost of deferred payments, such as pensions, lease obligations, and damages from contract breaches. A proper discounting framework requires selection of an appropriate discount rate, often reflecting the risk-free rate or adjusted market return for similar investments.

- **Compounding:** Compounding refers to the phenomenon where interest earns interest over successive periods, leading to exponential growth of capital. In the legal context, compound interest may be awarded in bad-faith insurance cases or long-running fiduciary breaches to account for the opportunity cost of withheld funds.

The standard compound interest formula is:

$$A = P \left(1 + \frac{r}{n} \right)^{nt}$$

where A is the amount accumulated, P is the principal, r is the interest rate, n is the compounding frequency, and t is the number of years. Compounding is essential in trust accounting, investment disputes, and evaluating the time-weighted value of obligations over decades.

Each of these principles is not merely abstract theory—they shape tangible legal outcomes. Whether evaluating lost earnings in a wrongful termination case, forecasting the financial implications of delayed payments in class actions, or constructing expert testimony in complex financial disputes, the TVM core principles serve as indispensable tools. The law, in recognizing the real-world effects of money across time, relies on these principles to ensure that economic justice is neither delayed nor distorted by temporal shifts in value.

Practical Example: Choosing Between Settlements

Consider the following legal scenario: A plaintiff is offered a choice between two settlement options in a civil lawsuit:

1. **Option A:** Receive $500,000 today as a lump sum.

2. **Option B:** Receive $700,000 in five years.

On its face, Option B appears more generous—offering an additional $200,000. However, the time value of money dictates that a dollar received today is not equivalent to a dollar received in the future. To evaluate the two choices, we must convert Option B's future value into today's dollars using the present value formula:

$$PV = \frac{FV}{(1+r)^n}$$

Assuming a discount rate of 6%, the present value of Option B is:

$$PV = \frac{700,000}{(1+0.06)^5} = \frac{700,000}{1.3382} \approx 523,080.72$$

Interpretation: Option B, when discounted, has a present value of approximately $523,081. This exceeds the $500,000 lump sum offered today. Thus, based purely on financial logic and assuming the plaintiff can wait and will receive the payment as promised, Option B is superior.

But wait—other considerations matter:

- **Risk of Default:** If there is any uncertainty about the defendant's ability or willingness to pay after five years, Option A may be safer.

- **Liquidity Needs:** If the plaintiff requires immediate funds for medical treatment, relocation, or debt repayment, the immediate cash of Option A may outweigh the higher long-term value of Option B.

- **Tax Implications:** Depending on how the settlement is structured, taxes may apply differently to lump sums versus structured payments.

- **Personal Investment Strategy:** If the plaintiff can invest the $500,000 and generate returns exceeding 6%, Option A could ultimately outperform Option B financially.

This practical example demonstrates how the time value of money is not just a theoretical construct—it is central to real-world legal decision-making. Plaintiffs, attorneys, judges, and mediators must all consider financial modeling to ensure equitable outcomes. Courts often request expert economic testimony to validate the fairness of settlement structures. Forensic economists employ these calculations routinely to advise clients on long-term implications of accepting or rejecting delayed compensation.

Broader Application: This kind of analysis extends well beyond tort settlements. The same principle applies when comparing:

- Installment-based breach-of-contract remedies vs. accelerated damages.

- Pension plans with annuity options vs. lump sum distributions.

- Periodic lease payments versus up-front buyouts in commercial real estate.

Every such decision implicates the time value of money and calls for precision. In complex litigation, opposing experts may battle over the correct discount rate, expected inflation, or projected investment returns. The assumptions embedded in these models can swing damages valuations by millions of dollars.

Ultimately, the TVM framework helps the legal system transform abstract future rights into present-day realities, quantifying justice in terms courts can calculate—and litigants can understand.

Lump Sum vs. Annuity: Strategic Choices for Lottery Winners

Winning the lottery presents recipients with a life-altering financial choice: **receive a lump sum payout now or an annuity paid out over multiple years**. Each option carries distinct advantages, risks, and growth opportunities depending on the individual's goals, risk tolerance, and investment acumen. This decision is more than just about math—it is about legacy, freedom, discipline, and risk governance.

Lump Sum Payout Strategy

With a lump sum, the recipient gains immediate access to a large capital base. While this option may result in a smaller total nominal payout due to discounting by the lottery commission and taxes, it offers unmatched flexibility and the potential for accelerated wealth creation through compounding returns, portfolio optimization, and alternative investments.

Example: A $100 million jackpot offers a $55 million lump sum after taxes and fees. Here's how that sum could be strategically grown across various investment avenues:

1. **Investment in a Closed Corporation (Private Equity):** The winner could purchase a controlling interest in a high-growth private company—such as a regional logistics firm, fintech platform, or biotech startup. By providing capital for expansion and taking an active governance role, returns in excess of 25–30% annually may be achievable. Over 5 years:

$$FV = 55,000,000 \times (1 + 0.30)^5 \approx 204,090,015$$

   The advantage here is the potential to influence strategy directly and benefit from operational scaling, often overlooked by public markets.

2. **Diversified Stock Market Portfolio:** A traditional strategy might involve a globally diversified portfolio with allocations across U.S. equities, international markets, and fixed-income assets. Managed using dollar-cost averaging and risk-adjusted indexing, assuming a conservative 9% annual return:

$$FV = 55,000,000 \times (1 + 0.09)^{10} \approx 130,093,879$$

   With professional wealth management and low-fee ETFs, this method balances growth with liquidity.

3. **Speculative Assets – Cryptocurrency and Commodities:** Allocating a modest portion (e.g., 10–15%) of the lump sum to high-volatility assets like Ethereum, Bitcoin, lithium, uranium, or carbon credits could generate asymmetric returns. If a $5 million investment in crypto grows 20x during a bull market:

$$5,000,000 \times 20 = 100,000,000$$

This strategy requires sharp entry/exit timing and high tolerance for volatility, but may yield exponential growth.

4. **Alternative Yield Investments:** The winner could allocate $10 million to alternative investments such as peer-to-peer lending, invoice factoring, music royalties, or litigation finance. With proper risk controls, yields of 12–15% are plausible, especially when backed by assets or secured legal claims.

5. **Angel Network Formation:** By starting or joining a syndicate of angel investors, the winner can support early-stage innovation and tap into equity upside, often with low entry points and preferential terms via convertible notes or SAFE agreements.

Annuity Option Strategy

Annuities provide a steady income stream over time—e.g., $3.3 million per year for 30 years in the case of a $100 million jackpot. While this guards against impulsive financial decisions and ensures long-term liquidity, inflation and currency devaluation may erode purchasing power unless strategic action is taken. However, the annual disbursement still offers multiple paths for intelligent compounding and generational planning.

Three advanced strategies to grow annuity-based wealth:

1. **Layered Investment Allocation:** Each year's payout can be divided into risk-based tiers to mitigate volatility:

- 50% into inflation-protected U.S. Treasury bonds (TIPS) or laddered municipal bonds.

- 30% into a broad ETF-based stock index fund (e.g., S&P 500, MSCI World).

- 20% reserved for venture capital participation, pre-IPO equity, or Series A startup rounds.

This three-layer architecture creates a hedge against inflation while maintaining long-term capital appreciation.

2. **Dynamic Real Estate Acquisition:** Allocate each year's annuity toward acquiring rental properties in high-growth metro areas or gentrifying neighborhoods. A $3.3 million annual income could easily acquire 6–10 multi-family units per year. Over 15 years, this approach creates a massive real estate empire generating passive rental income and capital appreciation. Combining tax advantages like depreciation, 1031 exchanges, and leverage accelerates portfolio growth.

3. **Constructing a Personal Investment Trust:** The annuitant may establish a revocable or irrevocable family trust to receive and manage each payment. This entity reinvests funds using:

- Institutional strategies such as tax-loss harvesting and dividend reinvestment.

- Global arbitrage across currency markets or emerging economies.

- Hedge fund or quant strategy exposure via feeder

funds.

This transforms passive cash into a living financial
organism that compounds generational wealth.

Summary Consideration

- **Lump Sum:** Best for recipients with financial
  discipline, access to top-tier advisors, and an appetite
  for market risk. It offers higher short-term growth
  potential and liquidity for bold entrepreneurial ventures.

- **Annuity:** Best for recipients seeking stable, long-term
  income with built-in safeguards against financial ruin.
  The annuity structure supports consistent reinvestment
  and minimizes impulsive wealth destruction.

Ultimately, the **time value of money** remains central to this
decision. Lump sum choices front-load opportunity and invite
dynamic strategy. Annuities provide a rhythm of sustainable
wealth, allowing thoughtful planning and compounding.
Either can build a legacy—if paired with wisdom, discipline,
and a sound financial framework.

Judicial Endorsement of TVM Principles

The **time value of money (TVM)** is not merely an
economic abstraction—it is a principle deeply embedded in
the legal system's approach to awarding monetary damages,
especially in cases involving long-term financial harm. Courts
throughout the United States have consistently recognized
that compensation for future losses must reflect the
present-day value of money to ensure that the injured party
receives a fair and equitable award. Failing to account for this

would distort the actual economic impact, potentially leading to either overcompensation or undercompensation.

Federal Recognition: The *Pfeifer* Decision

One of the most authoritative federal acknowledgments of the time value of money comes from the United States Supreme Court in the landmark case *Jones & Laughlin Steel Corp. v. Pfeifer*, 462 U.S. 523 (1983). In Pfeifer, the Court addressed the appropriate method of calculating lost future wages for a permanently injured worker under maritime law. The Court unequivocally held that damage awards for future economic loss must be reduced to their present value:

> "The calculation of damages must reflect the time value of money, since a lump-sum payment today has the capacity to earn interest and grow over time. Present value ensures that the injured party is made whole—no more, no less—without unfairly penalizing or enriching either party."
> *(Pfeifer, 462 U.S. at 537)*

The Court's holding laid out a framework for courts and juries to use when applying discounting methodologies to future income streams. The opinion also highlighted the tension between simplicity and precision, ultimately encouraging courts to adopt discounting practices that align with prevailing financial standards while maintaining fairness.

Lower Federal Court Applications

Federal appellate and district courts have echoed Pfeifer's logic in numerous cases involving personal injury, wrongful death, and breach of contract. For example, in *Chesapeake &*

Ohio Ry. Co. v. Kelly, 241 U.S. 485 (1916), the Supreme
Court had already laid the foundation for using present value
in tort litigation, noting that failure to discount future
earnings would result in unjust enrichment. Subsequent
rulings have emphasized that actuarial evidence and economic
expert testimony are admissible and often necessary to guide
juries on present value calculations.

State Court Recognition and Jury Instructions

The principle of present value has also permeated state law.
Many state courts require juries to discount future damages
to present value as part of their deliberations. To facilitate
this, standardized civil jury instructions in numerous
jurisdictions include explicit language instructing jurors on
how to factor in the time value of money.

- **California:** Judicial Council of California Civil Jury
  Instructions (CACI) No. 3904B requires jurors to
  reduce future economic damages to present cash value,
  defined as "the amount of money that, if invested
  reasonably today, would provide the plaintiff with the
  same amount of money they would have received over
  time in the future."

- **Florida:** Florida Standard Jury Instruction 501.07
  similarly advises jurors to "reduce any future damages
  to present value by considering the interest that can
  reasonably be earned on the amount awarded." The
  Florida Supreme Court has affirmed this instruction in
  multiple appellate rulings.

- **New York:** CPLR § 5041 governs the structured

judgment statute and mandates that future damages in excess of $250,000 be paid in annuity form, explicitly requiring a present value calculation of future economic loss.

These statutory frameworks and jury instructions underscore that present value calculations are not optional—they are judicially required to ensure fairness and alignment with both economic and legal standards.

Methodologies Approved by the Courts

Courts have approved multiple methodologies for calculating present value in litigation contexts:

1. **Discounting with a Net Rate:** Some courts accept the "net discount rate" approach, which assumes that inflation and interest rates will roughly cancel out, allowing a simplified single rate (e.g., 2%–3%) to be applied.

2. **Separate Inflation and Discount Rates:** Others require separate consideration of wage growth or inflation trends alongside interest rates, especially when expert testimony supports these figures.

3. **Use of Government Bonds:** Several courts approve using the rate of return on risk-free assets—such as U.S. Treasury bonds—as a conservative proxy for discounting.

4. **Expert Testimony:** Expert witnesses, often forensic economists or actuaries, are routinely permitted to testify about appropriate discount rates and present

value computations, so long as their methodology satisfies standards under *Daubert* or *Frye*.

Challenges and Legal Controversies

While the application of TVM is well-settled in principle, several controversies arise in practice:

- **Disputes Over Discount Rates:** Plaintiffs and defendants often clash over the appropriate rate to apply—plaintiffs may favor a lower discount rate to increase present value, while defendants argue for higher rates to reduce awards.

- **Inflation-Proofing:** In jurisdictions where inflation is rising rapidly, courts may need to address whether inflation-adjusted damages should be awarded before applying discounting.

- **Structured Settlements:** When annuity-based settlements are proposed, judges may need to independently assess whether the proposed structure adequately reflects the present value of the damages agreed upon.

Implications for Legal Professionals

Attorneys must understand the mechanics of discounting and present value calculations to:

- Prepare and challenge expert witness testimony effectively.

- Structure settlements that hold up under judicial scrutiny.

- Avoid appellate reversal due to erroneous damage awards.

- Advocate for or contest the appropriateness of proposed discount rates and inflation assumptions.

In sum, **judicial endorsement of the time value of money is both universal and evolving**, shaped by financial principles, case law precedent, expert testimony, and jury instruction policy. Mastery of this concept is essential for accurate damage modeling, effective trial advocacy, and principled resolution of complex financial claims.

Compounding Frequency and Real-World Applications

A foundational concept within the time value of money (TVM) framework is **compounding frequency**—the number of times interest is applied to a principal sum within a given time period. The frequency of compounding dramatically impacts the future value of an investment or obligation, especially over long time horizons. Understanding how this factor operates is essential for lawyers, economists, and financial analysts involved in damage modeling, settlement structuring, and asset valuation.

The general compound interest formula that incorporates frequency is:

$$FV = PV \times \left(1 + \frac{r}{m}\right)^{n \times m}$$

Where:

- FV: Future value of the investment or amount,
- PV: Present value or principal amount,
- r: Nominal annual interest rate (as a decimal),
- m: Number of compounding periods per year,
- n: Number of years.

Illustrative Comparison of Frequencies

Consider an investment of \$10,000 at an annual interest rate of 8% over 10 years, with various compounding frequencies:

- **Annual:** $FV = 10,000 \times (1 + 0.08)^{1}0 \approx 21,589.25$

- **Quarterly:** $FV = 10,000 \times \left(1 + \frac{0.08}{4}\right)^{10 \times 4} \approx 22,080.40$

- **Monthly:** $FV = 10,000 \times \left(1 + \frac{0.08}{12}\right)^{10 \times 12} \approx 22,196.40$

- **Daily (365):**
  $FV = 10,000 \times \left(1 + \frac{0.08}{365}\right)^{10 \times 365} \approx 22,255.74$

- **Continuously:** $FV = 10,000 \times e^{0.08 \times 10} \approx 22,255.78$

These examples illustrate that **the more frequent the compounding, the greater the accumulation**, though marginal gains diminish at higher frequencies.

Legal Relevance of Compounding Frequency

Compounding frequency directly affects damage calculations, settlement valuation, and interest accrual under judgment awards. It also arises in statutory interest mandates and prejudgment/postjudgment interest assessments. Here are several key areas where courts and legal professionals engage with this concept:

1. **Structured Settlements:** Annuities paid to plaintiffs in tort litigation often assume monthly or quarterly compounding in determining how much is needed to fund long-term payments. The choice of compounding frequency alters the size of the annuity premium significantly.

2. **Judgment Interest:** State and federal laws sometimes specify interest rates and compounding frequencies on money judgments. For instance, some jurisdictions apply simple annual interest, while others require semiannual or daily compounding. These differences can amount to tens of thousands of dollars in long-duration cases.

3. **Loan Disputes and Usury Laws:** Many consumer protection statutes limit the annual percentage rate (APR) that lenders can charge. Compounding frequency plays a key role in distinguishing between lawful and usurious interest practices.

4. **Contractual Interpretation:** In commercial disputes, ambiguities about compounding frequency in loan contracts, leasing agreements, or investment memoranda can lead to litigation. Courts often examine the expressed or implied compounding terms to determine the amount owed.

Business Applications: Internal Rate of Return (IRR) and Net Present Value (NPV)

Professionals in finance and corporate law routinely assess compounding frequency when calculating:

- **IRR:** The discount rate that makes the net present value of a cash flow stream equal to zero. The internal compounding assumption affects the interpretation of IRR and can distort project comparison if frequency is not standardized.

- **NPV:** When evaluating capital investments, the NPV of expected cash inflows and outflows depends on the assumed compounding frequency. Choosing monthly over annual discounting can make or break the profitability outlook for a venture.

Consumer Finance and Mortgages

For everyday consumers, compounding frequency is embedded in almost every significant financial transaction, including:

- **Mortgages:** Typically compounded monthly. A mortgage with a 6% APR compounded monthly results in significantly higher total interest than the same APR compounded annually.

- **Credit Cards:** Often compound interest daily, which dramatically increases the total amount owed if balances are not paid in full.

- **Savings and Investment Accounts:** Banks advertise APY (Annual Percentage Yield), which reflects the effects of compounding on nominal APR rates. Consumers must understand how their interest is compounded to make informed choices.

Continuous Compounding in Theory and Practice

While most real-world applications use discrete compounding, the concept of **continuous compounding**—where interest accrues at every infinitesimal instant—is foundational in theoretical finance and advanced modeling:

$$FV = PV \times e^{rt}$$

This exponential growth model underpins pricing models in derivative markets, such as the Black-Scholes equation for option valuation. It also plays a role in legal-economic modeling involving perpetuities and stochastic cash flows.

Implications for Forensic Economics

Forensic economists must select an appropriate compounding frequency when testifying on damages:

- **Too simplistic an assumption** (e.g., annual compounding only) may understate future losses.

- **Overly aggressive compounding** may inflate damages and face challenge under Daubert or Frye standards.

- Experts must **match the compounding assumptions** to the real-world behavior of the financial instruments involved—such as quarterly earnings reports, monthly pension payments, or daily trading returns.

Conclusion

Compounding frequency is not a trivial detail—it is a material driver of financial outcomes. Whether applied in calculating investment returns, modeling tort damages, negotiating settlements, or interpreting judgment interest statutes, frequency determines how wealth accumulates or obligations expand over time.

Legal professionals, economists, and advisors must be alert to its implications and apply it with precision to avoid costly errors or misrepresentations in litigation, arbitration, or financial planning.

So Far

The time value of money bridges the gap between economic reasoning and legal application. Understanding TVM equips professionals to evaluate damages, structure settlements, interpret long-term obligations, and analyze business transactions from a mathematically sound perspective. The rest of this chapter will explore how to apply these principles using present and future value calculations, adjusted for inflation and economic reality.

11.2   Present Value (PV)

Definition

Present value refers to the current worth of a sum of money that is to be received in the future, discounted at a specific interest rate. It enables comparison between sums received at different times.

Formula

$$PV = \frac{FV}{(1+r)^n}$$

- PV: Present Value

- FV: Future Value

- r: Discount rate (expressed as a decimal)

- n: Number of periods (usually years)

Example 1: Simple Present Value Calculation

Problem: What is the present value of $10,000 received 5 years from now, if the annual interest rate is 6%?

Solution:

$$PV = \frac{10,000}{(1+0.06)^5} = \frac{10,000}{1.3382} \approx 7,472.58$$

Answer: $7,472.58

Example 2: Present Value of a Legal Settlement

Problem: A court awards a plaintiff $500,000 to be paid in 10 years. If the discount rate is 4%, what is the present value of the award?

Solution:

$$PV = \frac{500,000}{(1+0.04)^{10}} = \frac{500,000}{1.4802} \approx 337,578.28$$

Answer: $337,578.28

11.3 Future Value (FV)

Definition
Future value is the amount a present sum of money will grow to over time when invested at a given interest rate.

Formula
$$FV = PV \times (1 + r)^n$$

Example 3: Future Value of an Investment
Problem: How much will $2,000 grow to in 8 years at a 7% annual return?

Solution:
$$FV = 2,000 \times (1 + 0.07)^8 = 2,000 \times 1.7182 \approx 3,436.40$$

Answer: $3,436.40

11.4 Consumer Price Index

Definition of CPI
The **Consumer Price Index (CPI)** is a statistical estimate constructed by governments to measure changes over time in the price level of a representative basket of consumer goods and services. These goods typically include housing,

transportation, food, healthcare, and apparel—categories that reflect a typical urban consumer's expenses.

CPI is expressed as an index number, which is a weighted average of prices relative to a base year. The base year is assigned a value of 100, and subsequent values show percentage increases or decreases in overall price levels. For example, if the CPI rises from 200 to 210, this indicates a 5% increase in prices over that period.

There are multiple variations of CPI. The most common in the United States are:

- **CPI-U:** Measures price changes for all urban consumers.

- **CPI-W:** Focuses on urban wage earners and clerical workers.

- **Core CPI:** Excludes food and energy prices due to their volatility.

Using CPI to Adjust for Inflation

Inflation reduces the purchasing power of money over time. To compare the real value of dollars between two different years, CPI adjustment is required. The formula to adjust for inflation using CPI is:

$$\text{Adjusted Value} = \text{Nominal Value} \times \left(\frac{\text{CPI (Target Year)}}{\text{CPI (Original Year)}} \right)$$

This allows us to answer questions such as: *How much would $1,000 from 1995 be worth in 2025 dollars?*

Adjusting for inflation is crucial in:

- Calculating real wage growth

- Evaluating historical investment returns

- Adjusting legal damages

- Drafting financial projections and pension formulas

- Economic policy and tax bracket adjustments

Example 4: Adjusting Historical Prices for Inflation

Problem: A product cost $1,000 in 1995. The CPI in 1995 was 152.4. The CPI in 2025 is 309.8. What is the price in today's dollars?

Solution:

$$\text{Adjusted Value} = 1{,}000 \times \frac{309.8}{152.4}$$
$$\approx 1{,}000 \times 2.0327$$
$$\approx 2{,}032.81$$

Answer: $2,032.81

Deeper Interpretation

In this example, the cost of living has essentially doubled over 30 years. A dollar in 1995 has roughly half the purchasing power of a dollar in 2025. This transformation affects everything from wage contracts and social security payments to the long-term valuation of settlements and judgments in court.

CPI in Legal and Economic Contexts

- **Tort Damages:** CPI is used by forensic economists to adjust historical earnings for inflation in wrongful death and personal injury cases.

- **Contract Claims:** Courts may allow CPI indexing to determine appropriate damages in breach of contract disputes involving long-term obligations.

- **Family Law:** Spousal and child support agreements may include CPI escalators to maintain standard of living over time.

- **Government Programs:** Social Security payments and tax brackets are periodically indexed to CPI to preserve purchasing power.

Cautions in CPI Usage

- CPI does not capture asset inflation (e.g., housing prices, stocks).

- CPI may differ by region and demographic group.

- Substitution bias and quality adjustments can lead to under- or over-estimation of real-world inflation.

Conclusion

The Consumer Price Index is a foundational metric in both economic analysis and legal compensation. It offers a standardized way to make time-based comparisons, ensuring that dollars from the past are properly contextualized in today's value framework. Whether assessing damages or preserving contractual fairness, CPI adjustment provides critical fairness and accuracy in financial assessments.

11.5   Combined PV

Conceptual Overview

Combining present value and inflation adjustment is essential in legal and financial analysis where damages span multiple time periods. This dual-layered adjustment is frequently encountered in lawsuits involving breach of contract, personal injury, long-term settlements, and trust litigation. Courts often require monetary values to be expressed both in real (inflation-adjusted) and present terms, especially when damages occurred in the past or are to be awarded in the future.

The general approach is:

1. **Inflation-adjust** the historical or future nominal value to reflect purchasing power in the target year using CPI.

2. **Discount** that adjusted value to today's dollars using an appropriate discount rate (reflecting investment alternatives, market risk, or statutory guidelines).

This ensures fairness, prevents overcompensation or undercompensation, and aligns with economic reality.

Example 5: Inflation-Adjusted Legal Damages

Problem: A breach of contract in 1990 caused damages worth $250,000 at that time. To present this value in 2025 dollars, use CPI values: 1990 CPI = 130.7, 2025 CPI = 309.8. What is the adjusted amount?

Solution:

$$\text{Adjusted Value} = 250{,}000 \times \frac{309.8}{130.7}$$
$$\approx 250{,}000 \times 2.369$$
$$= 592{,}578.42$$

Answer: $\boxed{\$592{,}578.42}$

Interpretation: The real value of a $250,000 judgment from 1990, when adjusted to account for inflation, represents a loss equivalent to nearly $600,000 in 2025 dollars. This transformation is vital in ensuring just compensation based on contemporary economic conditions.

Example 6: Present Value of a Future Inflated Sum

Problem: An injury settlement promises $1 million in 20 years. Assuming 2% annual inflation and a 5% discount rate, what is the present value of the inflation-adjusted future payment?

Step 1: Inflate Future Value to 2045 Purchasing

Power

$$FV_{\text{inflated}} = 1{,}000{,}000 \times (1.02)^{20}$$
$$\approx 1{,}000{,}000 \times 1.4859$$
$$= 1{,}485{,}947.40$$

Step 2: Discount to Present Value

$$PV = \frac{1{,}485{,}947.40}{(1.05)^{20}}$$
$$= \frac{1{,}485{,}947.40}{2.6533}$$
$$\approx 560{,}037.95$$

Answer: $560,037.95

Interpretation: The promise to pay $1 million in 20 years may appear generous. But once adjusted for 2% inflation and discounted at 5%, the present-day worth of that payment—*even if inflation is built in*—is approximately $560,000. This exemplifies why plaintiffs may prefer structured settlements or immediate lump sums, depending on expected inflation and prevailing discount rates.

Legal Context

Courts and economists frequently debate what constitutes the "correct" discount rate and inflation forecast. Legal precedents often defer to expert testimony or government sources like the Congressional Budget Office or U.S. Treasury rates.

In *Jones & Laughlin Steel Corp. v. Pfeifer*, 462 U.S. 523 (1983), the Supreme Court held that future damages should be reduced to present value to avoid unjust enrichment.

Courts have emphasized that both inflationary trends and interest rates must be transparently and reasonably modeled to reflect economic realism, particularly in personal injury and wrongful death contexts.

Takeaways

- Inflation alone may distort damage awards if not counterbalanced by discounting.

- Discounting without inflation adjustment underestimates real economic losses.

- Both steps together honor the legal obligation to "make whole" the injured party.

The fusion of present value and inflation adjustment provides a critical framework for lawyers, economists, and judges to align compensation with economic fairness and financial reality.

11.6   Answers to Practice Problems

1. **Present value of $100,000 in 15 years at 6% annual interest:**

$$PV = \frac{100,000}{(1+0.06)^{15}}$$
$$\approx \frac{100,000}{2.3966}$$
$$\approx 41,737.56$$

2. **Present value of $2,000/month for 10 years at**

5% annual interest compounded monthly:

$$PV = 2,000 \times \left(\frac{1 - (1 + 0.05/12)^{-120}}{0.05/12} \right)$$

$$\approx 2,000 \times 94.39$$

$$\approx 188,780$$

3. **Adjusted value of \$50,000 from 1980 to 2025 with CPI = 82.4 (1980) and CPI = 309.8 (2025):**

$$\text{Adjusted Value} = 50,000 \times \frac{309.8}{82.4}$$

$$\approx 187,738.83$$

4. **Future value of \$5,000 invested at 8% for 12 years:**

$$FV = 5,000 \times (1.08)^{12}$$

$$\approx 5,000 \times 2.5182$$

$$\approx 12,591$$

5. **Present value of \$300,000 in 5 years at a 4.5% discount rate:**

$$PV = \frac{300,000}{(1 + 0.045)^5}$$

$$\approx \frac{300,000}{1.2462}$$

$$\approx 240,705.23$$

6. **Future value of an annual investment of \$7,500**

for 20 years at 6%:

$$FV = 7,500 \times \left(\frac{(1+0.06)^{20} - 1}{0.06}\right)$$

$$\approx 7,500 \times 36.786$$

$$\approx 275,895$$

7. **Inflation-adjusted value of $10,000 from 1975 to 2025 (CPI 1975 = 53.8, CPI 2025 = 309.8):**

$$\text{Adjusted Value} = 10,000 \times \frac{309.8}{53.8}$$

$$\approx 57,590.70$$

8. **Present value of $1 million payable in 25 years, at 5%:**

$$PV = \frac{1,000,000}{(1.05)^{25}}$$

$$\approx \frac{1,000,000}{3.386}$$

$$\approx 295,287.82$$

9. **Real interest rate given nominal rate of 7% and inflation of 3%:**

$$r_{\text{real}} = \frac{1.07}{1.03} - 1$$

$$\approx 0.0388$$

$$\text{or } 3.88\%$$

10. **Present value of a perpetuity paying \$5,000 annually, discount rate = 4%:**

$$PV = \frac{5,000}{0.04}$$
$$= 125,000$$

11.7 Conclusion

To grasp the time value of money is to understand that justice, too, must be reckoned in temporal terms. Damages that stretch into the future or arise from the distant past must be brought into equilibrium with the present—not merely as a matter of arithmetic, but of fairness. Through discounting, compounding, and inflation indexing, we translate the abstract flow of time into tangible value, enabling courts and litigants to speak a common language of equivalence. These calculations are not sterile formulas—they are the architecture of restitution.

Yet numbers alone do not deliver justice. The courtroom is also a theater of human conduct, and economic valuation must sometimes bow to moral outrage. In the next chapter, we examine a case where dollars and decimals were not enough. In *Mathias v. Accor*, Judge Richard Posner confronts a different calculus: one that measures not loss, but deterrence; not compensation, but condemnation. There, the time value of money meets the time-honored power of punitive damages.

Chapter 12

Mathias v. Accor

12.1 Introduction

In the storied tradition of American jurisprudence, few
appellate opinions have wielded both narrative elegance and
doctrinal precision as powerfully as Judge Richard Posner's
opinion in *Mathias v. Accor Economy Lodging, Inc.*, 347 F.3d
672 (7th Cir. 2003). The case, involving the seemingly minor
tort of bedbug infestation in a discount motel, evolved into a
landmark articulation of the role punitive damages play in
deterring corporate misconduct. Posner, famed for pioneering
the law and economics movement, used the occasion to
critique Supreme Court doctrine, advance an economic theory
of punishment, and preserve a pragmatic framework for
justice.

This chapter explores *Mathias* not simply as a rejoinder to *State Farm v. Campbell*, 538 U.S. 408 (2003), but as a rich text that reveals Posner's broader commitment to fair dealing, market integrity, and the need to preserve justice within capitalism's transactional frameworks. Importantly, this chapter uncovers a factual misstatement in the case, one which, when corrected, deepens the moral gravity of Posner's reasoning and highlights his distinctive method of jurisprudence.

12.2 The Case Background

In *Mathias*, plaintiffs sued Accor's Red Roof Inn after suffering bedbug bites during a stay. Although compensatory damages were nominal—$5,000—the jury awarded each plaintiff $186,000 in punitive damages. The case was ripe for review in the wake of *State Farm*, where the U.S. Supreme Court stressed that punitive damages must bear a "reasonable relationship" to compensatory awards, often expressed as a single-digit ratio.

Judge Posner upheld the punitive award, asserting that such mathematical constraints misunderstand the deterrent purpose of punitive damages, especially in cases of widespread but low-dollar injuries. "The award of punitive damages... must serve the public purpose of deterring wanton and malicious conduct," he wrote. That public purpose would be thwarted if corporations could treat minor harms as a mere cost of doing business.

12.3   Logic & Judgment

Judge Posner's opinion in *Mathias* reflects more than an economic treatise on deterrence—it embodies a normative view that markets, while efficient allocators of resources, must be constrained by legal institutions that penalize exploitation and concealment. He emphasized that Accor's decision not to remedy the bedbug problem stemmed from a calculated economic judgment: that the cost of addressing the infestation exceeded the likely payout in damages.

This, in Posner's view, was exactly the type of rational negligence that punitive damages were meant to deter. In other words, the cost-benefit analysis that made it "cheaper to do nothing" had to be disrupted by a judicial counterweight. He argued that absent such deterrence, tort law would lose its capacity to discipline invisible harms that are real, widespread, and intentionally concealed.

12.4   *State Farm*

The Supreme Court in *State Farm* sought to impose constitutional limits on punitive damages by developing a set of guideposts, including a presumed single-digit ratio between punitive and compensatory awards. Posner dismissed this mechanical ratio as both impractical and unjust in cases like *Mathias*, where the defendant deliberately concealed harms from victims, most of whom would never litigate.

He reasoned that a $5,000 compensatory award could not realistically reflect the true harm—emotional distress, breach

of safety expectations, and systemic deception—suffered by
the plaintiffs. Nor could a low ratio deter a company that
profited substantially from underreporting or ignoring such
complaints.

12.5 An Obscured Misstatement

Upon further examination, commentators have noted a
factual misstatement embedded in the opinion. Judge Posner
wrote that Red Roof Inn was operating with a general
manager who had failed to inform higher-ups about the
infestation. In truth, documentary evidence from discovery
suggested that upper management had received direct notice
of the problem from multiple sources. The decision not to act
was not the result of managerial silence but of a strategic
decision by the corporation.

This clarification intensifies the moral culpability underlying
Accor's inaction. Rather than a failure of internal
communication, the case became an instance of systemic
disregard for consumer welfare. Posner's framework still
holds—but this detail sharpens the economic model's ethical
edge. It was not mere negligence; it was economic
opportunism at the expense of public health.

12.6 The Economic Rationale

Judge Posner stressed that bedbug infestations—like other
minor but offensive harms—pose unique challenges to
deterrence. Victims are unlikely to sue over small injuries, and

most will not pursue legal relief. A company that calculates it can quietly settle a few claims while saving money on mass remediation may rationally engage in concealment.

Economically, this results in what Posner called "under-deterrence." Unless the law permits heightened punitive damages, firms will build low damage payouts into their budgets as a routine externality. In effect, they will impose "small injuries on many," with impunity. The only counterbalance is to amplify the damages in the few cases that make it to trial, thereby correcting the structural deficit in deterrent power.

12.7 Jurisprudential Signal

Mathias is not simply a procedural affirmation of jury discretion; it is a jurisprudential signal. Posner signals to corporations that economizing on safety or honesty will trigger judicial interventions calibrated to correct their cost-benefit distortions. He asserts that judges must look beyond numeric formulas and assess whether the legal system incentivizes responsible market behavior.

His opinion also encourages trial courts to focus on patterns of corporate behavior—not just individual instances of harm. Courts can and should draw inferences from conduct that is repeated, concealed, and profit-seeking, even when the harm is nominal or symbolic.

12.8   Institutional Competence

Posner also defended the jury's role in determining punitive awards, cautioning against appellate courts substituting their judgment without strong justification. In his view, jurors are especially well-suited to determine moral blameworthiness and gauge the community's sense of outrage.

While economic logic demands efficiency, Posner's deeper insight was that moral outrage has economic utility: it conveys social disapproval and thus deters repetition. The jury is not just an instrument of retribution—it is a signaling device in the marketplace of behavior.

12.9   Legal Equilibrium

The notion of equilibrium is central to Posner's opinion. In the same way that markets equilibrate supply and demand, the legal system equilibrates incentives and duties. When wrongdoing is cheap, the law must adjust the price. The high punitive award in *Mathias* was not disproportionate—it was the precise cost necessary to reach an efficient deterrent point.

Here, Posner brings together economics, behavioral law and economics, and moral judgment into a unified method. He aligns the efficient markets hypothesis with social expectations, and shows that where market prices underrepresent risk or harm, legal damages must step in to re-price the transaction.

12.10 Broader Principles

While the case involves an unsavory infestation, Posner's opinion extends well beyond its facts. The doctrine applies to any case in which latent harms are distributed across a large population—such as data privacy violations, environmental pollution, false advertising, and deceptive financial products. In all such cases, the rationale of *Mathias* persists: the harm is not fully captured by the price of any single transaction.

12.11 Posner's Jurisprudence

Mathias v. Accor encapsulates Judge Posner's mature jurisprudence—a blend of narrative power, legal pragmatism, and economic modeling. It is storytelling with consequence, precedent with principle. It demands that law not just process disputes, but recalibrate social and economic systems toward greater fairness.

Moreover, the case stands as a critique of judicial formalism. Where the Supreme Court imposed a narrow ratio test in *State Farm*, Posner widened the lens, emphasizing proportionality not to damages alone, but to wrongdoing, concealment, and danger.

12.12 Conclusion

Judge Posner's opinion in *Mathias* demonstrates that a good judge must be more than a technician—he must be a realist, an economist, a moralist, and a guardian of civil society. The true harm in *Mathias* was not the bites. It was the breach of trust, the strategic concealment, and the degradation of accountability in a market governed increasingly by spreadsheets and spreadsheets alone.

In drawing from economics and moral philosophy, Posner reminded us that the law must evolve to meet the logic of the world it seeks to govern. In doing so, *Mathias v. Accor* endures not merely as bedbug jurisprudence, but as a milestone in the law's ongoing effort to preserve both justice and market dignity.

"Punitive damages are not a numbers game. They are a moral reckoning."
— Judge Richard Posner, paraphrased

Chapter 13

Posnerian Economics

13.1 The Economic Analysis

Judge Richard Posner, one of the most influential jurists and legal theorists of the 20th and 21st centuries, revolutionized the field of law by integrating economic reasoning into legal decision-making. As a judge on the U.S. Court of Appeals for the Seventh Circuit and a prolific academic, Posner championed the view that economic efficiency provides a rational and objective metric by which to evaluate legal rules, doctrines, and outcomes.

Foundations of Law and Economics

Posner's foundational work, particularly his seminal book *Economic Analysis of Law*, posits that much of common law

can be best understood as a system of rules that aim to
maximize societal wealth. He argued that torts, contracts,
and property law often evolve in ways that encourage efficient
behavior and minimize the total costs of accidents, breaches,
and disputes. His approach aligns with the Chicago School of
economic thought, which emphasizes market efficiency,
rational actors, and utility maximization.

Efficiency as a Legal Standard

In Posner's framework, efficiency—specifically, *Kaldor-Hicks
efficiency*—becomes a guiding principle for judicial
decision-making. Under this criterion, a legal rule is
considered efficient if those who benefit from it could
hypothetically compensate those who are harmed, leading to
a net gain in social welfare. This utilitarian foundation allows
for a cost-benefit analysis of rules and legal outcomes,
focusing less on abstract notions of justice and more on
practical consequences.

Applications Across Legal Fields

Posner applied economic reasoning across diverse areas of law:

- **Tort Law:** He argued that tort rules, such as strict
  liability and negligence, serve to minimize the sum of
  accident costs and prevention costs.

- **Contract Law:** He viewed breach of contract as an
  economically rational act when the cost of performance
  exceeds the benefit, provided that expectation damages
  are paid.

- **Antitrust Law:** Posner emphasized consumer welfare

and market efficiency, advocating for minimal
government intervention unless monopolistic behavior
clearly harms consumers.

- **Family Law and Criminal Law:** Even in
traditionally non-economic fields, he explored how
incentives, deterrents, and opportunity costs could
inform legal rules.

Forensic Economics in the Posnerian Tradition

The rise of forensic economics in litigation reflects Posner's
legacy. Courts now increasingly accept expert economic
testimony to resolve complex legal disputes. This includes:

- Quantification of damages in tort and contract disputes.

- Cost-benefit analysis in environmental and regulatory
law.

- Valuation of lost earning capacity in personal injury and
wrongful death cases.

- Economic modeling in class actions to demonstrate
predominance and commonality.

Posner's theoretical foundation legitimized the presence of
forensic economists in the courtroom, transforming legal
reasoning from abstract deliberation to empirical inquiry.

Critiques and Refinements

Despite its profound influence, Posner's economic analysis of
law has faced criticism. Critics argue that:

- It overlooks moral, distributive, and rights-based considerations in favor of utilitarian calculus.

- It assumes rational behavior in markets where power asymmetries and psychological biases abound.

- It commodifies law, reducing human relationships to economic transactions.

Posner acknowledged some of these critiques, particularly later in his career, where he adopted a more pragmatic approach and distanced himself from rigid law-and-economics orthodoxy.

Legacy and Continuing Influence

Posner's influence continues to permeate judicial reasoning, law school curricula, and the practice of forensic economics. His writings laid the intellectual groundwork for integrating economics into the legal system not merely as a tool for understanding markets but as a framework for interpreting contracts, assigning liability, and measuring harm.

His legacy lives on in modern courts' use of economic models to assess damages, class certification, antitrust violations, and regulatory costs. Forensic economists, often testifying in complex litigation, stand as living embodiments of Posnerian legal philosophy—experts translating normative legal disputes into quantitative analyses that judges and juries can comprehend.

As legal systems evolve in complexity and scale, Judge Posner's vision of an empirically grounded, economically rational jurisprudence remains both relevant and indispensable.

13.2 Opinions by Judge Posner

Judge Richard A. Posner's jurisprudence is renowned for its integration of economic analysis into judicial decision-making. His opinions frequently move beyond traditional legal doctrine to engage in rigorous cost-benefit assessments, game theory applications, and microeconomic modeling. This section highlights several influential opinions that exemplify his unique fusion of law and economics.

1. *Indiana Harbor Belt Railroad Co. v. American Cyanamid Co.*, 916 F.2d 1174 (7th Cir. 1990)

In this seminal decision, Judge Richard Posner applied economic reasoning to tort law, specifically the choice between strict liability and negligence in the context of hazardous materials transport. The case arose from a chemical spill involving acrylonitrile—a highly toxic and flammable substance—during the unloading of a railway tank car in an urban rail yard operated by Indiana Harbor Belt Railroad. The railroad sought to hold American Cyanamid, the shipper, strictly liable for damages caused by the leak.

Rather than defaulting to doctrinal distinctions between abnormally dangerous and ordinary activities, Posner reframed the issue through a law-and-economics lens. His opinion probed deeply into cost allocation, deterrence, and the economic rationale behind different liability regimes.

Negligence vs. Strict Liability: Economic Distinctions
Posner emphasized that strict liability should only be applied
when it leads to superior incentives for accident prevention.
He set out the following economic considerations:

- **Control and Incentives:** Since American Cyanamid
  had relinquished control over the transport at the time
  of the leak, imposing strict liability would not alter the
  shipper's behavior in a way that would prevent future
  harm.

- **Activity-Level vs. Precaution-Level Regulation:**
  Strict liability could cause firms to reduce or abandon
  socially useful activities (e.g., chemical transport), even
  when the risk can be adequately mitigated through
  precautionary measures by others.

- **Cheapest Cost Avoider Principle:** The railroad was
  in a better position to monitor train operations, detect
  leaks, and maintain yard safety. Therefore,
  negligence—a fault-based standard—better aligned
  liability with the party most capable of prevention.

Externalities and the Economics of Dangerous Goods
Posner's opinion analyzed the broader externalities associated
with transporting hazardous goods. He noted that chemical
transport is an essential component of industrial economies
and that the imposition of strict liability could lead to:

- **Underproduction of Valuable Goods:** If firms face
  excessive liability for remote harms they cannot control,
  they may curtail production or shift operations overseas,

with negative economic ripple effects.

- **Inefficient Routing and Urban Avoidance:**
  Companies might reroute shipments through longer or
  more rural paths simply to reduce liability, raising costs
  for everyone and introducing new risks in other regions.

- **Redundant Precautions:** If both shippers and
  carriers adopt duplicative safety measures, the marginal
  benefit of additional precautions may be outweighed by
  their cost, leading to Pareto inefficiency.

Institutional Competence and Tort Law Design

Posner further questioned whether courts were well-suited to
impose strict liability in industrial spill cases. He suggested
that:

- **Legislative and Regulatory Channels Are
  Preferable:** Congress and administrative agencies (e.g.,
  the Department of Transportation) are better equipped
  to impose and enforce safety standards tailored to
  specific industries.

- **Tort Law Should Not Deter Optimal Levels of
  Activity:** Judges must consider whether liability rules
  foster or hinder the socially optimal levels of hazardous
  activity, particularly when that activity serves vital
  economic functions.

Influence and Legacy   Posner's opinion in *Indiana Harbor
Belt Railroad* is widely cited in both tort law and
law-and-economics literature. It illustrates how economic
reasoning can:

- Clarify when strict liability is normatively appropriate.

- Encourage judicial restraint in expanding tort doctrines that could lead to excessive litigation.

- Emphasize empirical inquiry into who can reduce harm at the lowest social cost.

The case is now a cornerstone in law school casebooks, exemplifying the "cheapest cost avoider" theory popularized by Guido Calabresi and extended by Posner into a rigorous judicial framework. It also serves as a powerful demonstration of how economic theory can yield different outcomes than traditional legal analysis, particularly in complex industrial contexts.

Conclusion   Judge Posner's reasoning in *Indiana Harbor Belt Railroad Co. v. American Cyanamid Co.* goes beyond doctrinal formalism, applying economic efficiency as a constitutional principle of private law. His refusal to apply strict liability by rote—and instead advocating for a negligence standard grounded in rational deterrence and risk-cost minimization—has had a lasting influence on how courts and scholars understand liability in the industrial age.

> "And so with the dealer who sells a thousand doses of LSD on heavy blotter paper, the dealer who sells a thousand doses on light blotter paper, the dealer who sells the same number of doses on gelatin cubes, the dealer who sells the same number on sugar cubes, and the dealer who sells the same number in pure form: all these dealers are identically situated, so far as the purposes

animating the drug statute are concerned; all can
complain, therefore, that they are being sentenced
pursuant to an irrational scheme that denies them
the equal protection of the laws." — Judge
Richard Posner

2. *United States v. Marshall*, 908 F.2d 1312 (7th Cir. 1990) (en banc)

In this highly controversial case, the en banc Seventh Circuit
upheld a sentencing enhancement under the Anti-Drug Abuse
Act of 1986, which required that the weight of an entire
carrier medium—such as blotter paper containing LSD—be
included in calculating the quantity of drugs for sentencing
purposes. The majority reasoned that Congress had adopted
a clear statutory formula and that it was not within the
judiciary's role to question its rationality.

Judge Richard Posner issued a sharp and influential dissent,
arguing that the statutory method was economically illogical,
legally disproportionate, and morally suspect. By applying
economic principles to criminal law, Posner launched one of
the most powerful critiques of mandatory sentencing rules in
modern jurisprudence.

Core Economic Objection   Posner challenged the
statute's failure to distinguish between the active ingredient
(LSD) and the inert medium (blotter paper), leading to wildly
disproportionate sentencing outcomes. Two defendants
possessing chemically identical amounts of LSD could receive
dramatically different sentences based solely on the weight of
the paper. This violated basic principles of fairness,

proportionality, and economic efficiency.

- A defendant carrying 100 doses on thin paper might face a lighter sentence than someone carrying the same 100 doses on heavier paper.

- The economic value of LSD is derived from the dose, not the mass of its carrier. Thus, the sentencing rule bears no rational relation to either harm or market value.

Marginal Deterrence and Sentencing Rationality
Posner framed his dissent around the concept of *marginal deterrence*, a key idea in economic criminal law theory. The notion is that penalties should increase gradually with culpability to incentivize reduced harm. By failing to reflect culpability accurately, the law incentivized:

- **Bulk Transport Over Dose-Specific Transactions:** Distributors might prefer larger but more efficient delivery mediums, increasing public risk.

- **Inefficient Policing and Prosecution:** Law enforcement resources would be disproportionately focused on minor dealers who happen to carry heavier media, rather than high-level traffickers.

Economic Modeling of Harm and Utility   Posner's dissent included an economic model of optimal punishment. He suggested that the sentencing function should be a continuous and monotonic function of the market value or actual harm caused by the drug. Using basic cost-benefit logic, he showed that:

- Punishment that overestimates harm (e.g., due to paper

weight) produces over-deterrence and undermines legitimacy.

- Punishment that underestimates harm (e.g., in other drug contexts) allows profit-maximizing behavior by rational actors who internalize the penalty as a cost of doing business.

Normative and Legal Implications   While the majority deferred to congressional intent, Posner emphasized that courts must assess whether statutory formulas yield irrational or perverse results. He argued that legislative deference should not extend to plainly absurd outcomes—especially when those outcomes contravene constitutional principles of equal protection and proportionality in sentencing.

His dissent predicted a host of real-world distortions:

- **Disparate Sentencing Across Jurisdictions:** Depending on the medium used, otherwise similar defendants faced vastly different penalties, creating systemic inequity.

- **Manipulation of Sentencing Outcomes:** Prosecutors could strategically charge based on form rather than substance, encouraging tactical abuse of sentencing enhancements.

- **Erosion of Trust in Judicial Logic:** Lay observers would rightly view such discrepancies as legally incomprehensible and morally indefensible.

Influence on Policy and Reform Discourse   Though not adopted by the court, Posner's dissent remains one of the

most cited critiques of sentencing disparities in the federal
drug laws. His reasoning:

- Was cited in sentencing reform debates during the 1990s
  and 2000s.

- Informed proposals for the recalibration of the U.S.
  Sentencing Guidelines.

- Was referenced in multiple academic treatises and law
  review articles as a paradigmatic example of economic
  logic applied to penal statutes.

Conclusion In *United States v. Marshall*, Posner's dissent
transformed a seemingly narrow statutory interpretation case
into a foundational moment for law-and-economics in criminal
jurisprudence. He demonstrated that even the most routine
legal calculations—such as drug weight—have embedded
assumptions about deterrence, efficiency, fairness, and
legitimacy.

> "[O]r, in words, only if the harm to the plaintiff if
> the injunction is denied, multiplied by the
> probability that the denial would be an error (that
> the plaintiff, in other words, will win at trial),
> exceeds the harm to the defendant if the
> injunction is granted, multiplied by the
> probability that granting the injunction would be
> an error. That probability is simply one minus the
> probability that the plaintiff will win at trial; for if
> the plaintiff has, say, a 40 percent chance of
> winning, the defendant must have a 60 percent
> chance of winning ($1.00 - .40 = .60$). The

left-hand side of the formula is simply the
probability of an erroneous denial weighted by the
cost of denial to the plaintiff, and the right-hand
side simply the probability of an erroneous grant
weighted by the cost of grant to the defendant." —
Judge Richard Posner

His dissent remains a touchstone for reform advocates and
scholars who seek to blend rigorous economic reasoning with
humane legal principles. It exemplifies the capacity of
economic analysis to illuminate hidden irrationalities within
ostensibly objective legal systems.

3. *American Hospital Supply Corp. v. Hospital Products Ltd.*, 780 F.2d 589 (7th Cir. 1986)

In this pivotal Seventh Circuit decision, Judge Richard Posner
reshaped the legal framework for evaluating motions for
preliminary injunctions. The case involved a dispute between
two competitors in the medical supply industry: American
Hospital Supply Corporation and Hospital Products Limited.
The plaintiff sought to enjoin the defendant from interfering
with its exclusive distribution agreements, alleging tortious
interference and unfair competition.

Rather than relying solely on traditional equitable balancing,
which often appeared vague or subjective, Posner proposed a
groundbreaking analytical model derived from decision theory
and economic principles. He articulated a probabilistic
formula to evaluate whether a preliminary injunction should

issue:

$$\text{Probability of success} \times \text{Harm from denial}$$
$$\geq (1 - \text{Probability}) \times \text{Harm from granting}$$

This formula, borrowed from expected utility theory, quantifies the trade-offs inherent in interim judicial relief. It represents a major doctrinal innovation in how courts balance the harms and likelihoods at the early stages of litigation, transforming equitable discretion into a form of mathematical optimization.

The Economic Logic of the Formula At its core, the formula reframes the court's decision as an exercise in risk-weighted harm analysis. Each side of the inequality weighs the expected loss associated with an incorrect decision. The left side of the inequality represents the cost of erroneously denying relief when the plaintiff should win, while the right side measures the cost of erroneously granting relief when the defendant should win.

This economic formulation allows judges to:

- **Rationalize Uncertainty:** Courts rarely have perfect information at the preliminary stage. Posner's formula helps decision-makers cope with probabilistic legal outcomes.

- **Quantify Asymmetrical Harms:** The method accommodates situations where the harm to one party may vastly outweigh the harm to the other, even if the likelihood of success is relatively low.

- **Reduce Judicial Arbitrariness:** By converting intuition into a comparative framework, the model promotes transparency and internal consistency in equitable rulings.

Practical Impact on Judicial Behavior   Posner's opinion marked a shift toward greater economic literacy in procedural law. Lower courts increasingly adopted the formula—or at least its logic—in making preliminary relief determinations. It became common for district judges to articulate the likelihood of success numerically or semi-quantitatively, and to structure their reasoning in ways that mimicked cost-benefit logic.

Although the model does not eliminate all discretion, it invites courts to:

- **Estimate Harms with Economic Tools:** Judges now regularly consider opportunity costs, market disruptions, and quantifiable financial damages in preliminary stages.

- **Weigh Public and Private Interests with Precision:** The formula permits incorporation of externalities—such as patient care in this case—into the harm calculus.

- **Communicate Judgments to Appellate Courts:** The framework provides a structured rationale that makes appellate review of injunctions more principled.

Interdisciplinary Fusion: Law Meets Economics and Operations Research   Posner's formulation is not just a clever metaphor—it aligns with principles from operations research and decision theory used in business, military strategy, and public policy. His approach can be viewed as a legal analogue to cost-effectiveness analysis or Bayesian decision-making under uncertainty.

By fusing equitable jurisprudence with econometrics, Posner advanced a new kind of judicial reasoning, one that treats litigation as a series of investment decisions under risk constraints. This is especially appropriate in commercial disputes where legal errors carry substantial financial implications.

Criticism and Enduring Influence   Some legal scholars initially critiqued the formula as being overly reductionist or numerically impractical, especially in cases involving intangible rights or noneconomic injuries. Nevertheless, Posner acknowledged these limitations in the opinion, noting that the formula should guide, not dictate, judicial reasoning.

Despite these critiques, the formula has had lasting effects:

- **Cited Widely:** The decision is taught in federal courts courses and procedural textbooks nationwide, with over 1,000 citations across case law and scholarship.

- **Adopted Internationally:** Courts in the UK, Canada, and Australia have acknowledged the logic of Posner's analysis in their own preliminary relief standards.

- **Integrated Into Judicial Training:** Economic modeling for equitable relief now forms part of judicial education seminars and federal judicial center materials.

Conclusion   *American Hospital Supply Corp. v. Hospital Products Ltd.* remains a paradigmatic case of Posner's economic jurisprudence in action. It exemplifies his belief that law should borrow from the best tools of other disciplines to promote justice, efficiency, and coherence. By reengineering a centuries-old doctrine through the lens of economics, Posner did not merely clarify the law—he transformed its methodology.

Quote from the Opinion:

> "The task is to minimize the costs of error. A rule that ignores probabilities invites inefficient injunctions; a rule that ignores harms fails to protect important interests."

4. *Coasean Themes: Chicago Board of Realtors v. City of Chicago, 819 F.2d 732 (7th Cir. 1987)*

In this influential opinion, Judge Richard Posner applied Coasean economics and the logic of transaction costs to a constitutional challenge brought by landlords against the City of Chicago. The municipal ordinance in question introduced a wide array of regulatory restrictions on landlord-tenant relationships—governing the handling of security deposits, imposing deadlines for return of such deposits, regulating late fees, and dictating language disclosures in leases.

Posner, writing for the Seventh Circuit, found that the ordinance overstepped rational policy bounds and invalidated it on grounds of economic inefficiency and constitutional overreach. Rather than treating landlord-tenant regulation as a matter of traditional police power, Posner evaluated the law

through the lens of market consequences. He drew heavily on
the work of Ronald Coase, particularly the Coase Theorem, to
illustrate how legal rules can alter bargaining dynamics and
misallocate resources.

Key Economic and Legal Findings   Posner's opinion
highlighted several core points:

- **Regulatory Burdens Are Not Free:** While the city
  aimed to protect tenants, Posner argued that the
  compliance costs would ultimately be shifted to tenants
  themselves in the form of increased rent. He noted that
  markets internalize costs, and regulation that alters this
  equilibrium can harm the very group it purports to help.

- **Reduced Housing Quality and Supply:** Drawing
  from urban economics literature, Posner warned that
  overregulation would lead landlords to withdraw from
  the rental market, convert units to condominiums, or
  neglect maintenance. This would shrink the housing
  supply and degrade quality, especially in low-income
  neighborhoods.

- **Efficiency of Market-Based Allocation:** The
  opinion emphasized that voluntary exchanges in
  competitive markets are usually more efficient than
  command-and-control mandates. Posner maintained
  that tenants and landlords can negotiate lease terms
  without municipal micromanagement, provided there is
  no evidence of monopoly or fraud.

- **The Failure of Uniform Rules:** One of Posner's
  criticisms centered on the ordinance's inflexible,

one-size-fits-all approach. He noted that housing
markets are heterogeneous—what might be reasonable
for a luxury downtown apartment may be inappropriate
for a low-income efficiency unit in a different
neighborhood.

The Coase Theorem in Practice   The decision is
particularly notable for its clear and deliberate invocation of
the Coase Theorem. Posner observed that when transaction
costs are low, parties will negotiate toward efficient outcomes
regardless of initial legal entitlements. The implication was
that the ordinance disrupted this natural efficiency by
imposing artificial constraints on private bargaining, thereby
introducing inefficiency and deadweight loss.

Instead of enhancing tenant welfare, Posner predicted that
the regulation would result in:

- **Higher Transaction Costs:** Landlords would be
  forced to hire lawyers or compliance officers to interpret
  ambiguous clauses or face litigation risk.

- **Legal Ambiguity:** The ordinance's vague language
  created uncertainty about permissible practices, chilling
  the landlord's willingness to engage in ordinary market
  behavior.

- **Over-deterrence:** By punishing conduct that was not
  clearly exploitative, the ordinance might encourage
  landlords to exit the rental market or avoid riskier but
  necessary tenants.

Judicial Philosophy and Economic Realism   Posner's
opinion offered a pragmatic counterpoint to regulatory

idealism. He expressed a general skepticism toward legislative efforts to "correct" perceived power imbalances in private contracts without rigorous empirical justification. He challenged the assumption that landlords inherently exploit tenants, instead inviting policymakers to assess whether such regulations actually improve housing access, affordability, or stability in measurable terms.

By framing the ordinance as a type of price control, Posner placed it within a broader tradition of economically suspect policy tools—akin to rent control or minimum resale price maintenance—that are often politically popular but economically dubious. He wrote that the burden of proof should fall on the government to show that such regulations produce more benefit than harm, citing the lack of a cost-benefit study in the record.

Broader Implications and Legacy   The ruling had a ripple effect, not only shaping how courts reviewed landlord-tenant laws but also influencing how economic theory entered judicial discourse. It became a touchstone for:

- **Law and Economics Courses:** Frequently cited in casebooks and university curricula as a model application of Coasean reasoning to judicial decision-making.

- **Urban Policy Reform:** Urban economists and policy analysts referenced the opinion to critique well-meaning but counterproductive housing legislation.

- **Subsequent Jurisprudence:** Posner's approach was echoed in later cases analyzing wage laws, health

mandates, and business licensing—anywhere costs and
incentives could distort intended benefits.

This case exemplifies Posner's belief that economic analysis
belongs not just in academic journals, but in the courtroom.
It remains one of the clearest examples of a federal appellate
judge treating economics as a judicial tool—not merely to
evaluate damages or efficiency, but to assess the very
legitimacy of legislative action.

Quote from the Opinion:

"A growing body of empirical literature deals with
the effects of governmental regulation of the
market for rental housing. The regulations that
have been studied, such as rent control in New
York City and Los Angeles, are not identical to
the new Chicago ordinance, though
some—regulations which require that rental
housing be "habitable"—are close. The
significance of this literature is not in proving that
the Chicago ordinance is unsound, but in showing
that the market for rental housing behaves as
economic theory predicts: if price is artificially
depressed, or the costs of landlords artificially
increased, supply falls and many tenants, usually
the poorer and the newer tenants, are hurt. See,
e.g., Olsen, An Econometric Analysis of Rent
Control, 80 J.Pol.Econ. 1081 (1972); Rydell et al.,
The Impact of Rent Control on the Los Angeles
Housing Market, ch. 6 (Rand Corp. N–1747–LA,

Aug. 1981); Hirsch, Habitability Laws and the
Welfare of Indigent Tenants, 61 Rev.Econ. & Stat.
263 (1981)."

5. Patent, Antitrust, and Economics: *Asahi Glass v. Pentech Pharmaceuticals*, 289 F. Supp. 2d 986 (N.D. Ill. 2003)

Although this district court opinion was not issued from the
appellate bench, Judge Richard Posner, sitting by designation
in the Northern District of Illinois, authored a landmark
decision on the intersection of patent law, antitrust theory,
and economic efficiency. The case arose from a dispute over
the legality of a reverse payment settlement agreement
between Asahi Glass and Pentech Pharmaceuticals, involving
the alleged infringement of a pharmaceutical patent.

Reverse payment settlements—wherein a patent holder pays
an alleged infringer to delay entering the market—had long
sparked debate regarding whether such arrangements
constituted a form of anticompetitive market allocation. At
the time, critics argued that these settlements undermined the
pro-competitive goals of antitrust laws by preserving
monopoly pricing at the expense of consumers. Judge Posner,
however, offered a different lens.

Drawing heavily from microeconomic theory, Posner evaluated
the agreement not from a formalistic antitrust framework, but
through a pragmatic analysis of market incentives, litigation
risk, and innovation economics. He dismissed the complaint,
ruling that the reverse payment agreement did not necessarily

constitute an unlawful restraint of trade, and articulated
three core principles that continue to influence courts today:

- **Economic Justification of Reverse Payments:**
  Posner explained that paying a generic competitor to
  delay market entry is not inherently illegal. He argued
  that such payments may simply reflect the patent
  holder's desire to avoid costly litigation, rather than a
  scheme to divide the market. These payments, in his
  view, are a rational allocation of resources when
  litigation is uncertain and expensive.

- **Absence of Per Se Illegality:** Unlike traditional
  price-fixing conspiracies, which are per se illegal under
  the Sherman Act, Posner emphasized that patent
  settlements require a rule-of-reason approach. Without
  a clear showing of market foreclosure or exclusionary
  conduct, the mere fact of a payment does not establish
  antitrust liability.

- **Promotion of Innovation and Legal Efficiency:**
  Posner underscored the societal benefits of allowing
  parties to resolve disputes without prolonged litigation.
  He observed that discouraging such settlements would
  chill innovation and impose undue burdens on the court
  system. Settlements, he wrote, should not be penalized
  unless they have demonstrable anticompetitive effects.

To support these conclusions, Posner subtly invoked principles
of game theory, particularly the idea of suboptimal Nash
equilibria in the face of uncertain litigation outcomes. His
opinion suggested that in the high-risk, high-cost context of
pharmaceutical patent litigation, parties often rationally opt

for settlements to avoid mutually destructive outcomes. This perspective foreshadowed later academic and judicial work on the "Actavis problem"—the tension between patent law's exclusionary rights and antitrust's promotion of market competition.

Furthermore, Posner acknowledged the need for economic evidence in determining whether a settlement is anticompetitive in fact. He argued that the proper inquiry is not merely whether a reverse payment occurred, but whether the settlement as a whole caused consumer harm by delaying the introduction of lower-cost alternatives. This insight anticipated the Supreme Court's more nuanced approach in *FTC v. Actavis*, 570 U.S. 136 (2013), which cited similar concerns but allowed such cases to proceed under a rule-of-reason analysis.

In addition to its doctrinal implications, the opinion is a vivid example of how Posner blended doctrinal interpretation with empirical modeling. He framed the patent system as a legal mechanism intended to approximate optimal innovation incentives, and cautioned that misapplying antitrust scrutiny could disrupt the delicate balance between rewarding inventiveness and preventing monopoly abuse.

Ultimately, *Asahi Glass v. Pentech* remains a pivotal district court case that influenced the trajectory of antitrust law in the pharmaceutical sector. It illustrates Judge Posner's deep commitment to reconciling law with economics—where judicial reasoning is not only guided by precedent but also grounded in the efficient functioning of markets, rational actor models, and evidence-based policy analysis.

Quote from the Opinion:

> "A patent is a license to sue rather than a license
> to make, use, or sell. Settlements that reflect the
> probabilistic nature of patent litigation should not
> be presumed unlawful, lest we deter economically
> efficient behavior."

Conclusion: A   Legacy   of   Analytical Innovation

Judge Posner's body of work represents a transformation in
legal thinking—an interdisciplinary turn toward
quantification, incentives, and systemic analysis. His opinions
frequently include references to:

- Opportunity cost

- Marginal utility

- Asymmetric information

- Transaction costs

- Game theory

By treating law as a field amendable to empirical reasoning
and economic modeling, Posner not only redefined how judges
reason through hard cases but also legitimized the role of
forensic economists in shaping courtroom narratives.

13.3   His Influence

What began as an intellectual provocation in the pages of law reviews and federal opinions soon became doctrine. By the late 1980s and into the 1990s, the jurisprudence of Richard A. Posner had moved beyond iconoclastic innovation and matured into a national template—reshaping how courts, scholars, and litigants approached questions of liability, efficiency, and remedy. No longer merely an advocate of law and economics, Posner had become its chief architect and institutionalizer.

Antitrust: From Chicago School to Federal Canon

In the field of antitrust, Posner's early work with the Chicago School—alongside Robert Bork and George Stigler—fundamentally altered the enforcement landscape. His judicial opinions, particularly on the Seventh Circuit, emphasized consumer welfare, market efficiency, and rigorous economic modeling as the bedrock of antitrust analysis. This approach supplanted the older structure-conduct-performance paradigm, which had previously focused more on market concentration and firm size.

Through decisions such as *Blue Cross & Blue Shield United of Wisconsin v. Marshfield Clinic*, 65 F.3d 1406 (7th Cir. 1995), and *U.S. v. Syufy Enterprises*, Posner refined the application of economic logic to monopoly behavior and vertical restraints. The Supreme Court followed suit, adopting similar analytical frames in *Verizon v. Trinko*, 540 U.S. 398 (2004), and *Leegin*

Creative Leather Products, Inc. v. PSKS, Inc., 551 U.S. 877
(2007)—each echoing Posnerian reasoning, often without
attribution.

Tort and Damages: Efficiency as a Legal Compass

Posner's tort opinions, particularly in cases involving punitive
damages, became blueprints for state and federal courts. His
opinion in *Mathias v. Accor Economy Lodging, Inc.*, 347 F.3d
672 (7th Cir. 2003), articulated a coherent economic
justification for punitive awards—framing them not as moral
retribution, but as rational responses to underdeterrence
where compensatory damages were likely to be internalized as
mere costs of doing business.

Following this line of reasoning, numerous jurisdictions began
adopting Posner's economic test: Do punitive damages serve
an efficient deterrent purpose where compensatory awards
alone would not suffice? His framework was explicitly cited or
silently mirrored in opinions from California, New York, and
Texas courts, as well as in federal jurisprudence applying state
tort law under diversity jurisdiction.

Contracts and Commercial Law: The Rise of Rational Breach

Perhaps no doctrine better reflects Posner's imprint than the
widespread acceptance of the "efficient breach" theory in
contract law. First proposed in academia, the notion that
breaching a contract is not inherently wrongful if it leads to a
more efficient allocation of resources gained judicial traction

through Posner's opinions. In cases like *Lake River Corp. v. Carborundum Co.*, 769 F.2d 1284 (7th Cir. 1985), Posner critiqued penalty clauses not through the lens of fairness, but economic waste.

Over time, courts across the country began citing Posnerian logic when assessing liquidated damages, mitigation duties, and the measure of expectancy interest. Law students were taught to view contracts less as moral obligations and more as mechanisms for economic coordination—an approach traceable directly to Posner's bench.

Judicial Economy and Procedural Reform

Beyond substantive law, Posner reshaped judicial administration itself. A vocal critic of inefficiency in litigation, he advocated for active case management, streamlined pleadings, and the use of judicial resources in proportion to economic stakes. His influence led to broader acceptance of summary judgment, limits on discovery, and skepticism toward protracted trial processes—now embedded in the Federal Rules of Civil Procedure and mirrored in local court practices nationwide.

From Dissenting Visionary to Doctrinal Touchstone

The progression of Posner's influence follows a familiar trajectory in American legal thought: radicalism, resistance, assimilation, and orthodoxy. Where once his views were met with skepticism or seen as academic overreach, they are now embedded in the legal DNA of countless doctrines. Supreme

Court decisions, treatises, law school curricula, and everyday judicial reasoning reflect his fingerprints.

As the legal system increasingly values predictability, cost-efficiency, and data-informed decision-making, Posnerian economics has become not merely influential—but foundational. His method is no longer one voice in the conversation; it is the grammar of the modern legal dialect.

13.4   The Reckoning

Few jurists in American history have undergone as dramatic a public intellectual transformation as Judge Richard A. Posner. Over a career that spanned more than three decades on the United States Court of Appeals for the Seventh Circuit, Posner built an empire of logic, championing the primacy of economic efficiency as the north star of legal reasoning. But in his later years—and with even greater candor after his retirement in 2017—Posner began to question not only the contours of his own jurisprudence, but the very assumptions that had shaped his once-uncompromising worldview.

An Architect of Logic, a Student of Consequence

In the early and middle phases of his judicial career, Posner's decisions bore the hallmark of the Chicago School: dispassionate rationality, skepticism of regulation, and an unshakable faith in markets as engines of social welfare. His opinions were incisive, often scathing, and focused relentlessly on outcome optimization. He famously eschewed moral argumentation, favoring utility over virtue, and declared that judges should act as "pragmatic adjudicators," not philosophical theorists.

But over time, the limitations of this approach began to surface. Critics charged that Posner's framework underappreciated non-market values—such as dignity, fairness, or historical injustice—and that his abstraction often reduced complex human disputes to economic puzzles. To many, his method was brilliant but bloodless.

Late-Career Shifts: From Economic Rigor to Empirical Humility

In the final decade of his judicial service, Posner's writings and judicial behavior began to signal a pivot. He became increasingly vocal about the shortcomings of legal formalism and even began to question the sufficiency of economics as a comprehensive lens for adjudication. In interviews and opinions, he lamented the profession's obsession with precedent over consequences and began championing a more empirical, case-specific approach to judging.

In a 2016 interview, he remarked:

> "I pay very little attention to legal rules, statutes, constitutional provisions... A case is just a dispute. The job of a judge is to produce the best consequences."

This startling admission marked a shift from Posner the theorist to Posner the empiricist. He was no longer satisfied with the elegance of a model—he wanted proof of its real-world impact. Efficiency remained a concern, but he now seemed more alert to issues of accessibility, judicial arrogance, and the lived experiences of litigants.

Departure from the Bench and the Rise of Judicial Dissent

In 2017, Posner abruptly retired from the Seventh Circuit, citing growing frustration with the judiciary's treatment of pro se litigants. He believed that courts had become inhospitable to those without lawyers, treating them as procedural nuisances rather than citizens deserving of justice. This concern—rooted not in abstract theory, but in the human realities of the courtroom—marked the culmination of his philosophical shift.

Soon after retiring, Posner authored a short book titled *Reforming the Federal Judiciary: My Former Court Needs to Overhaul Its Staff Attorney Program and Begin Televising Oral Arguments*. It was a blistering critique not only of internal court practices but of the broader judicial culture. He took direct aim at his colleagues, lamenting what he viewed as intellectual complacency, bureaucratic opacity, and the moral detachment of judges from the people they serve.

Post-Judicial Reflections: From Legal Technocrat to Public Ethicist

Since stepping down, Posner has become more introspective, even contrite. He has admitted that some of his earlier opinions lacked sufficient compassion or failed to capture the nuances of human vulnerability. While he has not disavowed

law and economics, he has reframed it as a tool among
many—not a singular philosophy of justice.

In lectures and interviews, he has emphasized the importance
of humility in judging and the danger of judicial ego. The
once-combative critic of "legalese" now champions clarity not
merely for elegance, but for accessibility. He has advocated
for self-represented litigants, spoken out against rigid
originalism, and expressed growing concern over structural
inequalities in the legal system.

In one of his final essays, Posner wrote:

> "The confidentiality of the judicial process would
> not matter greatly to an understanding and
> evaluation of the legal system if the consequences
> of judicial behavior could be readily determined.
> If you can determine the ripeness of a cantaloupe
> by squeezing or smelling it, you don't have to
> worry about the produce clerk's mental processes."

The Evolution of a Legacy

Posner's late-career and post-retirement reflections do not
erase his earlier contributions, but they do complicate them.
His journey reveals a restless intellect willing to evolve—even
to repudiate parts of its own legacy. It suggests that Posner's
greatest insight may not be the supremacy of economic
reasoning, but the necessity of revision: that no model,
however brilliant, is immune to the demands of reality,
empathy, or change.

In this light, Posner's legacy is not a monument to theory, but a mirror to the law itself: capable of refinement, receptive to experience, and forever unfinished.

13.5   Posnerian Horizon

No single chapter can fully capture the kaleidoscopic mind of Richard A. Posner. Though we have traced the main currents of his economic jurisprudence—through landmark opinions, theoretical innovations, and his shifting public philosophy—there remain tributaries less explored but no less vital.

Posner's influence extended deeply into intellectual property, administrative law, and even the philosophy of language. He wrote extensively on copyright law, proposing that optimal duration and enforcement should be governed not by natural rights but by the incentivization of creative output. In matters of administrative law, he was unafraid to question the competence of agencies, suggesting that courts should not defer blindly to technocratic decision-making when it lacks cost-benefit justification. Even in judicial writing itself, Posner advocated for radical clarity, stripping decisions of arcane Latinisms and verbose obfuscation in favor of a style both precise and democratic.

He was also a relentless book reviewer, using the pages of the *New Republic*, *The Atlantic*, and *New York Times* to evaluate not only legal texts but fiction, biography, and science—applying the same incisive logic to Hemingway as he did to Holmes. For Posner, the law was never siloed; it was an open system, shaped and sharpened by the totality of human knowledge.

What we may have missed, then, is not a blind spot but a challenge: Posner was not content to remain a theorist, nor merely a judge. He demanded that every serious thinker become, in some form, a student of consequence. In that sense, his example is less a doctrine than a call to intellectual vigilance.

13.6 Conclusion

Richard A. Posner did not merely interpret the law; he reengineered its machinery. He saw legal reasoning not as a static inheritance of precedent but as a dynamic system governed by incentives, costs, and empirical consequences. From torts to contracts, from antitrust to procedure, his vision was totalizing: to ground justice in utility, to translate abstract rights into measurable outcomes, and to equip judges with the tools of economists.

Yet even this towering edifice was not immune to time. As Posner aged, he looked back at his own edifice with both pride and disquiet—seeing cracks where once he saw symmetry, and blind spots where once he saw logic. His shift from economic absolutism to pragmatic empathy reveals that the true genius of Posner was not in his models, but in his willingness to revise them.

With his legacy now woven into the fabric of American legal thought, we are left with both a map and a mirror: a map of how law and economics can inform justice, and a mirror reflecting the perils of abstraction without humanity.

We now turn from the architect to the arena. In the next chapter, we explore how economic analysis meets the unruly world of *Complex Cases*, where multiple plaintiffs, tangled causation, systemic harms, and probabilistic injury demand the most sophisticated tools of forensic economics. Here, Posner's legacy is not merely echoed but tested in the courtroom crucible.

Chapter 14

Complex Cases

14.1   FBI Investigations

Introduction

In the investigation and prosecution of white-collar crime, particularly in cases involving money laundering, corruption, monopolistic practices, and corporate collusion, the Federal Bureau of Investigation (FBI) relies heavily on the expertise of forensic accountants and economists. These professionals provide the analytical foundation necessary to trace illicit financial flows, identify concealed control relationships among corporate actors, and quantify illegal gains in complex commercial arrangements.

White-collar crime rarely presents as a single, isolated

transaction. Rather, it often occurs within complex and dynamic financial ecosystems involving shell corporations, offshore tax havens, front companies, and shadow banking networks. The movement of illicit funds, whether for purposes of money laundering, asset concealment, or bribery, is orchestrated across multiple jurisdictions and camouflaged behind layers of contractual formality, falsified accounting, and deliberate obfuscation. The forensic accountant's role is to pierce this veil of complexity.

The FBI's white-collar crime unit operates at the intersection of law, finance, and data analytics. Forensic accountants serve not only as technical experts but as investigative strategists, working alongside special agents, prosecutors, and intelligence analysts to reconstruct economic behavior, model suspicious transactions, and unravel schemes that would otherwise remain hidden. Their ability to translate raw financial data into legally actionable evidence is indispensable in securing indictments and convictions.

This importance is magnified in cases where companies maintain unique or "special" relationships with one another. These may include:

- **Parent–subsidiary structures** where corporate separateness is maintained in form but not in function.

- **Nominee-controlled entities** used to disguise ownership or evade regulatory scrutiny.

- **Contractually interdependent enterprises** whose dealings mask kickbacks, bid-rigging, or market manipulation.

- **International joint ventures** that serve as conduits for the movement of illicit capital.

In such cases, forensic accountants do more than examine ledgers and invoices. They construct economic timelines, map organizational networks, and model the flow of value across legal boundaries. They help determine whether a transaction served a legitimate business purpose or was designed to enable or conceal illegal conduct. Their work often involves:

- Reconstructing destroyed or incomplete accounting records;

- Linking electronic transfers to shell accounts and offshore banks;

- Testing the economic rationality of transactions through comparative analysis;

- Assessing the consistency of financial disclosures with operational realities.

When companies work together to dominate a market—through price-fixing, collusion, or coordinated scarcity—these relationships often take the form of oligopolistic cartels or informal monopolistic control. Forensic accountants are instrumental in identifying these structures and proving their economic effects. They measure:

- The artificial inflation or suppression of prices,

- The marginal loss to consumers or competitors,

- The illegal gains distributed among the colluding firms,

- The use of coordinated strategies to exclude competitors

or manipulate demand.

Additionally, forensic accountants frequently assist in the application of key statutes, including:

- **The Bank Secrecy Act (BSA)** and **Anti-Money Laundering (AML)** rules governing suspicious activity reports (SARs), currency transaction reports (CTRs), and due diligence obligations.

- **The Foreign Corrupt Practices Act (FCPA)**, particularly when U.S. companies or their foreign subsidiaries are involved in the payment of bribes to secure business.

- **The Sherman Act** and **Clayton Act**, which prohibit monopolistic conduct and anticompetitive mergers.

- **The RICO Act (Racketeer Influenced and Corrupt Organizations)**, which allows prosecutors to charge individuals or businesses engaged in a pattern of racketeering.

In sum, forensic accountants and economists form the backbone of the FBI's strategy in combating financial crime and corporate abuse. They bring clarity to opacity, transforming a tangled web of transactions and entities into a cohesive narrative of illegal enterprise. This chapter examines the techniques, tools, and legal principles that define their work in investigating fraud, collusion, and financial manipulation across the modern corporate landscape.

Hidden Financial Relationships

In complex litigation, especially in fraud, corruption, and racketeering cases, what appears to be a web of independent legal entities may in fact be a tightly coordinated financial organism. Forensic economists are often called upon to pierce the corporate veil, trace beneficial ownership, and map the true architecture of influence hidden beneath layers of formal separation. Their task is not simply to account for what is visible, but to uncover what has been deliberately obscured.

A superficial examination of company structures may reveal different names, addresses, and articles of incorporation. Yet beneath these distinctions may lie:

- **Common ownership or beneficial control**, where ultimate equity holders control multiple entities behind shell companies or trusts.

- **Strategic entity layering**, in which business structures are intentionally fragmented to frustrate transparency and hinder enforcement efforts.

- **Consolidated cash flow and revenue streams**, masked through circular transactions, intercompany loans, or trade-based money laundering tactics.

- **Influence networks**, where key individuals, often directors, executives, or shadow officers—exercise de facto control across several organizations.

- **Rotating partnerships**, with the same actors repeatedly appearing in different ventures, serving different formal roles but furthering a shared economic agenda.

- **Nominee structures**, in which intermediaries or strawpersons are used to disguise true ownership and beneficial interest.

- **Transfer pricing manipulation**, used to shift profits or losses between entities under common control to alter tax liability or hide gains.

- **Jurisdictional arbitrage**, exploiting differences in disclosure rules, banking secrecy, or incorporation laws to conceal ties across borders.

Through forensic methods—including network analysis, cross-referencing of bank records, digital communication audits, and subpoenaed internal documents, economists and accountants reconstruct the hidden economic reality behind the legal fiction.

These revelations often become dispositive in high-stakes litigation and criminal enforcement. Demonstrating that a nominally independent entity is in fact part of a unified scheme can:

- Establish *constructive control* for purposes of liability.

- Justify *piercing the corporate veil* under the alter ego doctrine.

- Support allegations of *fraudulent conveyance*, asset shielding, or conspiracy.

- Reveal *patterns of racketeering activity* under RICO or equivalent statutes.

- Enable tracing of *illicit enrichment* or proceeds of crime for forfeiture or restitution.

In sum, the forensic investigation of hidden financial relationships transforms a static snapshot of corporate form into a dynamic map of financial behavior. It is through this lens that law and economics merge, not in abstraction, but in the gritty, granular, and often global pursuit of truth behind the paper trail.

Tracing Laundered Funds and Corporate Layering

Money laundering often involves disguising the origin, ownership, or destination of funds. Forensic accountants employed by the FBI follow the money trail by:

- Tracing **multi-jurisdictional transfers** through SWIFT codes, correspondent banks, and offshore entities.

- Analyzing **phantom invoices, false loans, and service contracts** used to justify intercompany payments.

- Detecting **over- or under-invoicing schemes** between related companies (a hallmark of trade-based money laundering).

- Using forensic software to link **recurring transaction patterns, shell layers, and account signatories**.

They often identify red flags such as unexplained cash deposits, round-dollar amounts, or rapid inflow and outflow of funds through newly formed corporate entities.

Forensic Accountants in Antitrust and Market Control Cases

When the FBI investigates companies suspected of controlling markets through monopolistic or oligopolistic behavior, forensic economists are critical in establishing:

- **Unlawful price coordination** among peer-level competitors.

- **Market allocation, bid rigging, or supply restriction** strategies used to reduce competition.

- **Predatory pricing** followed by recoupment phases to destroy rivals.

- **Shared profit pools or cartel bonus structures** linked to performance targets.

They examine industry-wide cost data, internal pricing forecasts, historical price movements, and inter-firm communications. Forensic economists compare these with established economic models to detect anticompetitive behavior.

Valuing Illicit Gains and Asset Forfeiture

Beyond identifying wrongdoing, forensic accountants help quantify its financial impact. This work supports:

- **Restitution orders** for defrauded victims.

- **Civil and criminal forfeiture actions** under RICO

or money laundering statutes.

- **Parallel tax investigations** by reconciling unreported income and business expenses.

They reconstruct income statements, balance sheets, and undisclosed ledgers to calculate the amount of money illegally obtained or concealed, often under conditions where the official records have been manipulated or partially destroyed.

Courtroom Support and Visualization

In complex cases, forensic economists and accountants assist not only with analysis but also with presentation. They prepare visual aids and testify in court to explain how:

- **Money moved through multiple shell companies** or foreign accounts.

- **Control was exerted** through interlocking directors or cross-ownership.

- **Profits were distributed** among conspirators or reinvested in legitimate enterprises.

Their ability to reduce intricate financial maneuvers into digestible charts and flow diagrams often proves decisive in persuading juries and judges.

Illustrative Examples

Case studies serve as the crucible in which forensic techniques are tested, applied, and ultimately translated into courtroom persuasion. While theory provides the framework, examples breathe life into that architecture, showing how abstract tools

confront real-world complexity. What follows are expanded
illustrations of how forensic economics and accounting
illuminate hidden misconduct, pierce legal formalism, and
empower prosecutors, regulators, and litigators.

Example 1: Trade-Based Money Laundering Scheme in the Textile Industry

The FBI, in collaboration with the Department of Homeland
Security and international banking regulators, initiates an
investigation into a network of textile importers suspected of
laundering narcotics proceeds on behalf of a South American
cartel. The scheme centers on a series of transactions
involving the overpayment for fabric and garment shipments
sent from controlled entities in Southeast Asia. Though the
shipments appear routine, the invoices are grossly inflated and
routed through shell companies.

Forensic accountants are brought in to dismantle the illusion
of legitimacy. Their work involves:

- Identifying **invoice mismatches** across customs
  declarations, bank transfer records, and internal
  purchase orders—highlighting repeated overvaluation of
  goods.

- Tracing **payment flows** through correspondent banks
  and offshore jurisdictions including the British Virgin
  Islands and Panama, noting patterns of circular fund
  transfers indicative of layering and integration phases of
  laundering.

- Comparing invoiced prices to **global market indices
  and benchmark pricing databases** (e.g., PIERS,

Import Genius, WTO customs data) to demonstrate
egregious mispricing that cannot be justified by quality,
volume, or logistics.

- Conducting **Benford's law analyses** on numerical
  entries to flag statistical anomalies inconsistent with
  organic commercial activity.

- Mapping relationships between company officers,
  directors, and beneficial owners across jurisdictions to
  show a web of **related-party entities** created for
  obfuscation.

The forensic report ultimately provides a compelling narrative:
a closed-loop laundering circuit disguised as global trade.
Prosecutors use this evidence to indict under anti-money
laundering statutes, resulting in asset seizures and the
dismantling of a major transnational laundering platform.

Example 2: Monopolistic Control in the Technology Sector

A joint task force between the FBI's Antitrust Division and
the DOJ Economic Analysis Group launches a multi-year
investigation into a dominant software platform suspected of
engaging in predatory pricing and exclusionary practices
aimed at smaller rivals in the cloud productivity space.

Forensic economists are tasked with evaluating the economic
impact and legality of the firm's conduct under both Section 2
of the Sherman Act and state-level unfair competition laws.

Their analysis involves:

- Performing **time-series regression analysis** of pricing behavior to detect below-cost sales over sustained intervals, adjusted for customer acquisition cycles and promotional norms.

- Reviewing **internal corporate strategy memos**, quarterly planning decks, and executive communications which reveal deliberate efforts to undercut competitors, followed by aggressive price increases post-market exit.

- Constructing **counterfactual market models** to estimate what pricing and innovation trajectories would have occurred had competition remained intact—thus quantifying harm in terms of consumer surplus loss.

- Examining **barrier creation tactics** such as exclusive bundling agreements, most-favored-nation clauses, and the use of interoperability restrictions to raise switching costs.

- Modeling **network effects and lock-in** using simulations to demonstrate that the company's market power extends beyond price manipulation to structural entrenchment.

The findings inform a high-profile antitrust lawsuit, resulting in a consent decree mandating pricing transparency, structural divestiture of a product line, and third-party compliance monitoring for five years. The case sets a new benchmark for algorithmic market abuse detection.

Example 3: Healthcare Fraud through Phantom Billing and Overutilization

In a major federal healthcare fraud case, forensic accountants and health economists are enlisted to investigate a multi-clinic medical enterprise suspected of submitting millions of dollars in fraudulent Medicare and Medicaid claims. Whistleblower reports allege "phantom billing" for procedures never rendered, along with coercive overutilization of diagnostic imaging and outpatient procedures.

The forensic team:

- Reconciles **billing codes with patient appointment logs**, staff rosters, and medical device usage logs to expose statistically impossible procedure volumes.

- Applies **outlier detection algorithms** to CPT and ICD-10 code frequencies, benchmarking against regional and national averages to identify fraud clusters.

- Investigates **patient records for signature duplication, ghost entries, and forged physician authentication**, often confirmed through handwriting analysis and metadata audits.

- Conducts **network analysis** of physicians, billing specialists, and management to reveal shared incentives and quota-driven fraud schemes.

- Quantifies **economic impact to the government** using historical claims denial rates and actuarial loss estimation models.

The investigation culminates in a multi-count indictment under the False Claims Act, the Anti-Kickback Statute, and the federal RICO statute. Over $45 million in fraudulent billing is documented, and forensic analysis becomes central to the prosecution's case.

Example 4: Environmental Damages and Corporate Externalities

A forensic environmental economist is retained in a civil class action against a multinational chemical company accused of illegally discharging industrial waste into a watershed. The community alleges decades of undisclosed contamination leading to elevated cancer rates, reduced property values, and ecological collapse.

The expert's role includes:

- Estimating **property value diminution** through hedonic regression models incorporating contamination exposure as a disamenity factor.

- Quantifying **health-related damages** using statistical correlation between pollutant concentration and epidemiological data, calibrated for demographic and geographic variables.

- Calculating **restoration costs** based on ecological remediation scenarios and projected timelines.

- Uncovering **internal risk assessments and cost-benefit memoranda** showing corporate awareness and willful inaction.

- Valuing **loss of ecosystem services**—such as groundwater purification and biodiversity—through contingent valuation and replacement cost methods.

The analysis supports a $300 million settlement, mandating clean-up, medical monitoring, and environmental restitution.

These illustrative examples are not merely theoretical. They represent the intersection of data, method, and law. They show how forensic economics transcends static accounting to illuminate the patterns, incentives, and harms that animate the most complex and consequential disputes of our time.

Conclusion

Forensic accountants and economists serve as the backbone of financial investigation in FBI-led cases involving complex commercial structures, especially when layered corporate control and financial misdirection are at play. Whether tracking illicit profits through shell entities or exposing collusion in market pricing, they translate numbers into narratives of misconduct. Their work makes it possible to dismantle sophisticated financial crimes that would otherwise remain obscured behind layers of legal formality and economic complexity.

14.2 Horizontal Privity

Forensic Economists & Horizontal Privity

Horizontal privity arises in commercial law when two or more parties operate at the same level of the supply or distribution chain. Unlike vertical privity, which connects parties in a buyer-seller or manufacturer-retailer relationship, horizontal privity concerns co-manufacturers, competing distributors, or

parallel vendors who are not in a direct contractual
relationship with the plaintiff but are nonetheless part of the
same transactional ecosystem.

In traditional warranty and product liability law, horizontal
privity was historically required to allow a plaintiff to recover
from a third-party seller or manufacturer. Over time, courts
have relaxed this requirement, particularly where foreseeable
reliance, joint venture agreements, or networked supply chains
blur the boundaries between horizontal and vertical actors.

Horizontal Disputes

Forensic economists contribute substantially to cases involving
horizontal privity by mapping out the financial and
operational interdependence among parallel actors in a
market. Their work helps courts and litigants understand how
competitors or co-participants in a market scheme may be
jointly responsible for causing economic harm.

Common scenarios include:

- **Collusion and Price-Fixing:** When competing firms
  at the same market level coordinate prices, limit output,
  or divide territories, forensic economists use market
  simulations, pricing models, and antitrust damage
  theories to measure the impact of collusion on
  consumers and competitors.

- **Joint Liability in Defective Product Distribution:**
  In cases where a defective product is distributed by
  multiple peer-level parties, such as co-packagers or
  co-distributors, forensic economists help determine each

party's share of the economic loss.

- **Loss of Market Share:** Plaintiffs may allege that coordinated actions among horizontal competitors caused measurable damage to their business. Economists evaluate market behavior, customer attrition, and lost revenue using regression analysis, benchmarking, and historical performance data.

Demonstrating Economic Nexus Among Horizontally Related Firms

To establish liability among horizontally related parties, plaintiffs must demonstrate that their injuries stemmed from concerted or parallel conduct. Forensic economists are instrumental in this effort by:

- Identifying **patterns of parallel conduct** that suggest collusion rather than coincidence.

- Performing **counterfactual analysis** to estimate what would have occurred had defendants acted independently.

- Establishing **common economic incentives** or market positions that facilitated cooperation among competitors.

- Modeling **interlocking financial interests** or shared gains derived from harmful acts.

Their findings may also support arguments for joint and several liability or equitable apportionment of damages based on economic contribution to the harm.

Case Example: Horizontal Collusion in the Food Industry

Imagine a group of competing dairy processors accused of coordinating supply restrictions to drive up wholesale milk prices. Although no direct contracts exist between the plaintiffs (grocery retailers) and each individual defendant, plaintiffs allege harm due to elevated input costs.

A forensic economist might:

- Compare price trends before, during, and after the alleged conduct.

- Use econometric tools to test whether prices exceeded competitive benchmarks.

- Quantify pass-through costs to retailers and ultimately to consumers.

These findings support the claim that horizontally situated defendants collectively distorted market outcomes, satisfying the functional equivalent of privity in tort-based recovery.

Conclusion

While horizontal privity is less often a strict legal barrier in modern commercial litigation, understanding the financial and operational linkages among co-level parties is crucial in allocating responsibility and calculating damages. Forensic economists provide the analytical framework to link horizontally related entities to economic outcomes, thereby reinforcing causation, liability, and fair apportionment in complex legal disputes.

14.3 Vertical Privity

Forensic Economists and Vertical Privity

Vertical privity refers to the legal relationship between parties in a direct chain of distribution, such as manufacturers, wholesalers, retailers, and end consumers. It stands in contrast to horizontal privity, which involves parties at the same level of commerce. In product liability, warranty claims, and commercial disputes, vertical privity often determines whether a plaintiff may recover from upstream entities in the supply chain, particularly when the transaction occurred through intermediaries.

Historically, strict privity rules limited claims to parties in direct contractual relationships. However, modern commercial jurisprudence has gradually eroded the privity requirement, especially where implied warranties, third-party beneficiary doctrines, or tort theories (such as negligent misrepresentation or failure to warn) come into play.

The Role of Forensic Economists in Vertical Relationships

Forensic economists play a pivotal role in analyzing economic harm and value transmission along vertically integrated or chained corporate structures. Their expertise is vital in identifying how costs, prices, profits, and losses flow between layers of the distribution system—and how upstream conduct impacts downstream economic outcomes.

In litigation, this expertise is often employed in the following contexts:

- **Defective Product Chains:** When a component manufacturer's defect causes systemic product failure, forensic economists evaluate the financial impact on assemblers, distributors, retailers, and consumers.

- **Supply Chain Disruptions:** In breach of contract claims or force majeure disputes, economists quantify lost profits or increased costs at each stage of the vertical chain.

- **Vertical Price Controls and Resale Price Maintenance:** In antitrust cases, economists assess whether upstream firms exerted unlawful control over downstream pricing, and whether such controls distorted competitive dynamics.

- **Licensing and Franchise Disputes:** Economists evaluate royalty structures, economic coercion, and dependence in vertical franchisor-franchisee arrangements.

Tracing Economic Harm Through the Supply Chain

To demonstrate liability and quantify damages in vertically privity-based disputes, forensic economists typically:

- Construct **input-output models** to follow the flow of goods, services, and payments.

- Perform **but-for analysis** to compare actual outcomes against a hypothetical scenario absent the wrongful conduct.

- Use **cost pass-through models** to determine how upstream overcharges or defects affected downstream pricing or margins.

- Evaluate **diminution in goodwill or enterprise value** for downstream firms harmed by upstream actions.

These approaches are especially useful in class action contexts, where a defect or illegal practice originates at the top of the chain but harms a broad class of indirect purchasers or franchisees.

Case Example: Vertical Antitrust Enforcement in the Tech Industry

Consider a scenario where a global technology manufacturer mandates resale prices to downstream distributors, limiting their ability to compete on pricing. Retailers bring suit, alleging lost market share and diminished margins due to the vertical price restraints.

A forensic economist might:

- Analyze sales records across distributors to detect pricing rigidity or price floors.

- Model consumer demand responses under alternative (unconstrained) price scenarios.

- Estimate overcharges or margin compression experienced by the retailers.

- Determine whether upstream controls were consistent with a strategy of market foreclosure or collusion.

This analysis supports a theory of anticompetitive harm grounded in vertical privity and informed by empirical economic modeling.

Conclusion

Vertical privity remains a cornerstone concept in commercial litigation, particularly in product liability, franchise disputes, antitrust enforcement, and breach of contract cases. Forensic economists help courts and litigants trace economic causality through vertically linked firms, thereby illuminating how conduct at one level reverberates across the entire distribution chain. Their work supports equitable allocation of damages, reinforces legal theories of liability, and provides critical clarity in otherwise opaque corporate relationships.

14.4 Multi-Party Litigation

Overview of Complex Commercial Relationships

In modern commercial litigation, particularly where multiple legal entities operate within an intertwined business framework, establishing the nature and function of the relationships between those entities is foundational. These complex relationships are not merely organizational—they are legal, financial, contractual, and operational. The identification and analysis of these relationships significantly

influence both the establishment of liability and the
methodology used to calculate economic damages.

Such disputes often arise from contract breaches, fiduciary
misconduct, fraudulent transfers, or statutory violations (such
as antitrust laws or securities regulations), and they tend to
involve an intricate web of related corporate forms. These
forms may include parent corporations, wholly or partially
owned subsidiaries, sister corporations under common control,
joint ventures, partnerships, and layered holding companies
with cross-border affiliations.

Understanding these relationships is critical because liability
may not be confined to the legal entity that executed the
wrongful act. Plaintiffs may allege that harm was enabled or
exacerbated by a network of related entities that were either
direct participants in the misconduct, benefited unjustly, or
failed in their oversight or fiduciary duties. Such allegations
often give rise to theories of joint and several liability,
conspiracy, aiding and abetting, or veil-piercing.

Types of Commercial Relationships Relevant to Litigation

- **Parent–Subsidiary Structures:** Where a parent
  company dominates the operations of a subsidiary to
  such an extent that the subsidiary lacks true
  independence, the parent may be held liable for its
  conduct—particularly under the "alter ego" or
  "instrumentality" doctrines.

- **Affiliated and Sister Companies:** Corporations
  under common ownership or control may share

liabilities or engage in coordinated conduct. Disputes may arise when liability is sought to be spread across these entities.

- **Joint Ventures and Strategic Partnerships:** Contractual relationships between companies to collaborate on defined goals (e.g., co-development, co-marketing) often come with mutual obligations. Breach by one party may affect the other's economic performance or reputation.

- **Special Purpose Entities (SPEs) and Shell Companies:** Frequently used in finance, real estate, and IP licensing, these entities may be exploited to shield assets, disguise transfers, or obfuscate liability. Courts may scrutinize their legitimacy and disregard their separateness if abuse is shown.

Role of Forensic Economists in Untangling Corporate Webs In these environments, forensic economists and forensic accountants serve as essential experts. They assist counsel and the court in mapping out the financial relationships, cash flows, and operational interdependencies among related business entities. Their work involves:

- **Tracing intercompany transactions**—identifying whether payments, loans, royalties, or dividends were used to enrich or capitalize affiliates in a way that contributed to the plaintiff's harm.

- **Assessing control and influence**—evaluating whether a parent or controlling company effectively directed the decisions of its subsidiaries or partners, especially in relation to the wrongful conduct.

- **Quantifying shared gains or losses**—calculating how multiple entities profited jointly from fraudulent activity, contract breaches, or regulatory evasion.

- **Modeling economic loss**—developing damage models that apportion responsibility based on each entity's role and benefit in the overarching transaction or scheme.

Forensic economists also assist in rebutting opposing narratives that attempt to isolate liability to a single party while concealing the broader structural or financial ecosystem in which the harm occurred.

Legal Doctrines Intersecting with Complex Commercial Relationships   Several legal theories become central in these disputes:

- **Veil Piercing and Alter Ego:** Plaintiffs may attempt to disregard corporate separateness when a company is undercapitalized, lacks formal governance, or is used as a conduit for the parent's business.

- **Civil Conspiracy and Aiding and Abetting:** In tort or fraud cases, economic experts help establish joint conduct or knowledge among affiliated entities contributing to a coordinated harm.

- **Unjust Enrichment:** Where one entity benefits economically from another's wrongdoing without direct participation, economists can quantify that enrichment and trace its flow through layered corporate channels.

- **Constructive Fraudulent Transfers:** Forensic

economists often analyze whether a financially
distressed company improperly transferred assets to
related entities for less than fair value, particularly in
insolvency or bankruptcy contexts.

Examples of Complex Litigation Scenarios   Consider a
cross-border technology licensing dispute: a U.S. plaintiff
alleges that its licensee breached an exclusive agreement by
sublicensing patented material through a subsidiary
incorporated in the Cayman Islands. The sublicensee then
commercialized the product through a European distributor
also owned by the same parent.

Forensic economic analysis might reveal:

- The revenue and profits of each link in the distribution
  chain.

- Internal royalty rates, management fees, or cost-sharing
  agreements among the affiliates.

- Coordinated financial planning or performance bonuses
  tied to the success of the infringing product.

- The degree of operational and financial integration
  across borders.

Such analysis helps identify each defendant's role in the
economic harm and can support equitable apportionment,
disgorgement remedies, or treble damages in statutory claims.

Conclusion   In sum, the modern commercial landscape is
characterized by strategic complexity and layered
interdependence. Forensic economists bring clarity to that
complexity, illuminating how related entities interact, transfer

value, coordinate behavior, and, sometimes, collude to avoid liability. Their work is not only critical for damages assessment but also for proving the factual and financial predicate for legal liability in multi-party commercial litigation.

Parent Companies, Subsidiaries, and Affiliates

Corporate structures are often complex by design. A parent company may own multiple subsidiaries, some of which serve as operating companies while others hold assets or manage intellectual property. In litigation, piercing the corporate veil or assigning joint liability requires a careful analysis of:

- **Operational control**: Did the parent exert direct control over the subsidiary's decisions?

- **Financial interdependence**: Are the books consolidated? Were funds commingled?

- **Shared management or resources**: Do the entities share officers, employees, or branding?

- **Alter ego theory**: Is the subsidiary essentially a facade for the parent's operations?

Forensic economists and accountants play a key role in untangling these relationships by analyzing organizational charts, governance documents, intercompany transactions, and internal communications.

Horizontal and Vertical Privity in Commercial Claims

In contract and tort law, the doctrine of privity defines the legal relationship required to sue or be sued. In multi-party disputes:

- **Vertical privity** refers to direct contractual or transactional relationships—such as between a manufacturer and a wholesaler.

- **Horizontal privity** involves parties on the same level in the supply chain—such as two distributors or co-manufacturers.

Establishing privity is essential for claims involving breach of warranty, negligence, fraud, and economic loss. Courts may reject claims if the plaintiff lacks sufficient legal connection to the defendant, unless an exception—such as third-party beneficiary status or reliance—is shown.

Forensic experts assist attorneys by reconstructing the chain of contractual relationships, supply flows, and financial transfers. They help determine who paid whom, under what terms, and whether certain parties exerted undue influence or breached obligations in a way that caused measurable harm.

Forensic Accountants in Corporate Fraud, Corruption, and Embezzlement

Forensic accountants and economists are indispensable in complex litigation involving financial misconduct. Their investigative and analytical skills are used to uncover and prove:

- **Corporate fraud**: Inflated revenues, falsified expenses, or misreported liabilities.

- **Corruption and kickbacks**: Unrecorded payments, vendor manipulation, or bribery schemes.

- **Embezzlement**: Unauthorized withdrawals, diversion of funds, ghost employees or vendors.

- **Money laundering or asset hiding**: Use of offshore accounts, shell entities, or related-party transactions.

They analyze general ledgers, bank statements, payroll systems, audit trails, and financial statements to detect irregularities. In class actions or shareholder suits, they quantify the financial impact of the fraud across all affected parties.

Causation and Economic Linkage

One of the most critical roles of a forensic economist is to demonstrate the **economic nexus** between the wrongful conduct and the plaintiff's damages. In multi-party commercial cases, this often involves:

- **Tracing cash flows** across companies to identify enrichment or dissipation.

- **Modeling lost profits** or business interruption caused by the conduct of one or more defendants.

- **Analyzing market share impact** in cases involving collusion, price fixing, or monopolistic behavior.

- **Valuing stolen or diverted assets**, including intellectual property or trade secrets.

Forensic experts apply statistical tools, financial models, and industry data to reconstruct economic harm, distinguish it from unrelated losses, and apportion damages across culpable parties.

Illustrative Scenario

Suppose a pharmaceutical company (PharmaCorp) sues a competitor and its overseas subsidiary, alleging misappropriation of proprietary formulas and interference with contract manufacturers. The lawsuit names three entities:

- **BioSynth International, Inc.** (the direct competitor),

- **BioSynth Holdings, Ltd.** (parent company),

- **BioSynth Asia Pte. Ltd.** (the entity accused of misappropriation).

PharmaCorp must establish that all three companies operated in concert or under unified control. A forensic economist may assist by:

- Tracing the licensing of trade secrets across entities.

- Analyzing internal royalties, management fees, and supply chain records.

- Assessing the revenue generated from products incorporating the misappropriated IP.

- Estimating damages for lost market share or unjust enrichment.

Their work supports claims for fraud, breach of fiduciary duty, and civil conspiracy, helping the plaintiff overcome defenses based on corporate separateness or lack of direct contract.

Conclusion

In commercial cases involving multiple parties, corporate layers, or opaque financial arrangements, forensic economists and accountants are critical to building the evidentiary and economic foundation of the case. Their ability to clarify inter-entity relationships, establish financial linkages, and quantify damages transforms complex litigation into actionable legal strategy. By combining economic theory with investigative precision, they help courts and juries see through the smoke and mirrors of modern corporate wrongdoing.

14.5   Anti-Competitive Harm

Efficient Markets Hypothesis (EMH) in Economic Analysis

The Efficient Markets Hypothesis (EMH) is a foundational theory in financial economics which posits that asset prices in a competitive market reflect all available and relevant information at any given time. The implication of this theory is that no individual actor can consistently achieve abnormal profits without assuming additional risk, because prices instantaneously incorporate public data. While originally applied to securities markets, EMH has broader relevance in assessing competitive behaviors and information flow within commercial ecosystems.

From the perspective of forensic economics, EMH provides a theoretical framework for analyzing how market distortions, such as collusion, monopolistic abuse, or fraudulent misrepresentation, disrupt the natural allocation of resources and pricing accuracy. When markets fail to reflect true value due to hidden or manipulated conduct, injured parties across the economic spectrum may suffer calculable damages.

Anti-Competitive Behavior and EMH Disruption

Anti-competitive behavior undermines the assumptions underpinning EMH by creating artificial constraints on price formation, information dissemination, and resource distribution. These behaviors include, but are not limited to:

- **Price Fixing:** Agreements among competitors to fix, raise, or stabilize prices.

- **Market Allocation:** Dividing markets geographically or by customer type to limit competition.

- **Bid Rigging:** Collusive arrangements that undermine the integrity of competitive bidding processes.

- **Monopoly Leveraging:** Using dominant market power in one sector to stifle competition in another.

Such actions create asymmetric information environments and skew market prices, harming competitors, consumers, and even investors who rely on the fidelity of price signals.

Forensic Economists in Collusion and Market Abuse Cases

Forensic economists play a critical role in proving economic harm resulting from violations of antitrust law and anti-competitive practices. These professionals apply advanced tools from econometrics, game theory, industrial organization, and financial analysis to decipher complex behaviors and market patterns. Their multifaceted responsibilities encompass both qualitative assessments and quantitative modeling that collectively shed light on concealed or coordinated behavior intended to subvert competitive norms.

- **Market Structure Analysis:** Forensic economists analyze the composition of industries suspected of anti-competitive behavior. They examine market concentration through metrics like the Herfindahl-Hirschman Index (HHI), calculate entry and exit barriers, assess firm interdependence, and investigate whether conditions are ripe for tacit or explicit collusion. In monopolistic and oligopolistic settings, forensic economists trace the conduct and capabilities of dominant players, such as exclusive contracting, bundling, and predatory pricing.

- **Event Studies:** In matters involving securities fraud or the economic impact of public revelations (e.g., news of an antitrust investigation), event studies help determine whether abnormal price movements occurred following

disclosures. Forensic economists isolate the abnormal
return associated with a specific announcement date by
controlling for market movements and firm-specific risks
using models like the Capital Asset Pricing Model
(CAPM) or multifactor regressions. These studies
reinforce Efficient Markets Hypothesis (EMH)-based
arguments that prices incorporated distorted or hidden
information.

- **Damage Quantification:** Once liability is established,
forensic economists are tasked with computing
compensatory damages. They model what plaintiffs
would have earned or saved in a "but-for" world absent
the alleged misconduct. Techniques include regression
analysis, benchmarking against unaffected peer firms,
input-output modeling, and lost profits estimation. In
price-fixing cases, economists calculate overcharges by
comparing observed prices to those predicted under
competitive conditions, accounting for cost inputs,
demand elasticities, and temporal factors.

- **Simulation Modeling:** Forensic economists develop
counterfactual simulations to replicate market behavior
under lawful conditions. By simulating how market
shares, pricing, and consumer choices would have
evolved absent anti-competitive interference, experts
illustrate harm and apportion damages across the
affected economic landscape. These simulations often
require integration of behavioral economics, discrete
choice models, and dynamic competition theories.

- **Cartel Detection and Communication Analysis:**

In collusion cases, forensic economists may also analyze communication records, meeting frequencies, or patterns of signaling between alleged conspirators. Techniques like time-series clustering and natural language processing (NLP) applied to email or chat logs can uncover synchronized conduct or coded communications aimed at coordinating illegal behavior.

- **Geographic and Product Market Definition:** In both merger reviews and antitrust prosecutions, defining the relevant market is a critical task. Forensic economists delineate the boundaries of competition based on cross-price elasticities, customer substitution patterns, and regional pricing discrepancies. Accurate market definition affects the outcome of liability findings and informs damage calculations.

These sophisticated methodologies are especially powerful in class actions or multi-district litigation (MDL) where multiple plaintiffs allege systemic market manipulation across sectors. Forensic economists support these claims with compelling empirical evidence that distinguishes lawful competition from unlawful coordination, revealing the economic footprints of collusion in both direct and indirect forms.

Case Example: EMH Disruption in the Pharmaceutical Sector

In a landmark case involving price-fixing by a network of major generic drug manufacturers, forensic economists were tasked with analyzing the widespread economic consequences of collusive behavior across the entire pharmaceutical supply chain. The manufacturers, despite the competitive appearance of the generic market, engaged in covert agreements to maintain artificially elevated prices for commonly prescribed medications. This conduct disrupted the foundational principles of the Efficient Markets Hypothesis (EMH), which posits that asset prices reflect all publicly available information and adjust swiftly to new data.

The forensic economic investigation had to account for a range of nuanced challenges: drug formularies vary by institution; wholesale acquisition costs differ based on volume discounting; and rebates negotiated by pharmacy benefit managers (PBMs) often lack transparency. The economists assembled a multi-layered modeling framework to uncover both the direct and ripple effects of the pricing conspiracy.

The economic team undertook several key analytic procedures:

- **Benchmark Price Regression Analysis:** Utilizing a dataset of thousands of drug transactions across comparable therapeutic classes, economists conducted panel regression analysis to compare the prices of collusively priced generics against a control group of unaffected or competitively priced drugs. Covariates included drug class, manufacturer reputation, regulatory approval date, active pharmaceutical ingredients, and volume metrics.

- **Overcharge Estimation Across Plaintiffs:** Damages were calculated for three tiers of plaintiffs:

  1. *Hospitals and Clinics:* Economists aggregated purchase order data from institutional buyers and

measured cost differentials over time.

2. *Insurers and PBMs:* Experts evaluated inflated reimbursement schedules and formulary design restrictions stemming from the manipulated market.

3. *Government Payors:* Economists modeled taxpayer losses from Medicare, Medicaid, and VA procurement inflated by collusive pricing algorithms.

- **Market Share Reallocation and Exclusion Harm:** Beyond price effects, forensic economists evaluated the competitive harm to non-colluding generic manufacturers who were squeezed out of distribution contracts. Using market penetration metrics and formulary access data, they showed how exclusionary agreements and rebate traps shifted demand away from low-cost providers, violating antitrust norms and reducing long-run market efficiency.

- **Structural Break Tests and Price Cointegration Analysis:** To empirically test for market anomalies, time-series tests were employed to detect structural breaks in pricing patterns coinciding with key dates of conspiratorial conduct. Cointegration models demonstrated artificial correlation among prices that should have remained independent under competitive conditions.

- **Pass-Through Modeling:** Economists assessed how much of the overcharge was passed through to end consumers. Using elasticity data and claims records, they showed how price inflation led to higher copayments, increased premiums, and delayed treatment adherence among patients.

- **Violation of EMH Assumptions:** The economists demonstrated that the price signals generated by collusive activity created widespread misinformation in the market. Investors, actuaries, and analysts relying on apparent market signals were misled, creating capital misallocations, underpricing of risk, and loss of trust in pharmaceutical cost projections.

In court, these findings bolstered a sweeping legal theory that the manufacturers' conspiracy did not merely raise drug prices in isolation—it distorted a foundational component of market operation: price transparency. By undermining the EMH in a sector where transparency is already challenged by non-public rebates and opaque pricing structures, the cartel created cascading inefficiencies that harmed every node in the healthcare ecosystem.

The expert testimony provided by forensic economists was essential to establishing systemic harm across direct purchasers, third-party payors, competitors, and consumers. Their multidisciplinary approach combined financial theory, regulatory policy, statistical rigor, and market behavior analysis, ultimately supporting certification for a multi-billion-dollar class action and driving regulatory reforms in drug pricing transparency.

14.6   Conclusion

These cases illustrate that forensic economists are not just peripheral witnesses, they can be determinative. Their analyses provide the empirical substance courts demand when evaluating class certification, liability models, and damage quantification. As economic modeling techniques evolve, their alignment with legal doctrines continues to shape the trajectory of complex litigation in critical ways.

The Last Word

The Efficient Markets Hypothesis offers a powerful lens through which forensic economists can evaluate the economic consequences of anti-competitive conduct. By demonstrating how collusion and monopolistic practices create information asymmetries and distort pricing mechanisms, forensic experts provide the empirical evidence courts require to assign liability and award damages. Their work not only reinforces economic theory but also ensures accountability in cases where artificial market manipulation produces widespread harm across multiple commercial relationships.

Yet, in many of these cases, the harm is not confined to a single plaintiff or corporate counterparty, it ripples outward, affecting thousands, sometimes millions. When the contours of injury stretch beyond the scope of individual litigation, the legal system must evolve to meet the complexity and scale of the wrongdoing. It is here that the analytical power of forensic economics finds new expression in collective redress.

We now turn to the domain of *Class Action Litigation*, where aggregate harm meets procedural innovation, and the tools of economic analysis become indispensable in certifying classes, estimating damages, and shaping equitable remedies at scale.

Chapter 15

Class Action Litigation

15.1 Introduction

Class action litigation allows individuals with common claims to join together to sue as a collective entity. This form of litigation is particularly useful in situations where individual claims may be too small to justify separate lawsuits but collectively represent significant harm. Class actions promote judicial efficiency and protect defendants from inconsistent obligations, while offering a mechanism for redress to large groups of similarly affected individuals.

In federal court, class actions are governed by Rule 23 of the Federal Rules of Civil Procedure. This chapter explores the legal prerequisites for class certification and how forensic economists play a vital role in establishing, quantifying, and managing the economic underpinnings of class-wide harm.

15.2 Economic Commonality

Under Rule 23 of the Federal Rules of Civil Procedure, plaintiffs seeking class certification must meet four fundamental prerequisites under subsection (a): numerosity, commonality, typicality, and adequacy of representation. These elements ensure that the proposed class is cohesive enough to be treated as a collective for purposes of litigation. For cases brought under Rule 23(b)(3), which is frequently applied in economic, antitrust, and securities litigation, two additional criteria must be satisfied: that common questions of law or fact predominate over individual ones, and that the class action mechanism is superior to other forms of adjudication.

These legal standards impose a significant evidentiary burden on plaintiffs. Courts are not bound to accept class-wide theories at face value; instead, plaintiffs must present concrete, class-wide methodologies that align with the legal theory of liability. In this context, forensic economists have emerged as indispensable contributors to class certification efforts. They develop and apply rigorous economic models to demonstrate that the harm experienced by class members is not only systemic but also measurable using shared data and assumptions.

The Role of Forensic Economists in Establishing Commonality

In class action litigation, "commonality" refers to the existence of questions that can be resolved on a class-wide basis. This was clarified and heightened in the landmark case *Wal-Mart Stores, Inc. v. Dukes*, where the U.S. Supreme Court held that claims must be bound together by a common contention capable of class-wide resolution. Forensic economists help meet this standard by showing that the economic impact of the defendant's conduct affected all—or nearly all—class members in materially similar ways.

Key tools employed include:

- **Descriptive and Inferential Statistics:** Used to analyze patterns in data that suggest systemic harm or disparity.

- **Econometric Modeling:** Allows economists to isolate the impact of alleged misconduct (e.g., price-fixing or wage discrimination) while controlling for other variables.

- **Uniform Metrics:** Construction of standardized harm metrics that apply uniformly across the proposed class.

Demonstrating Predominance Under Rule 23(b)(3)

The "predominance" requirement under Rule 23(b)(3) of the Federal Rules of Civil Procedure is one of the most exacting hurdles a proposed class must overcome. Unlike the

commonality standard under Rule 23(a), which asks whether
there is at least one shared question of law or fact,
predominance demands a more rigorous showing: that the
shared questions are not just present, but that they
substantially outweigh any individual issues that might arise
during litigation.

Courts interpret this requirement through a practical lens,
asking whether adjudication of the common issues will resolve
a significant portion of each class member's claims. In this
context, the testimony and methodologies provided by
forensic economists are indispensable. These experts are often
the linchpins in demonstrating that liability and damages are
not only provable across the class using common evidence, but
that doing so is the most efficient and equitable mechanism
for resolution.

The Legal Importance of Predominance

Predominance is not merely a procedural gatekeeper; it
defines the legal architecture of a class action. In antitrust,
securities fraud, consumer protection, and employment
discrimination cases, if plaintiffs cannot demonstrate that
common economic methods can address harm and liability on
a class-wide basis, the case will almost certainly be dismissed
at the certification stage. This has been reinforced by key
Supreme Court rulings such as *Comcast v. Behrend* and
Wal-Mart v. Dukes, both of which clarified the evidentiary
thresholds required for predominance.

How Forensic Economists Support Predominance

Forensic economists provide empirical grounding to legal claims. Their models serve three critical functions:

- **Class-Wide Damage Models:** Economists develop regression models, structural equations, or econometric simulations that quantify economic harm across all class members using a single methodology. These models rely on variables that are common to all transactions—such as purchase dates, product types, geographic region, or exposure to a misrepresentation—allowing them to quantify overcharges, lost wages, or reduced product value for the entire class.

- **Shared Liability Frameworks:** Economic experts demonstrate that the underlying conduct—such as price-fixing, market manipulation, or systemic employment discrimination—affects all members similarly. By using transaction-level data, payroll records, or pricing matrices, forensic economists can show that the misconduct operates at a structural level, not merely through individualized or discretionary actions.

- **Counterfactual Market Reconstructions:** One of the most persuasive techniques involves building a "but-for" world—an economic model of what prices, wages, or returns would have looked like absent the alleged misconduct. These models create a baseline that applies equally to all class members and then measure deviations to calculate harm. This technique is often visualized through line graphs comparing actual versus predicted values across time.

Advanced Techniques Used in Modern Litigation

To meet the demands of courts applying Daubert scrutiny at
the certification stage, forensic economists increasingly rely on
sophisticated methodologies, including:

- **Fixed-Effects and Random-Effects Panel Models:**
  Control for variables within firms, regions, or
  individuals over time, isolating the treatment effect of
  the defendant's conduct.

- **Machine Learning and Clustering:** Used to
  segment large datasets into comparable groups, identify
  trends, and confirm class-wide harm through
  unsupervised analysis.

- **Monte Carlo Simulations:** Employed to test the
  robustness of damage calculations under different
  assumptions or scenarios, ensuring the model's
  reliability and repeatability.

- **Geospatial Analysis:** In cases with a geographic
  component (e.g., real estate redlining or environmental
  contamination), spatial econometrics is used to
  demonstrate patterns of uniform exposure and effect.

Illustrative Case Examples

Antitrust – In Re: Auto Parts Antitrust Litigation:
Plaintiffs alleged that suppliers conspired to fix prices of
automotive components. Forensic economists developed
market-wide overcharge estimates based on transaction data
from all major manufacturers, showing that pricing structures

deviated systematically from competitive norms.

Consumer Class Actions – False Labeling of Organic Foods: In a nationwide class action, economists applied hedonic pricing models to determine how much consumers overpaid due to the false organic labeling. These estimates were based on national pricing trends and consumer surveys.

Employment Class Actions – Gender Disparity in Promotions: In a Fortune 500 company, forensic economists used multivariate regression to analyze promotion and pay records. They controlled for seniority, education, and performance ratings and still found statistically significant disparities. The uniformity of the pattern supported class-wide relief.

Judicial Reception of Economic Testimony on Predominance

Federal courts have increasingly scrutinized economic testimony under the twin lenses of Rule 23(b)(3) and Rule 702 (Daubert). The prevailing trend has been to require plaintiffs to present complete, trial-ready economic models, not merely promises of future development. Courts have ruled that a damages model that fails to distinguish between injured and uninjured class members, or that fails to track the legal theory of liability, will not support certification.

However, when forensic economists succeed in constructing rigorous, testable, and case-specific models, courts often find in favor of certification. Economic evidence has thus become the hinge upon which class action success turns.

Conclusion

Predominance is not just a procedural requirement—it is a data-driven inquiry into whether collective adjudication will work. Forensic economists bring clarity, consistency, and methodological rigor to this inquiry. Their tools, when properly aligned with the case's legal theory, allow courts to treat a group of claimants not as fragmented individuals, but as a singular voice united by common harm and shared evidence. In this way, forensic economic analysis does not merely support predominance, it often defines it.

Applications in Specific Case Types

The practical impact of forensic economic testimony is evident across a variety of litigation contexts:

Price-Fixing and Antitrust: In cartel cases, economists estimate overcharges by comparing prices during the alleged conspiracy period with prices outside that window or in unaffected control groups. For instance, in the generic drug pricing litigation, forensic economists used pooled regression models on thousands of transactions to prove a consistent markup attributable to collusion.

Employment Discrimination: In wage gap and promotion disparity cases, economists deploy multivariate regression analysis, controlling for relevant variables such as education, tenure, and department. When statistical disparities persist across large datasets, it becomes powerful evidence of a company-wide practice amenable to class-wide adjudication.

Consumer Product Litigation: When a product is falsely labeled (e.g., "organic," "all-natural," "Made in USA"), economists use tools like conjoint analysis, hedonic regression, and contingent valuation to estimate how much value consumers placed on the false attribute. These tools assess uniform economic injury even when individual purchase motivations vary.

Securities Fraud: Forensic economists apply the fraud-on-the-market presumption (from *Basic Inc. v. Levinson*) to demonstrate that misstatements impacted stock prices uniformly. Event studies measure how market prices reacted to corrective disclosures, supporting commonality and predominance in shareholder suits.

Healthcare and Insurance: In cases involving unfair reimbursement practices or denied claims, forensic economists evaluate claims data across insurers, hospitals, or healthcare providers. Algorithms are constructed to simulate proper reimbursement under lawful conditions and contrast those with actual payouts.

Model Validity and the *Daubert* Standard

Following the *Comcast v. Behrend* decision, courts increasingly apply *Daubert* scrutiny to economic models at the class certification stage. Forensic economists must ensure their methodologies are:

- **Empirically Verifiable:** Capable of being tested and peer-reviewed.

- **Legally Aligned:** Tailored to the specific legal theory under Rule 23(b)(3).

- **Robust Across Assumptions:** Validated through sensitivity testing and scenario modeling.

A model that does not directly correspond to the class-wide theory of harm may result in denial of certification, even if it is statistically sound.

Visualizing Class Harm

Forensic economists increasingly use visual analytics and data visualization tools to depict:

- Geographic heat maps showing market impact zones.

- Time-series plots comparing benchmark and observed prices.

- Flow charts tracing distribution chains and identifying overcharge pass-through.

Such visuals help both the court and jury grasp abstract economic arguments and reinforce the argument for commonality.

Summary

In sum, Rule 23 class certification hinges not only on legal arguments but on the strength and credibility of economic models used to measure class-wide harm. Forensic economists provide the backbone of this evidentiary showing, translating massive datasets into coherent, legally admissible narratives of shared injury. By rigorously establishing that harm is traceable, quantifiable, and common across all or most members, economists help bridge the gap between individual injury and systemic injustice—the very essence of class action litigation.

15.3 *Wal-Mart v. Dukes*

In *Wal-Mart Stores, Inc. v. Dukes*, 564 U.S. 338 (2011), the
Supreme Court denied class certification to over one million
female employees alleging gender-based employment
discrimination. The Court held that the plaintiffs failed to
satisfy Rule 23(a)(2)'s "commonality" requirement because
they did not demonstrate the existence of a uniform corporate
policy of discrimination. Instead, the plaintiffs relied on
decentralized decision-making by individual store managers,
which the Court concluded could not support a finding of
commonality under Rule 23.

This decision significantly raised the bar for proving
class-wide commonality, establishing that plaintiffs must
identify a specific policy or practice that ties all claims
together in a way that makes class treatment appropriate. In
the wake of *Dukes*, courts have scrutinized certification
motions with greater attention to the uniformity of harm and
the methodologies used to demonstrate such harm. As a
result, plaintiffs increasingly turn to forensic economists to
supply the statistical "glue" necessary to establish that all
class members experienced common injury from a centralized
employment or corporate practice.

Forensic economists deploy a range of advanced statistical
tools and empirical methods to demonstrate uniformity of
impact across diverse employees or claimants. These
techniques are designed to reveal whether disparities in

employment decisions—such as hiring, promotions, pay rates, or terminations—can be attributed to systemic patterns rather than random variation or isolated decisions.

Key economic methods include:

- **Hierarchical Linear Modeling (HLM):** Used to control for variables at different organizational levels (e.g., individual store performance, regional manager influence), allowing economists to detect consistent patterns of disparity that may not be visible in aggregated data.

- **Bayesian Inference:** Assesses the likelihood of discrimination by integrating observed data with prior expectations based on policy structure or known practices. This method provides probabilistic support for claims of systemic harm.

- **Cluster Analysis:** Segments employee populations into statistically similar groups to identify whether subsets of the workforce were disproportionately affected by adverse decisions. This helps establish subclasses and refine the scope of uniform impact.

- **Logistic and Multinomial Regression:** Models the probability of employment outcomes as functions of gender, tenure, location, and other factors, enabling precise estimation of discriminatory patterns.

- **Propensity Score Matching:** Matches similarly situated employees based on observed characteristics to isolate differences in treatment attributable solely to protected status (e.g., gender), thereby highlighting systemic bias.

These analytical strategies are typically supported by access to large-scale corporate databases containing employee records, compensation histories, promotion outcomes, and performance evaluations. Forensic economists clean, preprocess, and normalize these datasets to ensure valid comparisons and remove bias in estimation. Courts often require expert reports that not only present statistical findings but also justify methodological choices under *Daubert* standards for expert admissibility.

In *Dukes*, the plaintiffs' reliance on anecdotal evidence and a broad sociological theory of implicit bias failed to establish the rigorous, statistically demonstrable uniformity that Rule 23(a)(2) now demands. Future plaintiffs seeking certification in employment discrimination or similar cases must therefore lean heavily on forensic economic analysis to validate that a specific policy—whether explicit or de facto—produced measurable, class-wide harm.

Ultimately, the *Dukes* decision has reshaped the landscape of employment-related class actions. It has elevated the evidentiary burden on plaintiffs and created an essential role for forensic economists to supply the empirical rigor needed to link legal theory with measurable economic outcomes across large groups of individuals.

15.4   *Comcast v. Behrend*

In *Comcast Corp. v. Behrend*, 569 U.S. 27 (2013), the
Supreme Court reversed a lower court's decision granting class
certification in an antitrust case brought by cable subscribers
in the Philadelphia area. The plaintiffs alleged that Comcast
had engaged in anti-competitive clustering
practices—acquiring competitor cable systems in the
region—which reduced competition and allowed the company
to raise prices. While the plaintiffs advanced four different
theories of antitrust injury, the district court accepted only
one of those theories for purposes of class certification.
However, the damages model submitted by the plaintiffs'
expert economist did not disaggregate harm attributable
solely to the accepted theory. Instead, it measured aggregate
damages stemming from all four liability theories, making it
impossible to determine which portion of the harm stemmed
from the viable claim.

The Supreme Court ruled that such a mismatch rendered the
plaintiffs' economic model legally deficient for class
certification under Rule 23(b)(3). The decision emphasized
that a class must demonstrate that damages are "capable of
measurement on a classwide basis" and that the "model
purporting to serve as evidence of damages... must measure
only those damages attributable to that theory." Without
such specificity, the predominance requirement under Rule
23(b)(3) cannot be satisfied.

This ruling had a profound impact on economic expert
practice in class actions. Post-*Comcast*, plaintiffs must present

a robust, well-structured damages methodology that matches the accepted legal theory of liability and can reliably quantify damages across the entire class. The opinion has since become a cornerstone in defense motions opposing certification, often triggering pre-certification *Daubert* hearings and challenges to expert methodology.

15.5 Other Landmark Cases

While *Wal-Mart v. Dukes* and *Comcast v. Behrend* have defined much of the modern landscape for economic evidence in class certification, other cases—across various circuits and domains—have significantly contributed to the legal and methodological evolution of forensic economics in class actions. These decisions highlight the growing sophistication of courts in evaluating expert evidence, the critical role of econometric modeling, and the challenges of aligning legal theory with economic reality.

In re Urethane Antitrust Litigation (2016)

In this multidistrict litigation, plaintiffs alleged that major chemical manufacturers conspired to fix prices in the urethane market. The class certification hinged on whether common issues of injury and damages predominated over individual ones. The plaintiffs presented extensive economic analysis, including regression models that showed supracompetitive pricing during the alleged conspiracy period.

The Tenth Circuit upheld the $1.06 billion jury verdict, emphasizing that the classwide economic model, though not

flawless, was sufficiently reliable under *Daubert* and provided
a rational basis for jury calculation. The case affirmed that
antitrust class actions can succeed with robust economic
modeling, even where some individualized differences exist.

Tyson Foods, Inc. v. Bouaphakeo, 577 U.S. 442 (2016)

Tyson Foods involved a group of workers claiming unpaid
overtime for time spent donning and doffing protective gear.
Plaintiffs relied on statistical sampling and representative
evidence to establish average time worked, which Tyson
challenged as insufficiently individualized. The Supreme
Court held that representative evidence could be used in class
actions where each member could have relied on that same
evidence in an individual suit.

This decision reinforced the admissibility of economic and
statistical methodologies, especially time-and-motion studies
and sampling, as legitimate tools for demonstrating liability
and damages in class contexts, particularly under the Fair
Labor Standards Act.

In re Restasis (2022)

In this recent pharmaceutical case, a class of drug purchasers
challenged Allergan's delay of generic competition through
improper Orange Book listings and sham litigation. Plaintiffs
relied on economic experts to demonstrate how the delay
affected pricing, modeled generic entry scenarios, and
estimated damages through benchmark comparisons across
therapeutic classes.

The court certified the class, finding the economic methodologies credible, coherent, and tied to the theory of antitrust injury. This case reflects the growing role of health economists and pharmaceutical market modeling in complex class actions involving regulatory and intellectual property manipulation.

In re Google Digital Advertising Antitrust Litigation (Ongoing)

Though still pending as of this writing, the consolidated class actions against Google for its alleged monopolization of digital advertising markets highlight the future direction of class certification battles. Plaintiffs' economic experts are tasked with modeling platform dominance, pricing algorithms, and market distortion across a layered and opaque ecosystem. These cases underscore the rising demand for forensic economists adept in digital markets, platform economics, and network effects.

Taken together, these cases illustrate that class action litigation is not only a procedural innovation but a stage for the continual refinement of economic evidence. They demonstrate how judges increasingly act as arbiters of data credibility, weighing regression results, benchmark scenarios, and economic logic as they do legal precedent.

15.6   Conclusion

Class action litigation represents the judicial system's recognition that some harms transcend the individual. In these cases, where thousands or even millions suffer from a shared injury, the law turns to aggregation, and to the tools of forensic economics, to craft collective redress. This chapter has explored the critical interplay between expert testimony, statistical modeling, and procedural standards in shaping the success or failure of class certification.

We examined the doctrinal hurdles established by landmark decisions like *Dukes* and *Comcast*, and we looked to other pivotal cases that demonstrate how courts navigate the complex terrain of commonality, predominance, and damages estimation. Whether the issue is wage theft, price fixing, monopolistic behavior, or regulatory manipulation, the common thread remains the same: without sound economic evidence, the class action collapses into a scatter of individual claims.

Forensic economists, then, serve not just as quantifiers of harm but as architects of accountability in the collective sense. Their work undergirds the structural logic of class litigation, connecting the dots between legal theories and economic consequences, across vast datasets and varied jurisdictions.

As we move to the next chapter, *Interesting Cases*, we shift from the procedural battleground to the rich narrative of forensic application. Here, the numbers give way to stories. We dive into real-world examples where the abstract principles of law and economics take vivid, unpredictable, and often astonishing form.

Chapter 16

Interesting Cases

16.1 Forensic Economic Evidence

While Supreme Court decisions establish overarching legal standards, many of the most instructive and practical rulings on the use of forensic economic evidence emerge from lower federal and state courts. These cases reveal how trial and appellate courts scrutinize and rely upon economic experts in certifying classes, calculating damages, and assessing causation.

16.2   Martin Shkreli

Overview of the Case

Martin Shkreli, a former hedge fund manager and CEO of
Retrophin Inc., gained national notoriety for inflating the
price of the life-saving drug Daraprim by over 5,000%, but his
criminal conviction in 2017 stemmed from a broader pattern
of securities fraud and misuse of corporate funds. The charges
focused on his management of MSMB Capital and MSMB
Healthcare, two hedge funds he founded and operated, as well
as his fraudulent appropriation of Retrophin's assets to repay
disgruntled investors. Prosecutors alleged that Shkreli
repeatedly lied to investors about the performance of his
hedge funds, covered up losses with money from new
investors, and misused Retrophin's public company funds to
satisfy personal obligations and legal settlements. Forensic
economics served as a vital tool in unraveling the web of
misrepresentation and financial manipulation at the heart of
the case.

Tracing Misappropriated Funds

A central and complex task for forensic economists in the
prosecution of Martin Shkreli was the meticulous tracing of
capital as it moved across a network of interrelated entities.
The case involved a sophisticated pattern of financial
deception that spanned hedge funds, a publicly traded
biopharmaceutical company, and personal accounts. Forensic
economists employed a battery of investigative tools to
untangle the movement of funds and uncover hidden patterns

of misappropriation, commingling, and obfuscation.

At the heart of their analysis was a forensic reconstruction of transaction chains involving MSMB Capital, MSMB Healthcare, and Retrophin Inc. Economists leveraged historical bank statements, corporate general ledgers, wire transfer records, and investment account ledgers to establish a comprehensive chronological mapping of financial flows. In many instances, transactions were routed through intermediary accounts or disguised under misleading labels to conceal their true nature.

Using advanced fund flow analysis, transaction sequencing algorithms, and relational data modeling, the forensic team identified a number of problematic financial maneuvers, including but not limited to:

- **Circular Transfers:** Economists detected a pattern of capital being transferred between MSMB Capital and Retrophin and then funneled back to Shkreli's personal or related accounts, indicating possible self-dealing.

- **Disguised Settlements:** Several payments made under the guise of "consulting agreements" were actually settlements to former hedge fund investors, undisclosed to shareholders and unsupported by any legitimate consulting services.

- **Shell Account Laundering:** Funds were sometimes passed through shell corporations and newly created entities to launder the transaction's origin or destination, complicating the appearance of impropriety to casual reviewers.

- **Asset Diversion:** Public company assets were used to repay private hedge fund debts, effectively transferring risk from Shkreli to the shareholders of Retrophin without their knowledge or consent.

Forensic economists also conducted time-series analysis to evaluate the temporal alignment of misleading public statements and subsequent financial transfers. They applied abnormal transaction detection methods to isolate transfers that deviated significantly from expected behavior based on historical corporate patterns. These red-flagged events were cross-referenced with internal communications and board resolutions to assess legitimacy.

Using forensic software and visualization tools such as i2 Analyst's Notebook and Tableau, economists generated highly detailed graphical representations of fund movement. These visual aids allowed the jury to follow the financial "breadcrumb trail" through dozens of accounts and entities, illustrating how misappropriated funds were disguised through layers of legal complexity.

Additionally, forensic economists examined metadata associated with electronic financial records, including IP access logs, transaction timestamps, and approval hierarchies, to assess who initiated or authorized questionable transfers. This digital forensic layer supported conclusions about Shkreli's direct involvement in structuring and executing illicit financial maneuvers.

To further strengthen the case, economists built counterfactual financial models to simulate what Retrophin's financial condition would have been had the misappropriated assets remained within the company. These models projected earnings, R&D expenditures, and shareholder equity, thereby quantifying the opportunity cost inflicted upon the company by Shkreli's diversion of funds.

Ultimately, the tracing of misappropriated funds by forensic economists was instrumental in the prosecution's ability to prove criminal intent and material misrepresentation. Their work provided the evidentiary backbone for charges involving securities fraud and conspiracy, demonstrating that the capital flows were not incidental but architected with precision and malice to defraud investors and enrich Shkreli at the expense of others.

Quantifying Investor Harm

Shkreli maintained throughout the trial that his investors ultimately made money and thus had not suffered any real financial harm. He pointed to the fact that, in several cases, investors were repaid more than they originally invested, often using funds diverted from Retrophin. However, forensic economists provided a comprehensive and multi-layered rebuttal to this narrative by introducing a robust framework for quantifying investor harm—one that extended far beyond net cash flow and into legal, economic, and ethical dimensions of fiduciary relationships, risk, and opportunity cost.

Forensic economists emphasized that real financial injury includes not only losses in absolute terms but also the violation of informed consent, misallocation of risk, and denial of lawful expectations under the investor agreement. They demonstrated that quantifying harm requires a broad understanding of capital stewardship, risk-adjusted returns, and fiduciary integrity.

Key components of their analytical framework included:

- **Opportunity Cost Modeling:** Forensic economists used historical investment data to calculate the returns investors could have reasonably expected had their capital been placed in comparable, properly managed funds or low-risk market indices. Monte Carlo simulations and regression-adjusted return expectations were applied to model a distribution of probable investor outcomes had Shkreli followed industry norms. This modeling revealed that, although some investors were repaid nominally more than their principal, the missed opportunity for consistent, market-based gains was significant.

- **Risk Exposure Analysis:** By reconstructing the portfolio composition and trading strategy of MSMB Capital and MSMB Healthcare, forensic experts revealed a pattern of extreme speculative investments, concentrated positions, and volatile short selling. These strategies were conducted without full disclosure to investors and often in contradiction to stated fund objectives. Economists presented Value at Risk (VaR) calculations and stress-testing scenarios to quantify how exposed investors were to systemic collapse—highlighting the mismatch between perceived and actual risk.

- **Temporal Misalignment of Returns:** Several of the returns used by Shkreli to argue that investors profited were traced back to Retrophin funds—not hedge fund profits. Forensic economists reconstructed the chronological sequence of investments and repayments, demonstrating that these repayments occurred years after the breach, undermining any claim of contemporaneous performance-based return. Time-adjusted cash flow analysis was used to present Net Present Value (NPV) harm to investors at the moment trust was breached.

- **Fiduciary Breach and Non-Economic Harm:** Forensic experts noted that in financial law, damages may be awarded not merely on the basis of lost profits but for the breach of fiduciary duty, deceit, and erosion of trust. They applied qualitative economic impact analysis to highlight how false reports, doctored performance statements, and concealed losses impaired investors' ability to make informed decisions. This harm, while not easily monetized, was supported through behavioral economics literature and investor testimony.

- **Forensic Cash Flow Mapping:** Economists created diagrams detailing how investor funds were used—many of which illustrated that money raised under the pretense of investment was diverted to cover unrelated personal expenses, settle private liabilities, or prop up Shkreli's failed ventures. This mapping invalidated the argument that successful investor outcomes exonerated misrepresentation at the outset.

- **Benchmarking Against Similar Funds:** To provide further context, forensic economists constructed a

composite benchmark using data from similar hedge
funds operating within the same period and sector. The
performance of MSMB funds was then compared against
these benchmarks using Sharpe ratios, Jensen's alpha,
and rolling return analysis. The contrast revealed that
MSMB's returns, when adjusted for volatility and
ethical compliance, were far inferior to what investors
could have obtained elsewhere.

- **Portfolio Theory Violations:** Experts also evaluated
  Shkreli's management through the lens of Modern
  Portfolio Theory (MPT). His concentration of risk, lack
  of diversification, and absence of hedging mechanisms
  violated the core tenets of fiduciary asset management.
  Forensic economists presented counterfactual diversified
  portfolios to illustrate the risk-adjusted gains investors
  were denied due to these violations.

- **Secondary Market Harm:** Economists further argued
  that Shkreli's deception caused ripple effects beyond
  direct investors. Misleading fund performance impacted
  subsequent capital inflows, distorted market perceptions
  of MSMB funds, and indirectly harmed third-party
  stakeholders including potential co-investors, brokerage
  firms, and underwriters who relied on falsified reports.

- **Longitudinal Behavioral Harm:** Drawing from
  empirical studies in behavioral finance, economists
  posited that the emotional and psychological toll of
  betrayal by a fund manager could impair investor
  decision-making in future financial endeavors. Expert
  testimony highlighted how prolonged litigation, stress,

and reputational damage amounted to a durable form of economic harm.

The damages were further contextualized using time-series economic models that tracked MSMB's actual performance relative to market indices such as the S&P 500, the Russell 2000, and hedge fund composite benchmarks. These comparisons, coupled with projections of counterfactual returns under lawful management, formed the evidentiary basis for asserting that real, measurable financial injury had occurred—regardless of the superficial outcome of repayment.

By integrating econometric modeling, risk analytics, ethical finance principles, and forensic tracing, the experts helped dismantle Shkreli's "no harm, no foul" defense. Their testimony underscored that fiduciary malfeasance cannot be excused simply because restitution was later paid—particularly when such restitution itself stemmed from further wrongdoing. Ultimately, forensic economics reframed the question from "Did they lose money?" to "Were they deceived, endangered, and deprived of lawful expectation?"—and the answer was unequivocally yes.

Economic   Modeling   of   Fraudulent Representation

A key aspect of the forensic economists' role was to disprove the credibility of Shkreli's reported financial performance. Economists used a variety of techniques to contrast claimed returns with plausible outcomes:

- **Risk-Adjusted Return Modeling:** Used to calculate

Sharpe ratios, standard deviation, and other measures inconsistent with the stated performance.

- **Scenario Simulations:** Economists generated hypothetical investment scenarios with similar risk profiles to highlight discrepancies in MSMB's reported success.

- **Bayesian Updating:** Applied to estimate how investor beliefs about fund safety would have shifted with truthful information.

These models demonstrated that Shkreli's hedge funds were built on a foundation of false confidence, strategic concealment of losses, and misaligned investor expectations.

Expert Testimony

Forensic economists were instrumental in making the financial intricacies of the case understandable to a lay jury. Through compelling visual exhibits, simplified analogies, and clear explanations, experts provided:

- **Infographics of Financial Flows:** Step-by-step breakdowns of fund transfers, showing how money was misdirected through a series of shell entities.

- **Damage Calculations:** Tables and charts that detailed the actual economic harm suffered by different categories of investors.

- **Narrative Economic Testimony:** Expert explanations of concepts such as fiduciary duty, portfolio diversification, and Ponzi-like mechanisms were vital for juror understanding.

Their testimony helped the jury distinguish between technical legality and economic deceit, leading to the conclusion that the investment structure was predicated on fraudulent misrepresentation.

Broader Economic Implications

The Shkreli prosecution stands as a milestone for how forensic economics can influence white-collar criminal trials. Several important implications emerged:

- **White-Collar Accountability:** The case set a precedent for holding executives criminally responsible for sophisticated but economically misleading conduct.

- **Application of Economic Concepts in Criminal Law:** Portfolio theory, forensic accounting, and economic harm modeling were presented as vital evidentiary tools.

- **Investor Protection:** The outcome reinforced legal standards that protect not just the outcome of investments, but also the transparency and ethical obligations underlying them.

Additionally, the case highlighted the limitations of relying solely on eventual returns to justify management actions, showing that the path taken and the rules followed matter significantly in the eyes of both law and economics.

Conclusion

The case against Martin Shkreli would have been far more difficult to prosecute without the aid of forensic economists.

Their work uncovered the financial infrastructure of fraud, quantified investor losses beyond surface-level gains, and dismantled the illusion of managerial success. Ultimately, forensic economics served as both a spotlight and a compass—revealing the hidden mechanisms of deceit and guiding the court toward a just outcome.

In re Urethane Antitrust Litigation, 768 F.3d 1245 (10th Cir. 2014)

This case involved allegations that major chemical manufacturers conspired to fix prices of urethane chemicals. The Tenth Circuit upheld a $1.06 billion jury verdict in favor of the plaintiff class, largely based on economic testimony. The plaintiffs' expert presented a damages model using multiple regression to estimate overcharges across a multi-year period. The court affirmed that:

- Regression models were an appropriate tool for showing class-wide injury and damages;

- Statistical imperfections did not preclude admissibility if the model reliably traced harm to the alleged conduct;

- Expert opinion may be sufficient to certify a class if it plausibly supports predominance under Rule 23(b)(3).

This case illustrates how juries and courts rely on forensic economists in highly technical antitrust cases to prove both causation and quantum.

Bouaphakeo v, Tyson Foods, Inc., 765 F.3d 791 (8th Cir. 2014)

Though ultimately reviewed by the Supreme Court, the class certification in this FLSA collective action was initially affirmed by the Eighth Circuit. Workers claimed they were not paid for time spent donning and doffing protective gear. Because Tyson had not recorded individual times, the plaintiffs' economist used average time estimates derived from a time-and-motion study.

The Eighth Circuit approved this representative evidence, highlighting that:

- Statistical averages could be used when an employer failed to keep individualized records;

- The forensic economist's regression and averaging techniques served as common proof of liability and damages;

- The methodology was consistent with standard economic practices and admissible under Rule 702.

This affirmed the permissibility of using expert-derived averages as a surrogate for individualized proof in wage-and-hour disputes.

In re High-Tech Employee Antitrust Litigation, 985 F. Supp. 2d 1167 (N.D. Cal. 2013)

This case involved allegations that companies like Google, Apple, and Adobe agreed not to poach each other's employees, thereby suppressing wages. Plaintiffs sought class certification for tens of thousands of affected workers.

The forensic economist's role included:

- Constructing a but-for world using counterfactual wage modeling;

- Running regression analyses that showed wage suppression linked to anti-solicitation agreements;

- Calculating aggregate damages across the workforce based on a statistically derived wage gap.

Judge Koh certified the class, crediting the expert's ability to model wage injury across job types, geographies, and employers using standard econometric tools.

In re Visa Check/MasterMoney Antitrust Litigation, 280 F.3d 124 (2d Cir. 2001), abrogated by *In re Initial Public Offerings Securities Litigation,* 2nd Cir.(N.Y.), December 5, 2006

This landmark case certified a class of millions of merchants alleging that Visa and MasterCard engaged in anticompetitive tying of debit cards to credit cards. Plaintiffs' forensic economist presented a model showing that:

- The tying arrangement inflated transaction fees;

- Damages could be measured through a common overcharge formula;

- Market-wide injury could be inferred using transaction data across class members.

The Second Circuit reversed the lower court's denial of certification and emphasized that courts should not prematurely reject expert models before full trial consideration unless clearly inadmissible.

Magical Cruise Co. Ltd. v Martins, 330 So. 3d 993 (Fla. 5th DCA 2021)

Case Overview

Parties & Background

Ana Maria Reis Martins, a former crew member aboard

Disney's Dream cruise ship, sued Magical Cruise Company Limited (doing business as Disney Cruise Line). She alleged:

Negligence under the Jones Act (46 U.S.C. s. 30104),

Wrongful refusal to reinstate her maintenance and cure benefits after she submitted medical records showing continued injuries, and

A punitive damages claim asserting that Disney's refusal was willful, arbitrary, or exhibited callous disregard.

Court's Decision The Florida Fifth District Court of Appeal issued its opinion on November 12, 2021, and denied rehearing on December 29, 2021.

> Dr. Anderson's calculations as to future medical expenses were unreliable because Ms. McKenzie merely assigned costs to a list of procedures and medications with no nexus between them and what Martins might actually need or how frequently she might need them. Despite this, Dr. Anderson bootstrapped those costs into a calculation of future medical expenses. This foundational failure rendered Dr. Anderson's testimony unreliable. *See Sanchez v. Cinque*, 238 So. 3d 817 (Fla. 4th DCA 2018) (affirming trial court's exclusion of expert's testimony where expert made assumptions not based on any facts contained in medical records). Ms. McKenzie's denial that she discussed the frequencies of Martins' needed medical procedures and medications or that she determined Martins'

employment capacity further undermines Dr. Anderson's testimony. Thus, Dr. Anderson's opinions as to future economic damages should have been excluded.

Outcome

The court affirmed in part, struck the punitive damages award, and remanded for a new trial on future economic damages. It also affirmed the denial of attorneys' fees in Martins's cross-appeal.

16.3   Influential Cases

While Supreme Court rulings such as *Daubert*, *Dukes*, and *Comcast* have framed the admissibility and utility of expert economic testimony, many influential precedents arise from lower courts where forensic economists have had a pivotal role in shaping verdicts and settlements.

Selected Cases

Key Non-Supreme Court Cases Involving Forensic Economic Evidence

Case	Court	Forensic Economist Role
In re Urethane Antitrust Litigation, 768 F.3d 1245 (10th Cir. 2014)	Tenth Circuit	Regression analysis established price-fixing overcharges. Economists' models helped uphold a $1 billion judgment despite *Daubert* challenges.
Perma Life Mufflers v. Int'l Parts, 376 F.2d 692 (7th Cir 1967)	Seventh Circuit	Expert economic testimony showed how vertical restraints injured downstream franchisees through lost pricing autonomy.
Apple Inc. v. Pepper, 846 F.3d 313 (9th Cir. 2017)	Ninth Circuit	Economists modeled App Store monopoly pricing. Analysis supported direct purchaser standing by showing harm to end-users.

(Continued)

Case	Court	Forensic Economist Role
In re TFT-LCD Antitrust Litig., 267 F.R.D. 583 (N.D. Cal. 2010)	N.D. Cal.	Economists used correlation and econometric techniques to support class certification in a global price-fixing cartel case.
In re Polyurethane Foam Antitrust Litig., 152 F. Supp. 3d 968 (N.D. Ohio 2015)	N.D. Ohio	Yardstick pricing models and market simulations quantified damages. Settlements exceeded $400 million.
DL v. District of Columbia, 302 F.R.D. 1 (D.D.C. 2013)	D.D.C.	Economic analysis quantified systemic loss of educational services. Expert input guided equitable remedies under IDEA.

(Continued)

Case	Court	Forensic Economist Role
In re Air Cargo Antitrust Litig., 06-MD-1775 (E.D.N.Y. 2014)	E.D.N.Y.	Economists constructed global models showing coordinated surcharges among international air freight carriers.

Significance in Legal Practice

These cases illustrate how forensic economists are not only essential in class actions and antitrust litigation but also increasingly relied upon in civil rights, regulatory, and tort litigation. Their ability to model aggregate harm, allocate damages, and validate causality has transformed complex litigation into data-driven legal proceedings.

Conclusion

Lower courts routinely treat forensic economists as indispensable in complex litigation. Whether establishing predominance in class certification, quantifying antitrust overcharges, or forecasting lost earnings, courts demand rigorous and case-specific economic modeling. These precedents underscore the high evidentiary value, and potential vulnerabilities, of forensic economic testimony in modern litigation.

16.4 U.S. Antitrust Law

Economic Foundations of the Sherman and Clayton Acts

The emergence of forensic economics in American antitrust law traces its roots to the passage of the Sherman Antitrust Act of 1890 and the Clayton Antitrust Act of 1914. These legislative milestones reflected increasing concern with market monopolies, cartels, and the abuse of economic power in the wake of rapid industrialization and the rise of trusts such as Standard Oil and U.S. Steel.

Economists were instrumental in laying the theoretical groundwork for antitrust legislation. Classical economic thinkers such as Adam Smith and later Alfred Marshall provided foundational concepts about market competition, consumer welfare, and the dangers of concentrated power. While not labeled "forensic economists" at the time, early academic economists advised lawmakers that monopolies reduced output, raised prices, and misallocated resources—arguing for laws that preserved competitive market structures.

The Sherman Act outlawed "every contract, combination... or conspiracy, in restraint of trade," while the Clayton Act targeted specific monopolistic behaviors such as price discrimination, exclusive dealing, and mergers that substantially lessened competition. These Acts represented a shift where economic theory began to directly shape statutory language.

The Rise of Economic Testimony in Antitrust Cases

Following the enactment of the Sherman Act in 1890 and the Clayton Act in 1914, the role of economists in legal proceedings expanded dramatically. Forensic economists emerged as indispensable expert witnesses in antitrust litigation, providing quantitative and theoretical frameworks to evaluate questions central to competition law. This included assessing market structure, defining relevant product and geographic markets, measuring market concentration using indices like the Herfindahl-Hirschman Index (HHI), estimating damages from anti-competitive conduct, and analyzing price and output distortions.

Courts increasingly turned to economic experts to interpret ambiguous statutory terms such as "restraint of trade," "monopolization," and "substantially lessening competition." Economic theory provided rigor where legal language was vague. For instance, in determining whether a firm had engaged in monopolization under Section 2 of the Sherman Act, courts began requiring a showing of market power and exclusionary conduct—both concepts necessitating economic analysis.

Major historical cases illustrate this shift. In *United States v. Aluminum Co. of America (Alcoa)*, 148 F.2d 416 (2d Cir. 1945), Judge Learned Hand's opinion relied heavily on economic reasoning to define the relevant market and evaluate Alcoa's dominance. Later, in *United States v. AT&T* (1982), forensic economists offered detailed economic models to demonstrate how AT&T's vertical integration and pricing strategies created barriers to entry and stifled competition. The breakup of AT&T into regional Bell companies was influenced in part by these analyses.

In modern practice, economists testify not only in cases of traditional monopolization, but also in merger evaluations under Section 7 of the Clayton Act. The U.S. Department of Justice (DOJ) and Federal Trade Commission (FTC) routinely rely on forensic economic models, including merger simulation, regression analysis, and critical loss analysis, to predict the likely impact of mergers on consumer welfare and market dynamics.

Moreover, the influence of economic testimony extends to judicial methodology. The use of the "rule of reason" in antitrust analysis—first articulated in *Standard Oil Co. of New Jersey v. United States*, 221 U.S. 1 (1911)—inherently invites economic balancing of competitive harms and benefits. Economists became vital in performing this balancing act.

The emergence of the Chicago School, led by scholars like Robert Bork, Richard Posner, and George Stigler, further entrenched economic analysis into antitrust jurisprudence. In cases like *Continental T.V., Inc. v. GTE Sylvania Inc.*, 433 U.S. 36 (1977), the Supreme Court adopted more economics-oriented reasoning, emphasizing efficiency over formalistic doctrines.

Today, forensic economists not only assist in litigation but also shape the regulatory frameworks governing competition policy. Their influence is seen in the DOJ/FTC Merger Guidelines, academic scholarship, and the growing integration of behavioral economics into antitrust law.

End-of-Section Problems

1. Define "market power." How do forensic economists measure it in antitrust cases?

2. Explain the Herfindahl-Hirschman Index (HHI). What thresholds suggest problematic concentration?

3. In *United States v. Microsoft Corp.*, what economic theories were used to determine monopolistic behavior?

4. Using a diagram, illustrate how monopolistic pricing creates deadweight loss and harms consumer welfare.

5. Describe how economic testimony influenced the outcome of the AT&T breakup.

Key Historical Cases Involving Economic Testimony

- **Standard Oil Co. of New Jersey v. United States**, 221 U.S. 1 (1911): One of the earliest cases interpreting the Sherman Act, this decision used economic reasoning to determine whether Standard Oil's size and conduct constituted unlawful monopolization. Although economists were not formally testifying yet, their writings heavily influenced Justice White's "rule of reason" doctrine.

- **United States v. American Tobacco Co.**, 221 U.S. 106 (1911): Decided the same day as *Standard Oil*, this case evaluated whether multiple entities acted in concert to reduce competition. The ruling relied on economic interpretations of market behavior.

- **United States v. Aluminum Co. of America**

(**Alcoa**), 148 F.2d 416 (2d Cir. 1945): Judge Learned Hand adopted a more technical economic analysis of market dominance and output restriction, essentially crafting an early form of economic market definition.

- **Brown Shoe Co. v. United States**, 370 U.S. 294 (1962): The Court emphasized the use of economic data, including market share and barriers to entry, to evaluate the anticompetitive effects of a merger. Economists testified to establish relevant market boundaries and competitive effects.

- **United States v. AT&T**, 552 F. Supp. 131 (D.D.C. 1982): In this landmark case that led to the breakup of AT&T, both government and defense called economists to analyze market power, barriers to entry, and consumer harm across telecommunications markets.

- **FTC v. Staples, Inc. and Office Depot, Inc.**, 970 F. Supp. 1066 (D.D.C. 1997): The Federal Trade Commission used extensive economic testimony and statistical demand estimation to show that the merger of Staples and Office Depot would result in higher prices for office supplies in specific geographic markets.

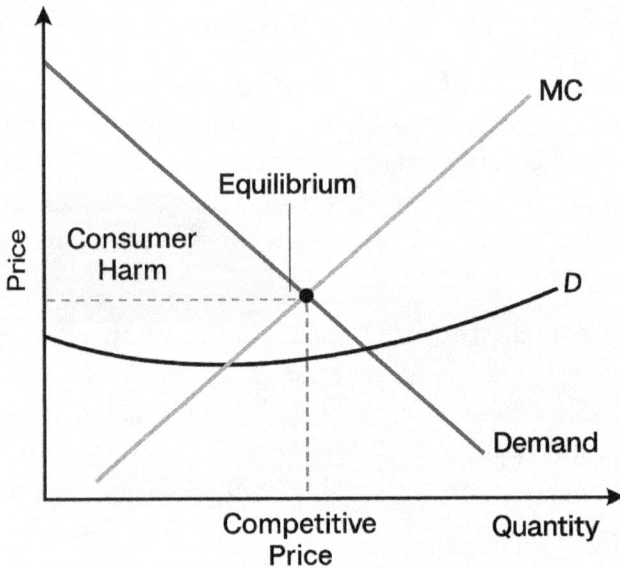

Figure 16.2: Illustration of Market Power, Output Restriction, and Consumer Harm

Institutionalization of Economic Expertise in Antitrust Law

Over the 20th century, the use of economists in antitrust law shifted from an occasional practice to a structural necessity. Today, economists are indispensable in:

- Defining relevant product and geographic markets

- Estimating the Herfindahl-Hirschman Index (HHI) to assess market concentration

- Conducting regression analyses to demonstrate price effects

- Estimating damages to consumers or competitors

- Modeling counterfactual scenarios ("but for" worlds)

Institutions like the Department of Justice's Antitrust Division and the Federal Trade Commission (FTC) now employ full-time economic staff and contract academic experts for litigation. Major antitrust consultancies, such as NERA Economic Consulting, Charles River Associates, and Compass Lexecon, routinely provide expert witnesses in merger review and monopolization cases.

Conclusion

Forensic economists have played a critical role in shaping both the development and enforcement of antitrust law. From the passage of the Sherman and Clayton Acts to modern-day merger analysis and monopolization doctrine, economists have provided courts with the quantitative and theoretical tools needed to interpret and enforce complex statutes. Their work continues to ensure that markets remain competitive, efficient, and fair.

End-of-Section Problems

1. What were the economic conditions that led to the passage of the Sherman Antitrust Act?

2. Define market power and explain how forensic

economists help courts measure it.

3. In the AT&T case, what economic arguments were used to justify the breakup of the company?

4. Draw a diagram showing how a monopoly restricts output and increases price compared to a competitive market.

5. Explain the Herfindahl-Hirschman Index and its use in merger analysis.

16.5   *U.S. v. Microsoft*

Although not a conventional class action, the landmark case of *United States v. Microsoft Corp.*, 253 F.3d 34 (D.C. Cir. 2001), remains one of the most consequential antitrust prosecutions in modern legal history. It exemplifies the indispensable role economic experts can play in high-stakes litigation involving monopolization, market power, and technological entrenchment. Filed by the U.S. Department of Justice and 20 state attorneys general, the case alleged that Microsoft engaged in anticompetitive conduct to maintain its monopoly over personal computer operating systems, particularly by leveraging its dominance in Windows to suppress competition from web browsers like Netscape Navigator.

The Economic Issues at Stake

At the heart of the litigation was a fundamental economic question: Did Microsoft's conduct harm competition, or

merely competitors? Prosecutors needed to demonstrate not
only that Microsoft held monopoly power, but that it
unlawfully maintained that power through exclusionary
tactics that reduced consumer welfare and stifled innovation.

This required more than legal theory—it demanded economic
modeling. Expert economists were tasked with analyzing:

- **Market definition and power:** Identifying the
  relevant market and proving that Microsoft had
  dominant control over operating system distribution,
  with barriers to entry so high as to prevent meaningful
  competition.

- **Predatory bundling:** Evaluating whether bundling
  Internet Explorer with Windows constituted a form of
  tying that foreclosed browser competition and chilled
  rival software development.

- **Network effects and lock-in:** Modeling how early
  adoption, application compatibility, and user familiarity
  created self-reinforcing dynamics that preserved
  Microsoft's position irrespective of product quality.

- **Consumer harm:** Estimating economic injury from
  reduced browser innovation, decreased pricing
  competition, and suppressed platform alternatives.

The Role of Expert Testimony

Several renowned economists played central roles on both
sides of the litigation. For the government, Professor Franklin
Fisher of MIT—an authority on industrial
organization—served as a chief economic expert. Fisher

argued that Microsoft's conduct was strategically designed to
eliminate nascent threats before they could mature into viable
competitive platforms. He emphasized that in technology
markets, the marginal cost of additional users is near zero,
but the value of the network increases exponentially—thus,
actions to block or delay early competition could have
long-term anticompetitive effects.

Microsoft, for its part, retained economists such as Richard
Schmalensee and later Robert D. Willig, who contended that
the company's behavior was pro-competitive and reflected
legitimate product improvement. They argued that consumers
benefited from the integration of Internet Explorer and that
rival browsers failed due to market preferences, not illegal
suppression.

Economic Legacy and Impact

The case ultimately resulted in a finding that Microsoft had
violated the Sherman Act. While the district court originally
ordered a breakup of the company, the remedy was
overturned on appeal, and a settlement was reached that
imposed structural and behavioral restrictions.

Nonetheless, the case had profound effects:

- It solidified the importance of economic evidence in
  monopolization cases, particularly in fast-moving,
  high-tech markets.

- It gave rise to renewed scholarship on network effects,
  tipping markets, and platform economics.

- It influenced global antitrust frameworks, as regulators

in the European Union and elsewhere initiated their own enforcement actions against Microsoft and other tech giants.

Perhaps most importantly, *United States v. Microsoft* demonstrated that economics is not merely supportive in antitrust litigation—it is foundational. In markets governed as much by code as by contract, expert economic insight becomes the court's lens into power, exclusion, and the cost of lost innovation.

Echoes Abroad: Microsoft in Europe and the Rise of Global Tech Antitrust

While the U.S. prosecution of Microsoft set an important precedent, the most sustained economic scrutiny of the company, and indeed of the broader technology sector, has taken place in the European Union. There, the European Commission has pursued a series of antitrust cases that illustrate how economic reasoning, market modeling, and expert analysis shape global regulatory strategies.

In **Microsoft Corp. v. European Commission** (2004–2009), the Commission found that Microsoft had abused its dominant position under Article 82 (now Article 102 TFEU) by:

- Refusing to provide interoperability information to rival server software vendors.

- Bundling Windows Media Player with the Windows operating system to the detriment of other media applications.

The Commission imposed a record fine of €497 million (later increased) and ordered Microsoft to disclose technical specifications and offer a version of Windows without Media Player. Economic experts were instrumental in evaluating the extent of harm caused by network foreclosure, the reduction in consumer choice, and diminished innovation.

The European actions reflected a broader shift: antitrust authorities increasingly relied on **structural economics**, including models of consumer behavior, software ecosystems, and path dependency. Economists played a central role in demonstrating that abuse in digital markets may not manifest through price increases, but rather through degraded competition, reduced quality, or manipulated defaults.

Apple and Amazon: New Frontiers in Economic Enforcement

Following the Microsoft blueprint, regulators worldwide have turned their attention to other tech giants—particularly Apple and Amazon—where platform dominance, vertical integration, and data asymmetries pose complex economic questions.

Apple: The European Commission has pursued several probes into Apple's App Store policies, particularly its 30% commission on digital goods and its alleged self-preferencing behavior. Economists have evaluated:

- Whether Apple's control over the iOS ecosystem creates a bottleneck for app distribution.

- The effect of in-app purchase restrictions on price competition and consumer choice.

- The potential for Apple to act as both gatekeeper and competitor, disadvantaging rival apps (e.g., Spotify, Epic Games).

These inquiries often turn on **two-sided market analysis**, where platforms serve both developers and users, and economic models must account for cross-group externalities and multi-homing behavior.

Amazon: Investigations by the European Commission, Germany's Bundeskartellamt, and the U.S. Federal Trade Commission have focused on Amazon's dual role as marketplace operator and competitor to third-party sellers. Forensic economists analyze:

- Amazon's use of non-public seller data to develop competing private-label products.

- Algorithmic self-preferencing in search rankings and "Buy Box" eligibility.

- Predatory pricing strategies and potential abuse of bargaining power over suppliers.

In 2022, the European Commission secured commitments from Amazon to reform its practices to avoid further fines, including structural separations in its logistics and data handling practices. These settlements stemmed from extensive economic modeling of platform dominance, data exploitation, and seller lock-in.

Toward a Global Economic Jurisprudence

These cases reflect an emerging **global convergence around economic antitrust enforcement** in digital markets. As the value chain moves from physical goods to data and algorithms, regulators increasingly rely on forensic economists not only to diagnose harm, but to design remedies.

Whether in Washington, Brussels, or Berlin, the message is clear: the modern antitrust courtroom is no longer dominated solely by legal argument. It is shaped by econometric regressions, platform dynamics, and incentive theory. And as the architecture of commerce becomes more virtual, the language of enforcement grows ever more mathematical.

16.6   Conclusion

The cases explored in this chapter underscore the extraordinary range and depth of forensic economics in action. Whether unraveling global laundering networks, dissecting collusive cartels, evaluating antitrust violations by multinational corporations, or quantifying the consequences of environmental destruction, these "interesting cases" illustrate the indispensable role of economic reasoning in modern legal proceedings.

Each case, while unique in its factual complexity, reveals a common pattern: behind every spreadsheet lies a story, and behind every economic model stands a human consequence. Forensic economists are called not merely to calculate, but to clarify—to illuminate hidden structures, quantify elusive harms, and render the abstract intelligible to courts and juries alike. Their work is where math meets motive, where theory confronts human behavior, and where justice demands precision.

But diagnosis is only the beginning. To convert economic insight into admissible evidence, and evidence into actionable damages, one must master the art and science of valuation. How do we calculate lost wages over a working lifetime? How do we convert pain into a number, or equity dilution into compensatory value? What methods govern business valuation, asset depreciation, or the present value of future loss?

In the next chapter, we turn to the analytical heart of forensic economics: *Valuation Techniques*. There, we will explore the quantitative frameworks that allow experts to move from narrative to number—and from economic theory to financial remedy.

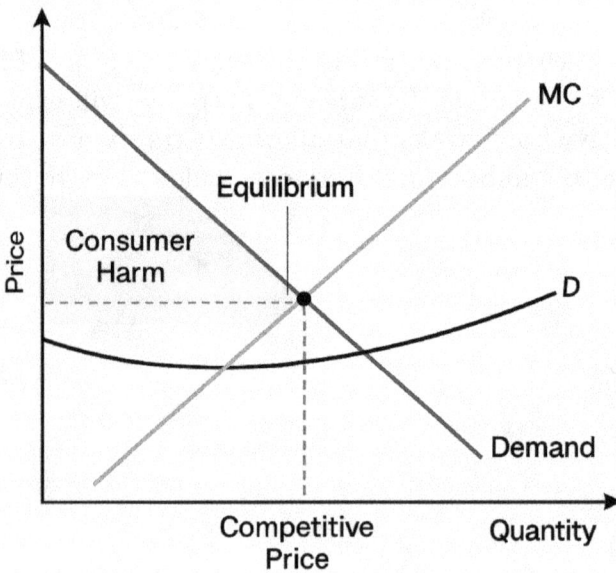

Market Power, Output Restriction, and Consumer Harm

Figure 16.1: Market Power and Deadweight Loss from Monopolistic Pricing

Chapter 17

Valuation Techniques

17.1   Introduction

This chapter explores quantitative valuation techniques used
in forensic economics to calculate damages, wages, lost
earnings, and consumer or employee harm. These
methodologies apply across personal injury cases, employment
discrimination litigation, and class action wage claims.

17.2   Valuation Techniques

Valuation lies at the heart of forensic economics. It is the
quantitative bridge between theory and remedy—the point at
which damage assessments, economic models, and legal claims
coalesce into actionable conclusions. Whether determining the

economic value of lost profits, environmental degradation,
wrongful death, or breached contracts, forensic economists
must select the right valuation method, justify its
appropriateness, and implement it with mathematical rigor.

This section explores several foundational valuation
techniques used in litigation and regulatory contexts,
illustrating their theoretical underpinnings, empirical
applications, and evidentiary standards.

Replacement Cost Method

The Replacement Cost Method estimates the value of a good,
service, or asset by calculating the cost required to replace it
with an equivalent in the current market. Often used in
insurance claims, infrastructure damage, or intellectual
property valuation, this method assumes that the value of the
lost or damaged item is equivalent to the cost of acquiring a
substitute of equal utility.

Forensic experts employing this method must:

- Identify a market substitute with comparable
  functionality, quality, and lifespan.

- Adjust for inflation, technological obsolescence, or
  improvements in replacement items.

- Consider logistical costs, depreciation, and regional
  market variability.

In legal contexts, this method is frequently deployed in
natural disaster cases, eminent domain proceedings, or
construction defect disputes. It is particularly effective when
market comparables are scarce or the damaged item is unique.

Market Valuation Method

The Market Valuation Method, or "comparative market analysis," determines value based on recent transactions involving similar goods or services. It relies on the core economic assumption that value is revealed through voluntary exchange. The strength of this method lies in its empirical transparency—if a product or asset routinely sells for $X, then that price provides a defensible anchor for damages.

Applications include:

- Valuing real estate, intellectual property, or vehicles in civil litigation.

- Determining the fair market value of securities, collectibles, or business interests.

- Benchmarking wage losses in employment disputes using labor market data.

The method requires meticulous adjustment for variation in quality, location, transaction conditions, and timing. Courts often demand that forensic economists disclose the number of comparables, their source, and the statistical methodology used to normalize differences.

Hedonic Valuation

Hedonic valuation employs regression models to estimate the value of intangible or composite goods by decomposing them into constituent characteristics. Most commonly used in labor economics, environmental valuation, and tort cases involving quality-of-life loss, this method quantifies the implicit prices of attributes such as risk, prestige, air quality, or scenery.

A typical hedonic wage regression model takes the form:

$$Wage_i = \beta_0 + \beta_1 \cdot Experience_i + \beta_2 \cdot Education_i$$
$$+ \beta_3 \cdot Risk_i + \beta_4 \cdot UnionStatus_i + \beta_5 \cdot Location_i + \epsilon_i$$

The coefficients (β values) represent the marginal value of each attribute. For example, β_3 reflects the wage premium required for working in a riskier job. By extending this approach to housing markets, economists can estimate the implicit value of safety, school quality, or pollution reduction.

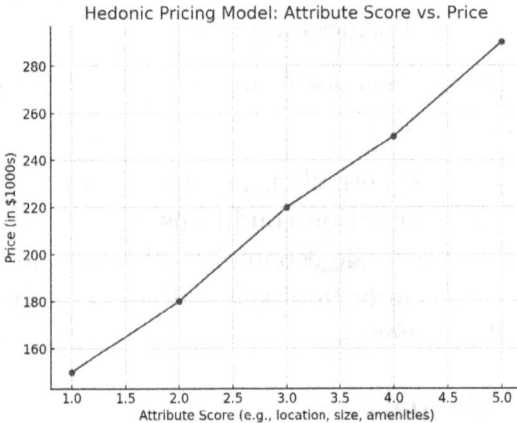

Figure 17.1: Example Hedonic Valuation Regression

Hedonic valuation is particularly valuable in wrongful death and environmental tort cases, where traditional market pricing is insufficient. Courts have accepted this technique to justify damage claims based on loss of enjoyment, aesthetic harm, or diminished quality of life.

Discounted Cash Flow (DCF) Analysis

DCF is a forward-looking valuation approach that estimates the present value of expected future cash flows. It is widely used in business valuation, lost profit calculations, and investment damages.

Key steps include:

1. Forecasting revenues, costs, and net income over a projection period.

2. Determining a terminal value to capture value beyond the projection horizon.

3. Selecting an appropriate discount rate based on risk and cost of capital.

4. Applying the discount factor to convert future earnings into present dollars.

DCF analysis is sensitive to assumptions about growth, discount rates, and capital structure. In litigation, forensic economists must justify their inputs using historical data, industry reports, and accepted financial theory (e.g., CAPM, WACC).

Contingent Valuation Method (CVM)

CVM is a survey-based technique used to estimate the monetary value of non-market goods, such as clean air, scenic vistas, or cultural heritage. Respondents are asked how much they would be willing to pay (or accept) to gain (or forego) a change in the good.

Though sometimes controversial, CVM is used in environmental law, resource damage assessment, and cost-benefit analysis of public projects. Proper design requires:

- Clear scenario framing and description of the good.

- Payment vehicle selection (e.g., tax increase, user fee).

- Sampling methodology and bias control (e.g., hypothetical bias, strategic bias).

Despite its limitations, CVM is often the only available tool when market analogs do not exist.

Comparative Critique and Selection

No valuation technique is universally applicable. Each carries its own assumptions, limitations, and evidentiary hurdles. The selection depends on the nature of the loss, data availability, jurisdictional precedent, and case theory. Often, forensic experts triangulate between methods to corroborate findings and improve robustness.

In the next sections, we will apply these techniques to practical litigation scenarios, illustrating how valuation transforms abstract economic harm into compelling legal argument.

17.3 Wage & Earnings

Wage and earnings analysis is a cornerstone of forensic economic assessment in personal injury, wrongful death, employment discrimination, and labor-related litigation. It enables the quantification of economic loss through the projection of past and future income streams. The valuation of wage loss is not limited to base salary alone; it encompasses the totality of compensation, potential for advancement, probability of continued employment, and duration of worklife.

This section provides an in-depth exploration of the tools, methods, and assumptions forensic economists use to estimate earnings capacity, calculate fringe benefits, and determine the worklife expectancy of individuals under various economic scenarios.

Earnings Capacity

Earnings capacity represents the expected income an individual could have earned over their working life but for an injury, death, or wrongful employment action. It includes base wages, commissions, bonuses, overtime, and often overlooked but economically significant fringe benefits. Forensic economists must build a comprehensive compensation profile using historical earnings records, tax documents, employer handbooks, and industry wage surveys.

Fringe benefits can comprise 25% to 40% or more of total compensation, and commonly include:

- **Health insurance:** Employer contributions to medical,

dental, vision, and life insurance plans.

- **Retirement plans:** Defined contribution (e.g., 401(k)) or defined benefit pensions, including matching contributions and vesting schedules.

- **Bonuses & stock options:** Performance-based incentives and deferred compensation mechanisms.

- **Paid leave:** Vacation, sick time, maternity/paternity leave, and personal days.

- **Educational assistance:** Tuition reimbursement, training stipends, or professional development funds.

In addition to direct benefits, economists may quantify indirect perks like discounted childcare, transportation subsidies, or wellness programs. Valuation of these benefits often draws upon employer cost data from sources such as the National Compensation Survey (NCS), conducted by the Bureau of Labor Statistics.

Expectancy Tables

Worklife expectancy refers to the statistically probable number of years a person is expected to remain in the labor force, accounting for probabilities of death, disability, unemployment, and retirement. This is not simply the difference between current age and retirement age, but a refined probabilistic estimate based on demographic and economic factors.

Key resources include:

- **U.S. Bureau of Labor Statistics:** Publishes labor

force participation and attrition rates stratified by age, gender, and education.

- **Social Security Administration (SSA):** Provides actuarial life tables to calculate survival probabilities.

- **Vocational Economic Tables:** Private actuarial tools that merge worklife expectancy with disability and dropout rates for injured populations.

Advanced worklife models may include adjustments for:

- **Occupation-specific attrition rates.**

- **Health status and comorbidities.**

- **Historical employment volatility or intermittent work patterns.**

- **Educational attainment and re-training potential.**

Wage Growth Projections

To convert projected earnings into present value, economists apply wage growth assumptions and discount rates. Growth assumptions are typically based on:

- Historical average earnings growth by industry and occupation.

- Inflation-adjusted productivity trends (real wage growth).

- Cost-of-living adjustments and collective bargaining agreements.

Discount rates, used to bring future values to present-day terms, are often based on:

- U.S. Treasury yields or risk-free rate assumptions.

- Blended rates derived from corporate bonds or annuity markets.

- Court-mandated fixed discount rates in some jurisdictions.

The net discount rate—the difference between assumed growth and discounting—has a profound impact on damage valuations. Small changes in this rate can significantly alter the present value of a multi-decade earnings stream.

Adjustments for Disruptions

Modern economic analysis must account for structural and episodic labor market disruptions. The COVID-19 pandemic, for instance, introduced new volatility into earnings trajectories, labor force participation, and remote work dynamics.

Forensic experts may now include:

- **Probabilistic adjustments** for future recessions or automation displacement.

- **Industry-specific sensitivity** to macroeconomic shocks (e.g., hospitality, healthcare).

- **Geographic labor elasticity** and access to alternative markets via remote work.

Economists often use Monte Carlo simulations or

scenario-based modeling to quantify the range of potential outcomes and provide courts with probabilistic damage estimates.

Application

Wage and earnings calculations are critical in:

- **Personal Injury and Wrongful Death:** Estimating lifetime lost income for plaintiffs or survivors.

- **Employment Discrimination:** Quantifying back pay and front pay due to wrongful termination, retaliation, or wage disparities.

- **Family Law:** Estimating earning potential for alimony or child support cases.

- **Breach of Employment Contract:** Calculating damages due to violation of tenure, commission, or severance terms.

In all cases, expert reports must be defensible, transparent, and anchored in peer-reviewed methodologies and reliable data sources. Economists may be cross-examined on assumptions, modeling techniques, and comparability of source data.

Conclusion

Wage and earnings analysis is far more than an arithmetic projection—it is a holistic exercise in economic realism. It blends actuarial probability, labor market economics, statistical modeling, and domain expertise. Whether projecting the upward arc of a promising career cut short or estimating the cumulative cost of unjust labor practices, forensic economists must transform data into credible, court-admissible insight.

In the chapters ahead, we further examine how these foundational tools combine with industry-specific models to assess business interruption, lost profits, and complex commercial damages.

17.4   Impact Models

Impact models are the analytical backbone of forensic economic analysis in cases involving systemic harm. These models quantify the economic effects of unlawful behavior—whether it be price-fixing, discriminatory pay practices, or anticompetitive conduct—on affected parties such as consumers, employees, or competitors. Unlike valuation techniques that focus on individual damages, impact models are often used in class-wide litigation, regulatory enforcement, and policy evaluation to measure aggregate effects.

At their core, impact models aim to answer a fundamental question: *What would economic outcomes have looked like but for the alleged misconduct?* By constructing counterfactual scenarios and measuring the deviation from actual outcomes, forensic economists provide courts with a credible, evidence-based narrative of harm. This section explores two major categories of impact models: those used in price-fixing and overcharge litigation, and those used to isolate wage disparities in employment discrimination cases.

Price Elasticity and Overcharges

In antitrust and consumer protection litigation, one of the primary goals is to estimate the amount consumers were overcharged due to illegal pricing behavior such as collusion, price-fixing, or deceptive marketing. Economists use the concept of price elasticity to model how buyers would have behaved under competitive market conditions.

Price elasticity of demand measures the percentage change in quantity demanded for a one-percent change in price:

$$\varepsilon = \frac{\%\Delta Q}{\%\Delta P}$$

In practice, economists estimate demand elasticity using time-series or panel data to model consumer behavior before, during, and after the period of alleged misconduct. The goal is to simulate what prices would have been in a competitive market and then calculate:

$$\text{Overcharge} = P_{\text{Actual}} - P_{\text{But For}}$$

$$\text{Total Harm} = \text{Overcharge} \times Q_{\text{But For}}$$

Where:

- P_{Actual}: observed market price during the conspiracy.

- $P_{\text{But For}}$: counterfactual price in the absence of collusion.

- $Q_{\text{But For}}$: projected quantity purchased absent overpricing.

Experts frequently use hedonic regressions, structural econometric models, or reduced-form difference-in-differences (DiD) estimators to build their counterfactual models. These methods help isolate the effect of anticompetitive conduct from broader market fluctuations, input costs, and seasonal trends.

Example: In a case involving a global auto parts cartel, forensic economists examined historical price trends, input cost volatility (e.g., steel, labor), and output trends in unaffected jurisdictions. The models showed that absent collusion, prices would have been 17–22% lower over a six-year period, leading to consumer overcharges in the hundreds of millions.

Employee Discrimination Impact Models

In employment litigation involving claims of racial, gender, or age discrimination, impact models are used to estimate whether protected classes receive materially different compensation or employment outcomes relative to similarly situated individuals. The key challenge is to control for legitimate explanatory factors (e.g., experience, education, tenure) while isolating the residual "unexplained" wage gap attributable to discrimination.

The most common tools include:

- **Linear Regression Models:** Ordinary Least Squares (OLS) is used to estimate the impact of demographic characteristics on wages or promotion likelihood, controlling for human capital variables.

- **Oaxaca-Blinder Decomposition:** A two-part model that decomposes the wage differential between groups into explained and unexplained components.

The decomposition formula is typically expressed as:

$$\text{Wage Gap} = (\bar{X}_m - \bar{X}_f) \cdot \beta + \bar{X}_f \cdot (\beta_m - \beta_f)$$

Where:

- $\bar{X}_m$ and $\bar{X}_f$: average characteristics (education, experience, etc.) of males and females.

- β_m and β_f: estimated return to those characteristics in male and female wage regressions.

- The first term represents the "explained" gap due to differences in characteristics.

- The second term represents the "unexplained" gap, often interpreted as potential discrimination.

Example: In a Title VII class action against a nationwide retail chain, economists used longitudinal payroll data to model starting pay, promotion rates, and bonus awards. After controlling for job title, education, tenure, and region, a statistically significant gender-based wage gap remained—strongly supporting the plaintiffs' claim of systemic bias.

Advanced Impact Models and Machine Learning

Modern forensic practice increasingly incorporates machine learning tools to enhance impact model performance. Random forests, gradient boosting machines, and LASSO regression have been applied in complex cases where traditional OLS may fail due to high-dimensional data or multicollinearity.

Example Applications:

- *Classification algorithms* to detect hiring bias across demographic groups.

- *Clustering techniques* to segment consumer harm based on purchase patterns.

- *Anomaly detection* in price histories to flag potential collusion episodes.

While courts still require models to be interpretable and statistically rigorous, these new techniques offer unprecedented capacity to analyze massive datasets and uncover subtle forms of economic harm.

Closing Impact Models

Impact models serve as the evidentiary engine behind some of the most complex and consequential litigation in modern law. By constructing counterfactuals and quantifying aggregate harm, forensic economists translate abstract allegations into measurable damages. Whether unveiling cartel-induced overcharges or revealing latent wage discrimination, these models give courts the analytical tools to see the unseen, and to restore equity where hidden imbalances once prevailed.

In the following chapter, we delve into the world of econometric testing, examining the statistical underpinnings that ensure these impact models withstand scrutiny from both opposing experts and the bench.

17.5 Conclusion

Valuation techniques are not merely mechanical exercises in arithmetic—they are the interpretive instruments by which forensic economists assign meaning, credibility, and legal weight to economic harm. From replacement cost to hedonic pricing, from discounted cash flows to contingent valuation, each method carries its own assumptions, strengths, and limitations. Their proper application demands both technical proficiency and contextual sensitivity to the nature of the harm, the availability of data, and the governing legal framework.

Earnings analysis, likewise, extends beyond the projection of wages. It invites a comprehensive accounting of benefits, worklife expectancy, and economic potential, accounting for risk, disruption, and the human dimensions of loss. Together, these tools provide courts with the numerical foundation to translate abstract injuries into tangible remedies.

Yet valuation models are only as strong as the data and assumptions upon which they are built. The credibility of expert testimony often turns on whether the methods used are statistically sound, empirically validated, and legally reliable. To that end, we now turn to the critical role of econometric testing, the set of statistical techniques that undergird, verify, and stress-test the models upon which modern litigation so often depends.

End-of-Chapter Problems

1. Describe the hedonic valuation technique and explain how it can be used in a wrongful death case.

2. What are the key inputs needed to calculate lost future earnings in a personal injury case?

3. How can regression analysis reveal wage discrimination in employment lawsuits?

4. Why is it important to consider fringe benefits in total earnings calculations?

5. Given the following data (provided in Appendix X), compute a simple wage regression model.

Suggested Readings

For those wishing to deepen their understanding of valuation methodologies, earnings analysis, and their application in litigation, the following readings are recommended:

- Clermont, W. R. (2025). *Foundations of Data Science and Statistics: Analytics Made Simple.* Fort Lauderdale: Self-published. Retrieved from https://www.amazon.com/dp/B0FK4F57H6. A practical and approachable guide to essential statistical concepts used in data science and economics.

- Smith, J. (2019). *Economic Damages and*

Compensation Models. New York: Aspen Press. An authoritative reference on damage calculation techniques used in torts, employment, and commercial litigation, with step-by-step modeling examples and case law applications.

- Fishback, P. V., Kantor, S. E., & Wallis, J. J. (2006). *Well Worth Saving: How the New Deal Safeguarded Home ownership.* Chicago: University of Chicago Press. Though historical in scope, this work illustrates hedonic valuation techniques and policy analysis in the context of housing markets and governmental interventions.

- Ward, M. A., & Thornton, R. J. (2008). *Regression Analysis and Damages Estimation. Journal of Forensic Economics,* 21(2), 123–145. A concise introduction to using regression techniques in the estimation of damages, with clear examples and discussion of admissibility under Daubert standards.

- National Bureau of Economic Research (NBER). Working papers on labor valuation, wage growth, and the economics of discrimination. Especially relevant are papers from the Labor Studies and Law and Economics programs, which include cutting-edge empirical research often cited in federal court decisions.

- Ireland, T. R., & Depperschmidt, C. L. (Eds.). (2021). *The New Forensic Economics.* Knoxville: Eastern Economic Association. A collection of modern essays and technical guidance from leading forensic economists on topics ranging from loss of earning capacity to structured settlements.

- U.S. Bureau of Labor Statistics. *National Compensation Survey (NCS)* and *Occupational Employment and Wage Statistics (OEWS)*. Essential primary data sources for benchmarking wages, estimating fringe benefits, and calculating geographic or industry-specific compensation.

Chapter 18

Econometric Tests

18.1 Introduction

Econometric analysis plays a central role in forensic economics. Whether estimating damages, testing causality, or identifying patterns of discrimination, statistical rigor is crucial. This chapter introduces the foundational econometric techniques and expands into forensic applications of survey and experimental designs in legal contexts.

18.2 Econometrics

Econometrics lies at the analytical core of forensic economics. It provides the statistical framework by which economists estimate relationships, test hypotheses, and quantify the

causal impact of real-world events—whether those events
involve lost earnings, discriminatory practices, overcharges, or
firm behavior. Courts increasingly rely on econometric
evidence to determine liability, certify classes, and assign
damages.

For forensic purposes, econometric analysis must be
transparent, replicable, and legally admissible under Daubert
or Frye standards. This requires careful attention not only to
model construction but also to variable selection, error
structure, diagnostics, and interpretability.

Linear Regression Analysis

Ordinary Least Squares (OLS) regression is the foundational
tool of applied econometrics. It estimates how a dependent
variable responds to changes in one or more independent
variables, holding all else constant. The general form is:

$$Y_i = \beta_0 + \beta_1 X_{1i} + \beta_2 X_{2i} + \cdots + \beta_k X_{ki} + \epsilon_i$$

Where:

- Y_i = outcome of interest (e.g., wages, prices, damages)

- X_{ki} = explanatory variables (e.g., education, injury
  status, firm size)

- β_k = coefficients estimating marginal effects

- ϵ_i = error term capturing unobserved factors

The goal is to estimate the values of β that minimize the sum
of squared residuals. The magnitude and sign of each β

provide evidence of whether and how each variable influences the outcome.

Example: In an employment discrimination case, economists might regress wages on gender, race, education, and tenure. A significant negative coefficient on the gender variable (after controlling for all other factors) may support a claim of unequal pay.

Dummy Variables and Categorical Data

To incorporate qualitative traits into regression models, economists use dummy variables—binary indicators representing category membership.

$$\text{Wage}_i = \beta_0 + \beta_1 \cdot \text{Male}_i + \beta_2 \cdot \text{Experience}_i + \beta_3 \cdot \text{Bachelor's Degree}_i + \epsilon_i$$

Where:

- $\text{Male}_i = 1$ if the individual is male, 0 otherwise.
- $\text{Bachelor's Degree}_i = 1$ if the individual holds a bachelor's degree.

These variables allow regression to control for group differences. In class action contexts, dummy variables may identify class membership (e.g., impacted vs. non-impacted consumers).

Caution: When working with categorical variables, avoid the dummy variable trap—perfect multicollinearity caused by including all categories.

Multicollinearity and Autocorrelation

OLS (Ordinary Least Squares) regression relies on a set of core assumptions that ensure unbiasedness, efficiency, and consistency of coefficient estimates. Among these assumptions, two of the most commonly violated in forensic economic modeling are multicollinearity and autocorrelation. Their presence can compromise both the reliability of statistical inference and the legal admissibility of economic testimony.

Multicollinearity

Multicollinearity arises when two or more explanatory variables in a regression model exhibit strong linear correlations. While multicollinearity does not bias the OLS estimates themselves, it inflates the standard errors of the estimated coefficients, making it difficult to assess their individual contributions to the dependent variable.

Sources:

- Including redundant variables (e.g., income and net worth).

- Dummy variable traps (e.g., including all categories of a categorical variable).

- Poorly scaled continuous variables (e.g., using both age and age squared).

- Model overfitting due to small sample size and many predictors.

Symptoms of multicollinearity include:

- Dramatic shifts in coefficient estimates with minor

changes to the model.

- A high R-squared value paired with few significant predictors.

- Unexpected coefficient signs (e.g., a positive relationship turning negative).

- Wide confidence intervals around estimated coefficients.

Detection:

- **Variance Inflation Factor (VIF):** A VIF above 10 typically signals multicollinearity.

- **Condition Index:** Values above 30 suggest collinearity problems.

- **Correlation Matrix:** Identifies near-perfect correlations between independent variables.

Legal Impact: In antitrust litigation, multicollinearity can obscure whether pricing is influenced by cost structures or anti-competitive coordination. Courts may reject regression models if experts cannot justify variable inclusion or explain statistical instability.

Solutions and Remedies:

- Remove or combine collinear variables.

- Use Principal Component Analysis (PCA) to reduce dimensionality.

- Increase sample size to offset collinearity's inflationary effect on standard errors.

- Use Ridge Regression as a regularization technique to stabilize estimates.

Autocorrelation

Autocorrelation refers to correlation between residuals (error terms) across observations, particularly over time. It violates the OLS assumption that the error terms are independently distributed, which leads to inefficient coefficient estimates and underestimated standard errors.

Typical forensic contexts:

- Time-series data in securities fraud cases (e.g., stock price manipulation).

- Longitudinal employment data used in backpay estimation.

- Serially correlated consumer purchasing behavior in false advertising or antitrust actions.

Symptoms of autocorrelation:

- Systematic patterns in residual plots (e.g., cycles or trends).

- Overstatement of significance (p-values too small).

- Inflated t-statistics despite poor model fit.

Detection:

- **Durbin-Watson statistic:** Values significantly below 2 suggest positive autocorrelation.

- **Breusch-Godfrey test:** More flexible test for

higher-order serial correlation.

- **Residual plots:** Visualization of residuals over time to detect trends or waves.

Corrective Measures:

- **Lagged Variables:** Introduce lagged versions of independent variables.

- **Generalized Least Squares (GLS):** Re-estimates coefficients allowing for serial correlation.

- **Newey-West Standard Errors:** Adjusts standard errors to remain valid in the presence of autocorrelation and heteroskedasticity.

- **Differencing:** Transform data into changes over time rather than levels.

Judicial Importance: In securities litigation, failing to correct for autocorrelation may lead to overstating the connection between an event and a price drop. This can lead to inflated damage estimates or class certification being denied due to unreliability of the event study.

Heteroskedasticity

Heteroskedasticity occurs when the variance of the residuals is not constant across all levels of the independent variables. This violates a key OLS assumption and leads to inefficient estimates and invalid standard errors, which in turn undermines the validity of hypothesis tests.

Legal Implications: In employment discrimination cases, heteroskedasticity may arise if wage variability increases with experience or tenure, especially across demographic groups. If not corrected, it can cause underestimation of damages or wrongful rejection of discrimination claims.

Symptoms:

- Fan-shaped residual plots (variance increasing with the predicted value).

- Over-rejection of the null hypothesis due to underestimated standard errors.

- Non-random pattern of residuals in a scatterplot.

Diagnostic Tests:

- **White's Test:** A general test for heteroskedasticity.

- **Breusch-Pagan Test:** Tests whether variance of residuals depends on independent variables.

- **Goldfeld–Quandt Test:** Splits data into two groups and compares variances.

Remedies:

- **Use Robust Standard Errors:** These correct standard errors without altering coefficient estimates.

- **Transform Dependent Variable:** Logarithmic or square-root transformations may stabilize variance.

- **Weighted Least Squares (WLS):** Gives lower weight to observations with higher variance.

- **Quantile Regression:** Useful for estimating effects across the distribution rather than the mean.

Practical Example: In wage and hour litigation, forensic economists may analyze income across workers with different hours, departments, or union status. If higher-paid workers exhibit more earnings volatility, uncorrected heteroskedasticity can result in flawed estimates of pay gaps or misclassification effects.

Conclusion

Multicollinearity, autocorrelation, and heteroskedasticity are the "silent killers" of forensic econometrics. Left unchecked, they erode the credibility of expert testimony, distort economic interpretation, and increase the risk of legal error. By identifying, diagnosing, and correcting these violations, forensic economists ensure their models withstand both statistical scrutiny and judicial challenge. The stakes are high—millions of dollars in damages or the fate of class certification may hinge on the rigorous handling of these foundational econometric threats.

Instrumental Variables (IV)

IV regression addresses endogeneity—when an independent variable is correlated with the error term, violating the OLS assumption of exogeneity.

$$\text{Wage}_i = \beta_0 + \beta_1 \cdot \text{Education}_i + \epsilon_i$$
$$\text{Instrument:} \quad \text{Proximity to College}_i$$

In this case, education is endogenous (possibly correlated with ability), but proximity to college is used as an instrument: correlated with education, uncorrelated with the error term.

Two-Stage Least Squares (2SLS) is the standard estimation procedure:

1. Regress the endogenous regressor on the instrument(s).

2. Use the predicted values in the main regression equation.

IV is commonly used in damages models when treatment effects are confounded or self-selected.

Panel Data and Fixed Effects

Panel data—observations over time for the same individuals or entities—allow economists to control for unobserved heterogeneity.

$$Y_{it} = \alpha_i + \beta X_{it} + \epsilon_{it}$$

Where:

- α_i = entity-specific effect (e.g., individual or firm fixed effect)

- t = time index

Fixed effects models control for all time-invariant characteristics of the entity, thus isolating the causal effect of time-varying variables.

Difference-in-Differences (DiD)

DiD is a quasi-experimental method used to evaluate the impact of policy changes, corporate conduct, or discriminatory practices.

$$Y_{it} = \alpha + \delta \cdot \text{Post}_t + \gamma \cdot \text{Treatment}_i + \beta \cdot (\text{Post}_t \times \text{Treatment}_i) + \epsilon_{it}$$

Where:

- β captures the treatment effect.

- $\text{Post}_t = 1$ for periods after the event.

- $\text{Treatment}_i = 1$ for affected group.

DiD is widely used in litigation involving labor law, antitrust enforcement, and regulatory impact.

Model Evaluation and Legal Standards

To be admissible under Daubert, econometric models must demonstrate:

- Testability

- Peer review and publication

- Known error rates

- General acceptance in the relevant field

Forensic experts must also:

- Provide thorough documentation of methods and assumptions.

- Conduct sensitivity analysis (e.g., how results change with alternative specifications).

- Validate models with out-of-sample predictions or robustness checks.

Conclusion

Econometric analysis transforms raw data into structured, probative evidence. When executed rigorously, it allows forensic economists to estimate causal effects, correct for bias, and make defensible inferences about damages, liability, or harm. Whether determining wage disparities, projecting lost profits, or assessing the impact of monopolistic behavior, econometrics is the critical bridge between economic theory and courtroom proof.

In the next chapter, we examine how market structure and competition shape the landscape in which these econometric tools are applied.

18.3   Statistical Testing

Statistical testing plays a foundational role in forensic economics, allowing practitioners to distinguish between random variation and meaningful patterns in data. In litigation, hypothesis testing is used to evaluate claims of discrimination, assess damages, test economic theories, and quantify whether observed outcomes differ from what would be expected under legal compliance or economic neutrality.

Statistical tests must be chosen carefully, justified with respect to the nature of the data, and interpreted with attention to Type I and Type II errors. In legal contexts, statistical results are often viewed through the lens of preponderance of the evidence, clear and convincing standards, or beyond a reasonable doubt, depending on the forum and the burden of proof.

Hypothesis Testing

Hypothesis testing is the process of evaluating a claim (the null hypothesis, H_0) against an alternative (H_1) based on sample data. A hypothesis is typically tested by computing a test statistic and comparing it to a critical value derived from a theoretical distribution (e.g., normal, t, chi-square).

Typical forensic applications include:

- **Testing wage equality:**

$$H_0 : \beta_{\text{gender}} = 0 \quad \text{vs.} \quad H_1 : \beta_{\text{gender}} \neq 0$$

  A statistically significant result suggests gender has a measurable impact on wages, supporting discrimination claims.

- **Comparing group means:** Paired or independent t-tests are used to compare means of two groups (e.g., wages before and after termination, pricing before and after alleged collusion, productivity before and after policy implementation).

- **Proportion tests:** Used to compare success rates across different groups, such as promotion rates among men and women or rejection rates by race in lending decisions.

- **ANOVA (Analysis of Variance):** Extends t-testing to multiple groups. For example, ANOVA can determine whether wage differences across departments or offices are statistically significant.

Key components of hypothesis testing:

- **Null Hypothesis** (H_0): typically a claim of no difference or no effect.

- **Alternative Hypothesis** (H_1): the hypothesis the analyst seeks to test.

- **Significance Level** (α): often set at 0.05; the threshold for rejecting H_0.

- **P-Value**: the probability of obtaining the observed result (or more extreme) if H_0 were true.

A p-value less than α leads to rejection of H_0, indicating statistical significance. However, statistical significance does not always imply practical or economic importance—a crucial point in litigation.

Chi-Square Tests and Contingency Tables

The chi-square test is a non-parametric statistical test used to determine whether an observed distribution of categorical data differs significantly from an expected distribution. It is especially powerful in cases involving class membership, hiring discrimination, voting access, or product selection.

In forensic settings, chi-square tests are commonly applied to:

- **Hiring Practices:** Comparing observed vs. expected hiring across demographic categories (e.g., gender, race).

- **Promotion Disparities:** Evaluating whether promotions are evenly distributed or show signs of disparate impact.

- **Product Mislabeling or Consumer Fraud:** Determining if certain defects or misrepresentations are statistically more likely in certain product batches or seller locations.

The test is based on the formula:

$$\chi^2 = \sum \frac{(O_i - E_i)^2}{E_i}$$

Where:

- O_i is the observed frequency.

- E_i is the expected frequency under the null hypothesis of independence.

A high chi-square value relative to the degrees of freedom suggests that the observed and expected distributions differ significantly.

Right-tailed Chi-Square Distribution

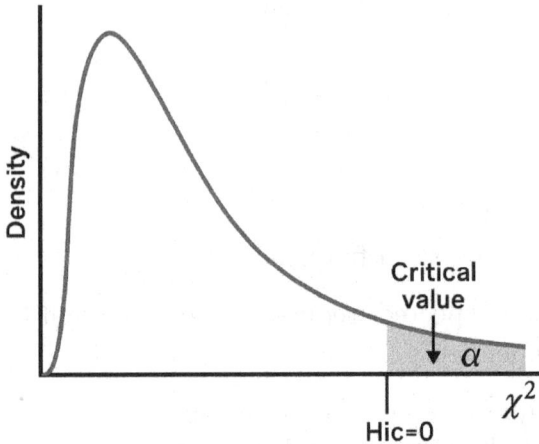

Figure 18.1: Expected vs. Observed Distributions in Title VII Litigation

Example: In a Title VII lawsuit, plaintiffs may argue that a company failed to hire a proportionate number of minority applicants. A chi-square test can evaluate whether hiring patterns are statistically inconsistent with the racial makeup of the applicant pool, strengthening claims of discriminatory intent or disparate impact.

Other Statistical Tests in Forensic Practice

- **Kolmogorov–Smirnov (K–S) Test:** Used to compare two sample distributions or test for goodness-of-fit. Applied in fraud detection or when testing distributions of payouts or returns.

- **Mann-Whitney U Test:** A non-parametric alternative to the t-test when normality assumptions are violated. Useful in wage disputes when sample sizes are small or data is skewed.

- **Wilcoxon Signed-Rank Test:** Compares matched pairs—useful for evaluating pre/post interventions when data is ordinal or non-normal.

- **Fisher's Exact Test:** Preferred for small-sample categorical analysis. Especially relevant in early-stage discovery when working with limited employment or consumer records.

- **Binomial and Poisson Tests:** Used in event studies, fraud detection, and environmental exposure litigation to determine whether observed event frequencies deviate from chance expectations.

Type I and Type II Errors in Legal Contexts

- **Type I Error (False Positive):** Rejecting the null hypothesis when it is actually true. In court, this equates to wrongly assigning liability.

- **Type II Error (False Negative):** Failing to reject the null hypothesis when the alternative is true. In court, this means failing to recognize actual wrongdoing.

- **Balancing Risks:** Legal standards of proof (e.g., "more likely than not" vs. "beyond a reasonable doubt") reflect society's chosen balance between these errors.

Courts may tolerate Type I errors more in civil contexts (where false negatives could perpetuate injustice), while criminal law places higher weight on avoiding Type I errors due to liberty concerns.

Conclusion

Statistical testing empowers forensic economists to convert anecdote into analysis and pattern into proof. From wage discrimination to product liability, statistical inference allows experts to identify discrepancies, measure disparities, and inform judicial outcomes with quantitative rigor. But with great power comes great responsibility: models must be valid, assumptions tested, and conclusions delivered with honesty and clarity.

In the next chapter, we explore how markets themselves can be modeled, interpreted, and used to infer competitive dynamics—a shift from micro-level inference to the structural forces that shape legal outcomes across entire sectors.

18.4   Survey and Experimental Techniques

Survey and experimental techniques occupy a crucial space in forensic economics, especially in cases where market data is incomplete, consumer intent must be inferred, or valuation hinges on preferences. These methods translate perception, behavior, and hypothetical decision-making into quantifiable economic value. They are commonly applied in intellectual property disputes, consumer class actions, antitrust enforcement, advertising fraud, and deceptive trade practices.

To be admissible in court, surveys and experiments must adhere to rigorous methodological standards, withstand statistical scrutiny, and be conducted with procedural transparency. Under the Daubert framework, courts assess whether the survey was conducted according to accepted principles, whether it has been peer-reviewed, and whether it maintains scientific integrity in execution and analysis.

Survey Design for Forensic Use

Surveys are often used to elicit consumer attitudes, measure confusion, assess reliance, or quantify demand for specific features. Whether used in Lanham Act claims, false advertising, or trademark dilution, a poorly constructed survey may be ruled inadmissible or given little weight.

Key principles in litigation-grade survey design include:

- **Random Sampling:** Participants must be drawn from a pool that reflects the target population. Convenience samples (e.g., friends or employees) are inadmissible in most contexts.

- **Stratification:** The sample should represent key demographic or behavioral strata (e.g., age, geography, buyer history) to avoid over- or under-representation.

- **Avoidance of Leading Questions:** Questions must be neutrally worded to avoid priming or anchoring effects that bias responses.

- **Pilot Testing:** Pre-tests help identify confusing phrasing, poor response categories, or dropout risks before full deployment.

- **Validation Procedures:** Cross-verifying survey
  responses with actual behavior (when available) or
  internal consistency checks.

- **Proper Documentation:** Full transparency about
  instruments, sampling frames, response rates, and
  cleaning procedures is essential for admissibility.

Example: In a false labeling case, a forensic economist might
survey consumers to determine whether the phrase "clinically
proven" materially influenced purchasing decisions. A
properly designed survey would randomize question order,
include control groups, and stratify by purchasing frequency.

Courts have both admitted and rejected surveys depending on
execution quality. In *Playboy Enterprises, Inc. v. Netscape
Communications*, the court dismissed a confusion survey for
failing to include proper controls. In contrast, in *McNeil-PPC,
Inc. v. Pfizer Inc.*, a consumer perception survey was
accepted after meeting accepted methodological standards.

Conjoint Analysis

Conjoint analysis is a statistical technique used to determine
how people value the individual components of a product or
service. It is especially powerful in intellectual property,
consumer protection, and damages estimation.

Forensic applications include:

- Estimating the premium consumers are willing to pay
  for a patented feature.

- Measuring the harm caused by deceptive or omitted claims.

- Modeling the substitution effect when a feature is removed or misrepresented.

Example: In a trademark case involving counterfeit products, a conjoint analysis might isolate the value consumers place on an authentic logo. Survey respondents are shown different combinations of product attributes, and statistical techniques (e.g., hierarchical Bayes, OLS, or maximum likelihood) estimate the marginal utility of each feature.

The results can be translated into:

- Willingness to Pay (WTP)

- Lost profits or consumer surplus

- Adjusted demand curves for damages modeling

Legal acceptance: Conjoint analysis has been accepted in cases such as *Apple v. Samsung* and rejected in others where it lacked transparency or failed to match real-world purchasing conditions. A court may exclude the method if the survey did not reflect actual market behavior or was overly speculative.

Experimental Designs

Experiments—especially randomized controlled trials (RCTs)—represent the gold standard for establishing causal effects. In litigation, however, full experimentation is often infeasible or unethical. Still, well-structured quasi-experiments and natural experiments can yield admissible and probative insights.

Experimental techniques in forensic settings include:

- **A/B Testing:** Comparing consumer response to two advertising treatments in online marketplaces. Used in platform manipulation or digital misrepresentation claims.

- **Field Experiments:** Deployed in discrimination studies (e.g., sending resumes with racially identifiable names to assess bias).

- **Lab Simulations:** Creating artificial marketplaces to study consumer behavior under controlled conditions.

- **Natural Experiments:** Leveraging real-world events (e.g., regulatory changes) as exogenous shocks to evaluate policy or business conduct.

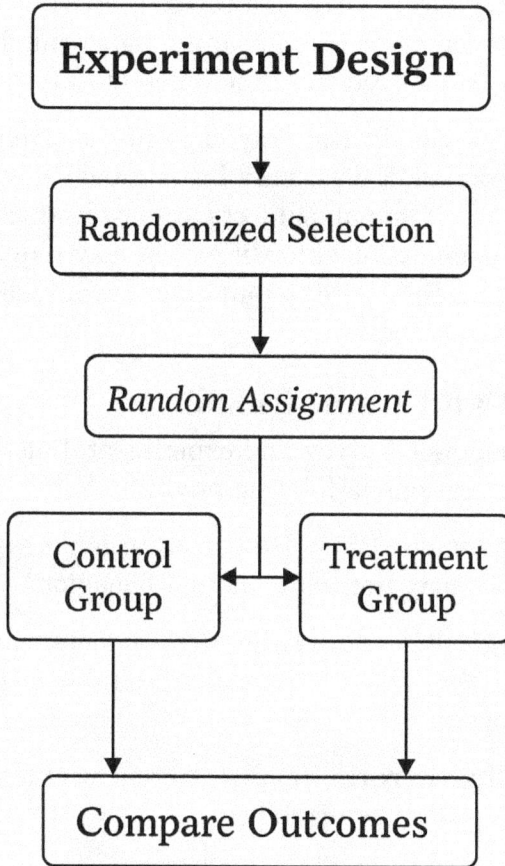

Figure 18.2: Structure of a Simple Randomized Control Trial

Example: In a digital false advertising case, forensic experts may use A/B testing to measure how different versions of a product listing affect conversion rates. If consumers exposed to misleading claims had significantly higher purchase rates, damages can be inferred from the differential response.

Ethical and legal limits: Any experiment involving deception or omission must pass Institutional Review Board (IRB) standards if human subjects are involved. Surveys or experiments commissioned for litigation may require disclosure under Rule 26(a)(2) and must avoid manipulative or suggestive framing.

Critiques and Limitations

Despite their power, survey and experimental methods face significant limitations in forensic practice:

- **Hypothetical Bias:** Responses to hypothetical questions may not match actual behavior.

- **Strategic Misreporting:** Respondents may give answers they think are socially desirable or helpful to the sponsor.

- **Sampling Errors:** Small or unrepresentative samples compromise generalizability.

- **Overcomplex Designs:** Surveys with too many attributes or choices can induce respondent fatigue or cognitive overload.

Best practice: Forensic economists should pre-register survey protocols when possible, apply robustness checks, and subject findings to peer validation or replication where feasible.

Techniques

Surveys and experiments serve as the bridge between economic theory and human experience. They allow economists to quantify preferences, assess causality, and test market hypotheses when transaction data alone cannot speak. When carefully designed, rigorously executed, and appropriately analyzed, these tools transform perceptions and behavior into empirical evidence fit for judicial scrutiny.

In the next chapter, we transition from behavioral elicitation to structural inference, examining how market power, collusion, and competitive effects are measured through market analysis.

18.5 Conclusion

Forensic economists use advanced statistical tools to uncover discrimination, test causality, and estimate impact. The scientific rigor of these techniques makes them powerful in both courtroom and policy settings.

End-of-Chapter Problems

1. Construct a regression model using hypothetical data to detect wage discrimination. Interpret your coefficients.

2. Explain why multicollinearity can undermine damage estimation models.

3. What standards must a forensic economist meet for survey evidence to be admitted under the Daubert standard?

4. Describe a case where instrumental variables would be necessary. What instrument would you propose?

5. Use a chi-square test to assess whether a company's promotion rate is independent of gender (data provided in Appendix Y).

Suggested Readings

- Wooldridge, J. (2020). *Introductory Econometrics: A Modern Approach*. Cengage Learning.

- National Research Council (2003). *The Polygraph and Lie Detection*. National Academies Press.

Chapter 19

Market Analysis

19.1   Introduction

Forensic economists are routinely called upon to evaluate
market dynamics, competitive behavior, and the pricing of
risk. This chapter surveys key tools for analyzing market
competition, insurance mechanisms, and risk-based pricing
models, all of which are crucial in antitrust, tort, and contract
litigation.

19.2   Market Structure

Understanding market structure is central to the forensic
analysis of competitive dynamics, monopoly power, collusion,
and market failure. Whether the issue is a merger, price-fixing

allegation, or monopolization claim, economists must delineate the market, assess concentration, and evaluate firm behavior using robust tools of microeconomic theory and empirical measurement.

Market Definition and Delineation

Defining the relevant market is the foundation of any antitrust inquiry. An improperly defined market can result in misleading conclusions about market power, competitive effects, and consumer harm. Market delineation involves identifying the boundaries within which firms compete, both in terms of product type and geographic reach.

Key Tools in Market Definition:

- **SSNIP Test (Small but Significant and Non-transitory Increase in Price):** The SSNIP test is the cornerstone of the hypothetical monopolist approach. It asks whether a firm could impose a price increase of 5–10% without losing sales to substitutes. If not, the market definition is too narrow and must be expanded to include close substitutes.

- **Cross-Price Elasticity of Demand:** Measures the responsiveness of demand for one product when the price of another product changes. High cross-price elasticity indicates strong substitution, supporting inclusion in the same market.

- **Critical Loss Analysis:** Compares the revenue lost due to a price increase with the revenue gained. If the loss in quantity outweighs the benefit of higher prices, the firm lacks market power in that definition.

- **Cluster Market Theory:** Recognizes that products or services often sold together (e.g., banking services, healthcare tests) may define a combined relevant market.

- **Real-World Evidence:** Includes customer switching patterns, internal company documents, pricing studies, and purchasing behavior—essential for courts evaluating the economic substance of a proposed market.

Legal Application: In cases such as *FTC v. Whole Foods Market*, the debate centered on whether natural/organic food stores constituted a separate product market. Courts used customer perception and substitution patterns to inform the final delineation. Forensic economists play a vital role in submitting expert declarations and empirical estimates to support or rebut proposed market definitions.

Concentration Measures

Once the market is defined, its structure must be analyzed to determine whether it is concentrated, fragmented, or transitioning. One of the most widely accepted tools for this is the Herfindahl-Hirschman Index (HHI), a measure of market concentration used by the U.S. Department of Justice and the Federal Trade Commission.

$$HHI = \sum_{i=1}^{N}(s_i \times 100)^2$$

Where s_i is the market share of firm i expressed as a

proportion (e.g., 0.25 for 25%).

Interpretation Guidelines:

- **HHI < 1500:** Unconcentrated market

- **1500 ≤ HHI < 2500:** Moderately concentrated

- **HHI ≥ 2500:** Highly concentrated market

Merger Policy Implications:

- If a merger increases the HHI by more than 200 points in a highly concentrated market, it raises significant competitive concerns and may trigger a presumption of illegality.

- Antitrust agencies use HHI changes in combination with econometric modeling and customer testimony to evaluate merger effects on price and innovation.

Example: A proposed merger between two regional hospital systems would raise the HHI from 2700 to 3100. Forensic economists might testify that the increase would significantly reduce patient choice and bargaining leverage for insurers.

Market Power, Output Restriction, and Consumer Harm

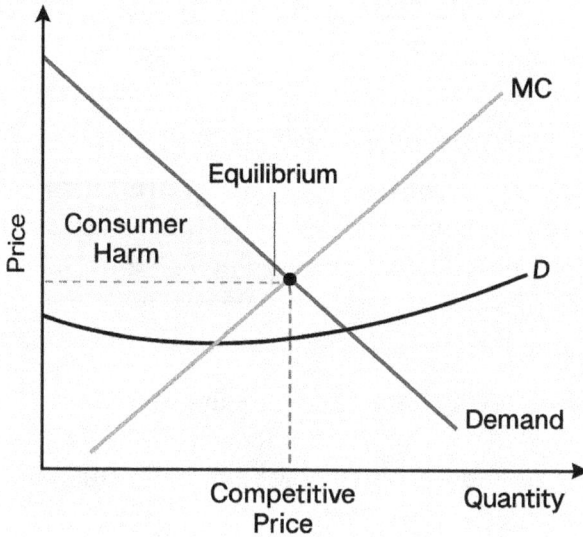

Figure 19.1: Impact of Market Concentration on Prices and Output

Game Theory and Strategic Behavior

In oligopolistic or concentrated markets, firms do not operate in isolation. Instead, they engage in strategic behavior, anticipating and responding to the actions of rivals. Game theory provides a structured way to model these interactions, including competitive strategies that may verge on collusion or monopolization.

Core Applications in Forensic Economics:

- **Tacit Collusion:** Without explicit agreement, firms may signal or coordinate on pricing, capacity, or output. Repeated game frameworks (e.g., Bertrand or Cournot models with repeated interaction) show how collusion can be sustained even without formal cartel agreements.

- **Predatory Pricing:** A dominant firm sets prices below cost to drive out competitors, expecting to recoup losses later through higher prices. Forensic models estimate the duration and depth of below-cost pricing and examine internal communications for strategic intent.

- **Entry Deterrence:** Incumbents may overinvest, flood the market, or tie up suppliers to raise barriers to entry. Strategic models show how such behavior reduces long-run consumer welfare.

- **Signaling and Commitment Devices:** Firms may make investments or public announcements that signal pricing discipline or punishment mechanisms.

Real-World Example: In the airline industry, economists have used game theory to analyze fare-matching systems and yield management tools that allow carriers to enforce tacit collusion. DOJ investigations into these markets have relied heavily on expert modeling of pricing behavior.

Additional Considerations in Market Structure

Beyond the three core areas above, forensic economists may be called upon to assess the following:

- **Vertical Integration:** Whether control over upstream or downstream firms restricts competition.

- **Platform Markets:** In tech and digital media, where two-sided markets (e.g., users and advertisers) complicate market definition and concentration analysis.

- **Network Effects:** Markets like social media or software may tip toward monopoly due to user interdependence.

- **Innovation Markets:** In mergers involving R&D-intensive sectors, the loss of future innovation must be considered alongside current market structure.

Example: In the Google Android antitrust litigation in the European Union, regulators and economists argued that bundling and default placement created an artificial advantage that entrenched market dominance, despite nominal competition.

Conclusion

Market structure analysis is the linchpin of modern antitrust and competition policy. It combines rigorous theory, real-world evidence, and strategic modeling to assess how firms compete, how markets evolve, and whether consumers are ultimately harmed. Forensic economists provide the tools

courts and regulators need to understand these
dynamics—not just at a snapshot in time, but over the arc of
competitive development.

In the next chapter, we explore how damages are calculated in
markets that are already distorted—how overcharges, lost
volume, and suppressed innovation are translated into
economic remedies that restore, deter, and correct.

19.3   Insurance Economics

Insurance plays a pivotal role in litigation involving damages,
liability coverage, and claims behavior. Forensic economists
are often called upon to analyze the incentives, market
failures, and behavioral responses embedded within insurance
markets. These analyses appear in tort disputes, subrogation
claims, health economics, employment law, and financial fraud
investigations.

Risk Pooling and Adverse Selection

At its core, insurance is a mechanism for transferring risk.
Individuals pay premiums into a pooled fund, which
compensates the unlucky few who experience losses. This
socialization of risk allows individuals and businesses to
reduce uncertainty and stabilize income or operational
continuity.

$$\text{Expected Loss} = \text{Probability of Event} \times \text{Cost of Event}$$

Risk Pooling: Works effectively when risk events are

independent and identically distributed. By the law of large numbers, the insurer can predict aggregate claims and set actuarially fair premiums. However, when risks are correlated (e.g., regional disasters or industry-wide cyber attacks), pooling fails to eliminate variability, and premiums rise significantly.

Adverse Selection: Occurs when individuals with higher risk profiles are more likely to purchase insurance, and insurers cannot perfectly distinguish between high- and low-risk applicants. Over time, the average risk in the pool increases, driving up premiums and forcing low-risk individuals out of the market—a classic "death spiral."

Forensic Application: In litigation over denied claims or coverage exclusions, forensic economists may show how underwriting models failed to price in adverse selection or how the insured party's risk profile diverged from the pooled assumption. In antitrust cases, such as those involving health insurance markets, they may demonstrate how market segmentation magnified adverse selection.

Quantitative Tools:

- Lorenz curves to measure inequality of risk distribution.

- Hazard models to estimate risk transition over time.

- Bayesian updating to revise risk estimates based on new claim information.

Moral Hazard and Claim Behavior

Moral hazard refers to the behavioral distortion that occurs when insurance reduces the marginal cost of risky behavior.

After obtaining coverage, insured parties may act less cautiously or even exaggerate losses, knowing they are financially protected.

Types of Moral Hazard:

- **Ex-Ante:** Increased risk-taking before a loss occurs (e.g., a business ignores fire code compliance after insuring property).

- **Ex-Post:** Exaggeration or falsification of losses after a claimable event (e.g., inflating the value of stolen items).

Litigation Contexts:

- Disability and Workers' Compensation claims often involve forensic evaluation of whether an insured had an incentive to remain injured or out of work.

- Health insurance fraud cases assess how co-pay structures and deductibles influence overutilization.

- First-party property insurance cases may involve overstated replacement costs or fabricated damages.

Econometric Tools:

- Difference-in-differences models comparing behavior before and after coverage begins.

- Regression discontinuity analysis around deductible thresholds.

- Utility maximization frameworks showing decreased marginal disutility from risky behavior post-coverage.

Economic Utility Shift:

Let $U(W)$ be the utility from wealth. The insured's decision can be modeled by expected utility:

$$EU = p \cdot U(W - L + I) + (1 - p) \cdot U(W - P)$$

Where:

- W: Initial wealth

- L: Loss magnitude

- I: Insurance indemnity

- P: Premium paid

- p: Probability of loss

This equation highlights how indemnification reduces disutility from a loss and may reduce the incentive to prevent it.

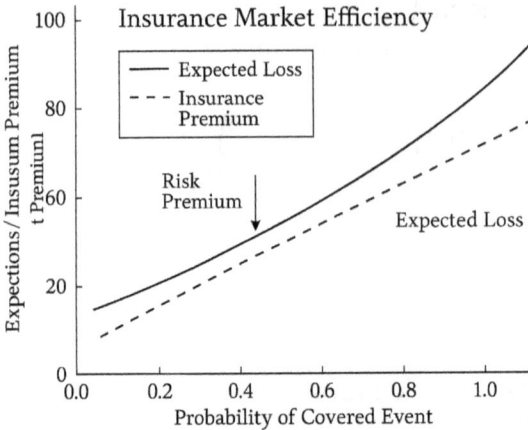

Figure 19.2:   Insurance, Expected Loss, and Premium Adjustment

Insurance Markets and Public Policy

Insurance markets often require regulatory oversight to remain functional. Asymmetric information and market power distortions can lead to under-insurance, overpricing, or denial of coverage for marginalized groups.

Legal and Regulatory Dimensions:

- **Bad Faith Litigation:** Insurers acting in bad faith (e.g., delay, denial, lowballing) may face punitive damages.

- **Rate Regulation:** In states like Florida or California, forensic economists may testify on whether rate increases are actuarially justified.

- **Risk Adjustment Mechanisms:** Used in health insurance exchanges to prevent adverse selection among competing insurers.

- **Subrogation Cases:** When insurers seek reimbursement from third parties, economists estimate net present value of recovery versus claim cost.

Example: In a post-hurricane litigation, an insurer may allege that property damage was due to flooding (not covered), while the plaintiff claims it was wind-related (covered). Forensic economists may be engaged to assess wind-versus-flood damage valuation using engineering reports and geospatial data, linking physical events to economic responsibility.

Reinsurance and Catastrophic Risk Modeling

At the institutional level, insurers themselves seek to manage risk through reinsurance—insurance for insurers. Reinsurance markets allow firms to cap losses from extreme events and stabilize premiums.

Catastrophic Modeling:

- Simulates aggregate losses under scenarios like pandemics, wildfires, cyberattacks, and climate events.

- Uses stochastic modeling, Monte Carlo simulation, and extreme value theory (EVT).

- Forensic economists use these models in mass tort claims and class actions involving distributed harm.

Example: In COVID-19 litigation, reinsurance contracts

were scrutinized to determine if business interruption losses were covered under force majeure clauses. Economists quantified total claims and tested statistical correlation between infection spikes and claim volume.

Conclusion

Insurance economics merges actuarial science, behavioral analysis, and public policy. Forensic economists illuminate the financial incentives and distortions introduced by coverage, pooling, and asymmetric information. Whether in individual disability disputes or global reinsurance arbitration, they provide the quantitative foundation upon which liability, damages, and justice are assessed.

In the next chapter, we extend our forensic lens into asset valuation and financial tools—exploring how present value, investment risk, and cost of capital shape the quantification of economic loss.

19.4 Risk Analysis

Risk is an inherent feature of economic life. In litigation, uncertainty affects the valuation of damages, the estimation of future earnings, and the calculation of liability. Forensic economists provide decision-makers with frameworks to quantify uncertainty, evaluate risk preferences, and present statistically grounded outcomes. This chapter explores the analytical core of risk analysis and its indispensable role in forensic economic modeling.

Expected Utility and Risk Aversion

At the foundation of modern risk theory is the concept of expected utility (EU). While expected value assumes a risk-neutral decision-maker, most individuals exhibit risk aversion—preferring a certain outcome over a risky one with the same expected payoff. This preference is captured by concave utility functions such as logarithmic or square-root transformations.

$$EU = \sum_{i=1}^{n} p_i \cdot u(x_i)$$

Where:

- p_i = probability of outcome i

- x_i = monetary value of outcome i

- $u(x)$ = utility function (e.g., $u(x) = \ln x$ for logarithmic utility)

Risk Aversion Metrics:

- **Arrow-Pratt Coefficient of Absolute Risk Aversion (ARA):**

$$ARA(x) = -\frac{u''(x)}{u'(x)}$$

- **Relative Risk Aversion (RRA):**

$$RRA(x) = -x \cdot \frac{u''(x)}{u'(x)}$$

Litigation Application: In settlement negotiations and
structured settlement design, forensic economists often assume
utility-maximizing behavior. Plaintiffs may reject lump-sum
awards if annuities offer superior risk-adjusted utility,
especially in wrongful death and catastrophic injury cases.

Monte Carlo Simulations

Monte Carlo simulations are a powerful stochastic tool for
modeling uncertainty. By repeatedly sampling from
probabilistic distributions of input variables, these simulations
generate a distribution of possible outcomes, rather than a
single deterministic estimate.

Process Overview:

1. Define input variables (e.g., wage growth, inflation,
   employment probability).

2. Assign probability distributions (e.g., normal,
   log-normal, triangular).

3. Perform thousands of simulations using random draws
   from each distribution.

4. Aggregate results to form a probabilistic forecast of
   outcomes.

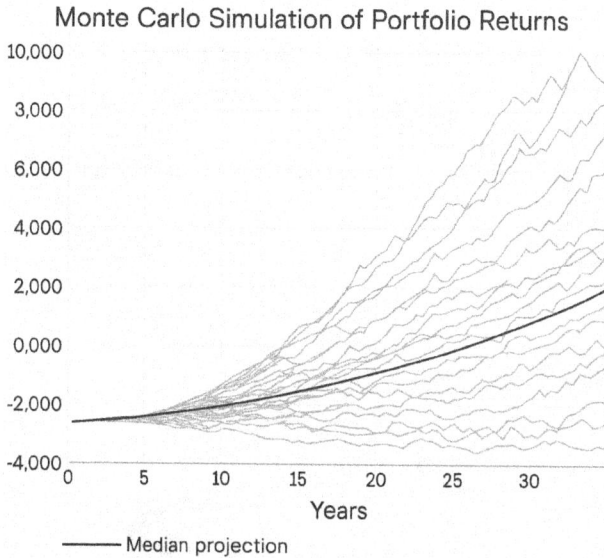

Figure 19.3: Monte Carlo Forecasting of Future Earnings

Forensic Context:

- **Wrongful Death Claims:** Simulate earnings trajectories under varying re-employment, health, and market conditions.

- **Class Action Allocations:** Distribute damages based on probabilistic claims verification.

- **Environmental Litigation:** Forecast cleanup costs and property value impairment under future regulatory scenarios.

Risk-Adjusted Discounting

While time value of money discounts future cash flows, risk-adjusted discounting adds an additional premium to reflect uncertainty. This is particularly relevant in damage valuation, investment loss cases, and contingent liability assessments.

$$PV = \frac{E(X)}{(1 + r + \rho)^t}$$

Where:

- $E(X)$ = expected value of cash flow

- r = risk-free rate

- ρ = risk premium

- t = number of time periods

Selection of Risk Premium (ρ):

- **Empirical Estimation:** Derived from market volatility, historical asset performance, or firm-specific beta coefficients.

- **Subjective Assessment:** Expert judgment based on industry risk, plaintiff profile, or economic volatility.

- **Litigation Example:** In investment fraud cases, economists estimate lost capital using risk-adjusted expected returns rather than naïve market averages.

Alternative Framework: Certainty Equivalent:

Instead of adjusting the denominator, analysts may use the certainty equivalent (CE) in the numerator:

$$PV = \frac{CE}{(1+r)^t}$$

Where:

$$CE = u^{-1}(EU)$$

This approach maintains a risk-free discount rate but reduces the projected cash flow to account for risk aversion.

19.5 Real-World Applications

Risk analysis plays a central role in diverse litigation contexts, where uncertainty governs outcomes, damages, and liability attribution.

- **Class Action Lawsuits:** Risk-adjusted market share models determine proportional recovery and apportionment of liability.

- **Auto Insurance Fraud:** Outlier detection using Benford's Law, frequency modeling, and random forest classifiers reveals fraudulent clusters.

- **Tort Claims:** Wage modeling incorporates probability of workforce reentry, morbidity, and residual functional capacity.

- **Financial Malpractice:** Monte Carlo models simulate portfolio outcomes under alternative fiduciary strategies.

- **Business Interruption Insurance:** Stochastic modeling assesses firm cash flow under variable recovery timelines and partial operation.

19.6 Conclusion

Forensic economists serve as translators between uncertainty and evidence, transforming probabilistic realities into structured insights that courts can rely upon. By employing tools such as expected utility models, Monte Carlo simulations, and risk-adjusted discounting, they expose the economic contours of litigation risk with mathematical precision. These techniques are especially vital in cases where outcomes hinge on contingent events, behavioral variability, or complex market dynamics.

Yet the value of forensic analysis is not limited to the modeling of uncertainty—it must ultimately culminate in the quantification of loss. In the next chapter, we move from the realm of market forecasting and risk analysis to the heart of legal remedy: the estimation of damages. There, the abstract yields to the concrete as models become measures of harm, restitution, and justice.

End-of-Chapter Problems

1. Define the SSNIP test and apply it to a hypothetical cell phone market.

2. Compute the HHI for a market where four firms hold 40%, 30%, 20%, and 10% shares. Interpret the result.

3. Explain how moral hazard can affect the behavior of insured parties in litigation.

4. Design a basic Monte Carlo simulation model to forecast lost income due to injury.

5. Analyze how the discount rate changes when a risky future income stream is involved.

Suggested Readings

- Carlton, D. W., & Perloff, J. M. (2015). *Modern Industrial Organization*. Pearson.
  A foundational text on the economics of competition, firm behavior, and market power, widely used in antitrust and regulatory analysis.

- Arrow, K. J. (1963). *Uncertainty and the Welfare Economics of Medical Care. American Economic Review*, 53(5), 941–973.
  A seminal paper that laid the groundwork for modern health economics, demonstrating how uncertainty distorts market behavior.

- Tirole, J. (1988). *The Theory of Industrial Organization*. MIT Press.
  A rigorous exploration of oligopoly theory, vertical integration, and strategic firm interaction—indispensable for forensic economists in competition law.

- U.S. Department of Justice and Federal Trade Commission. (2010). *Horizontal Merger Guidelines*. The official analytical framework used by enforcement agencies to evaluate the competitive effects of mergers, including HHI thresholds and market definition tests.

- Schmalensee, R., & Willig, R. D. (Eds.). (1989). *Handbook of Industrial Organization.* Elsevier.
  A comprehensive, research-level treatment of market structure, pricing, and entry dynamics authored by leading scholars in the field.

- Werden, G. J. (2002). *Identifying Market Power in Electric Generation. Antitrust Law Journal,* 70(2), 625–656.
  A specialized case study applying market power analysis to the energy sector, with methodological relevance to forensic practice.

- Train, K. E. (2009). *Discrete Choice Methods with Simulation.* Cambridge University Press.
  A key reference for economists working with consumer choice models and market segmentation, useful in merger simulation and product market definition.

Chapter 20

Damage Estimation

20.1 Introduction

This chapter introduces the economic methodologies used to estimate damages in civil litigation, including personal injury, commercial torts, contract breaches, and intellectual property (IP) infringement. Forensic economists serve as impartial analysts, converting injuries, losses, and market disruptions into monetary values. Their work frequently bridges legal narratives and financial evidence, providing courts and juries with empirically grounded frameworks for assigning liability and awarding compensation.

Beyond earnings losses, damage estimation encompasses goodwill impairment, lost enterprise value, royalty streams, and diminished market share. This chapter provides tools and examples for analyzing both individual-level harm and complex business scenarios, including how forensic economists determine the fair market value of patents, trademarks, copyrights, and trade secrets.

20.2   Damage Estimation

Types of Damages

Forensic economists typically calculate three categories of legal damages:

- **Compensatory Damages:** Measurable economic losses, such as lost wages, diminished profits, and incurred medical expenses.

- **Consequential (Special) Damages:** Secondary effects of the underlying harm, including long-term business interruption, delayed projects, and supply chain disruptions.

- **Punitive Damages:** Monetary penalties intended to punish egregious behavior and deter future misconduct. While not rooted in economic loss, economists may help evaluate proportionality or corporate capacity to pay.

Lost Earnings and Earnings Capacity

One of the most common damage scenarios involves the estimation of lost income due to injury, termination, or death. Economists use the present value formula:

$$\text{Present Value of Lost Earnings} = \sum_{t=1}^{T} \frac{E(W_t)}{(1+r)^t}$$

Where:

- $E(W_t)$ is expected earnings in year t

- r is the discount rate (typically derived from government bond yields or low-risk investment benchmarks)

- T is the number of lost working years

Adjustments may include:

- Work-life expectancy (using SSA or BLS tables)

- Fringe benefits (e.g., health insurance, retirement contributions)

- Inflation expectations

- Taxes and employment status

- Career trajectories or promotions likely absent the injury

Lost Earnings Time Series Analysis

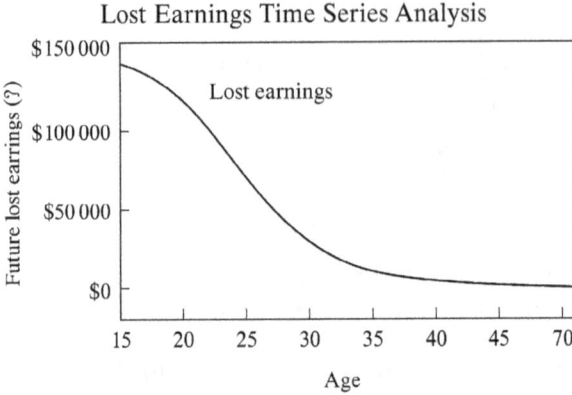

Figure 20.1: Present Value of Future Earnings: Pre- and Post-Injury

Case Example: In *Smith v. Transit Co.*, the plaintiff's injuries eliminated future earnings as an HVAC technician. Using vocational expert reports and actuarial life tables, the economist projected $2.1 million in lost income, adjusted for age, work-life expectancy, and re-employment possibilities.

Business Loss and Profitability Models

But-For Analysis

This approach compares actual financial results to a hypothetical world where the harm did not occur:

$$\text{Damages} = \text{But-for Profits} - \text{Actual Profits}$$

Inputs:

- Historical revenue and cost trends

- Industry benchmarks or competitor performance

- Disruption timelines and recovery phases

Contribution Margin Approach

Used when variable costs can be separated from fixed costs, and only incremental profits are relevant to damages.

$$\text{Contribution Margin} = \text{Revenue} - \text{Variable Costs}$$

Mitigation and Offsets

Plaintiffs have a duty to mitigate economic harm. Economists may estimate:

- Time required to find comparable employment

- Part-time income or severance packages

- Insurance benefits or disability payments

Failure to mitigate may result in substantial damage offsets. Forensic experts document job search efforts, labor market conditions, or employer rejections to support or rebut mitigation claims.

20.3 IP Valuation

Overview of IP Assets

- **Patents:** Time-limited exclusive rights over inventions or processes.

- **Trademarks:** Source identifiers like brand names and logos that carry consumer goodwill.

- **Copyrights:** Creative expressions (literary works, software, designs).

- **Trade Secrets:** Confidential business information offering competitive advantage (e.g., formulas, algorithms).

Valuation Approaches

1. **Cost Approach:** Measures how much it would cost to recreate the asset.

2. **Market Approach:** Looks at comparable transactions (e.g., licensing agreements, sale of IP portfolios).

3. **Income Approach:** Discounts projected cash flows the IP is expected to generate.

Royalty Relief Method (a subtype of income approach):

Estimates value based on the royalties a company avoids by owning the IP:

$$\text{IP Value} = \sum_{t=1}^{T} \frac{(\text{Revenue}_t \cdot \text{Royalty Rate})}{(1+r)^t}$$

Discounted Cash Flow (DCF) for IP

The DCF method is widely used in commercial litigation:

$$\text{IP Value} = \sum_{t=1}^{T} \frac{E(R_t - C_t)}{(1 + r)^t}$$

Where:

- R_t = projected revenue stream from IP usage

- C_t = costs directly attributable to the IP

- r = appropriate discount rate (may include risk premium)

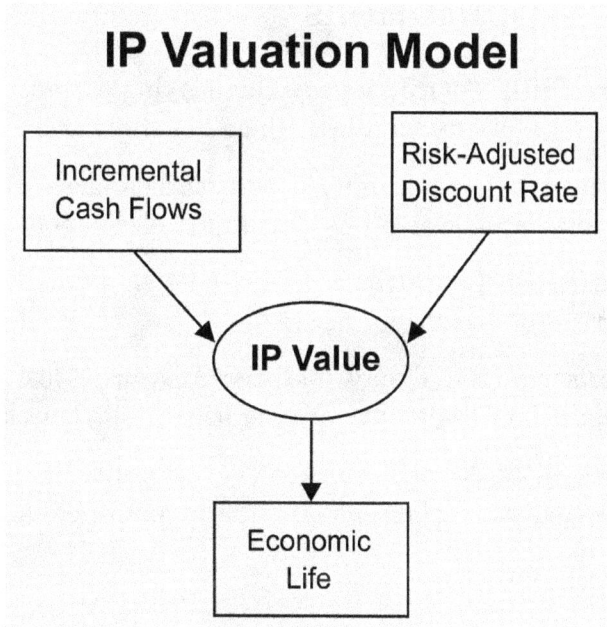

Figure 20.2: Intellectual Property Valuation via Discounted Cash Flow

Additional Considerations in IP Cases

- **Apportionment:** In patent cases, damages must often be apportioned to the value of the patented feature versus the whole product.

- **Unjust Enrichment:** Defendant's profits attributable to infringement, rather than plaintiff's losses.

- **Price Erosion:** How infringement forces lower pricing and reduces margins over time.

20.4 Applications

- **Wrongful Termination:** Quantifying earnings loss, bonus eligibility, and lost fringe benefits.

- **Patent Infringement:** Estimating damages using royalty rates, lost profits, or unjust enrichment models.

- **Franchise Disputes:** Valuing customer goodwill and territorial exclusivity losses.

- **Construction Delay Claims:** Measuring lost revenue from delayed openings or operational bottlenecks.

- **Breach of Non-Compete Agreements:** Evaluating diverted sales, client attrition, and loss of competitive advantage.

20.5 Conclusion

Damage estimation stands at the heart of forensic economics, transforming narratives of loss into quantifiable, defensible claims. From lost wages and business disruptions to royalty streams and goodwill impairment, these valuations are the currency through which courts assess justice in economic terms. By anchoring their analyses in rigorous models, transparent assumptions, and real-world data, forensic economists ensure their conclusions withstand cross-examination and judicial scrutiny.

Yet damages do not exist in a vacuum—they emerge from complex financial landscapes often marked by deception, distortion, or structural opacity. In the next chapter, we turn to the specialized financial tools that forensic experts deploy to investigate hidden transactions, uncover fraudulent schemes, and trace the economic footprints that underlie many modern legal disputes.

End-of-Chapter Problems

1. A plaintiff earned \$75,000/year and was projected to work 20 more years. If the discount rate is 4%, estimate the present value of lost earnings.

2. Explain the differences among cost, market, and income approaches to IP valuation.

3. In a copyright infringement case, what data would you request to conduct a DCF analysis?

4. In a breach of contract case, how would a but-for

scenario be structured?

5. Construct a graph showing lost profits over time and mitigation efforts.

Suggested Readings

- Fishman, S., & Jarosz, J. (2008). *Intellectual Property Damages: Guidelines and Analysis*. Wiley.
  A comprehensive resource offering methodologies and case studies for quantifying IP-related losses, including royalty analysis, lost profits, and apportionment.

- Pratt, S. P., & Niculita, A. V. (2008). *Valuing a Business: The Analysis and Appraisal of Closely Held Companies*. McGraw-Hill.
  Widely used by forensic experts, this text covers business valuation techniques, from DCF to market comps, with practical guidance for litigation contexts.

- Reilly, R. F., & Schweihs, R. P. (2004). *The Handbook of Business Valuation and Intellectual Property Analysis*. McGraw-Hill.
  Explores valuation strategies for both tangible and intangible assets, focusing on IP, early-stage ventures, and industry-specific damage models.

- Trugman, G. R. (2018). *Understanding Business Valuation: A Practical Guide to Valuing Small to Medium-Sized Businesses* (5th ed.). AICPA.
  A hands-on guide tailored to forensic valuation in legal proceedings, particularly useful for divorce, shareholder disputes, and commercial torts.

- Fannon, N. M., & Dunitz, J. A. (Eds.). (2010). *The Comprehensive Guide to Lost Profits and Other Commercial Damages* (Vols. 1–2). BVR.
  A multi-volume practitioner guide that explores damages in contract disputes, IP infringement, business interruption, and securities fraud.

- National Association of Forensic Economics (NAFE). Articles and conference proceedings on valuation standards, admissibility under Daubert, and current trends in damages estimation.

- Judicial Education Reference, Information and Technical Transfer (JERITT) Project Reports. Offers empirical insights and case studies on economic damages used in judicial training.

Chapter 21

Financial Tools

21.1   Introduction

Financial forensics is the investigative application of economic reasoning, accounting insight, and statistical tools to uncover irregularities and reconstruct the financial truth. In modern litigation, it serves not only to expose fraud and manipulation but also to elucidate complex asset structures, trace flows of illicit funds, and value obscured or misrepresented interests.

Forensic economists and forensic accountants often collaborate in matters ranging from white-collar crime and corporate malfeasance to divorce, partnership dissolution, and estate litigation. This chapter explores the most important analytical tools in financial forensics—how they function, when they are applied, and what kinds of evidence they produce for judicial consideration.

21.2 Core Tools

Bank Statement Reconciliation and Lifestyle Analysis

One of the most common forensic techniques is reconstructing an individual's financial profile using available bank records. By matching cash inflows and outflows over time and comparing them to tax filings, declarations, or known salary sources, experts identify:

- **Unexplained deposits or disbursements:** Frequent indicators of hidden income or illicit transfers.

- **Cash skimming or underreporting:** Especially common in cash-heavy businesses.

- **Structuring (smurfing):** Fragmenting large deposits to evade federal reporting thresholds.

- **Lifestyle inflation:** When expenditures exceed reported income, this discrepancy signals potential fraud.

This analysis is foundational in cases involving embezzlement, divorce, and tax evasion.

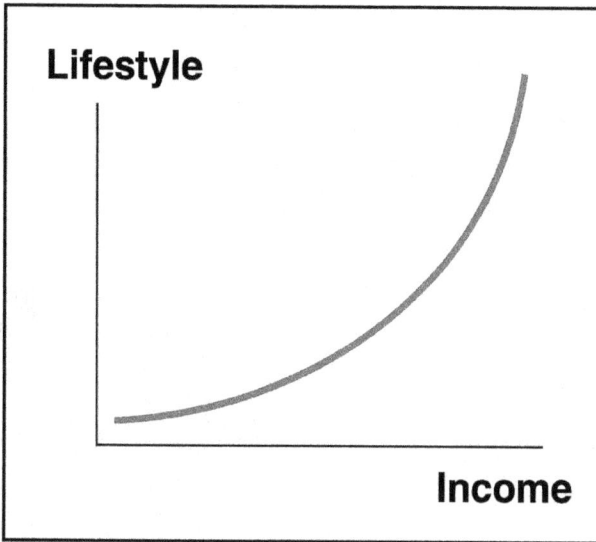

Figure 21.1: Lifestyle Expenditures vs. Reported Income

Beneish M-Score and Financial Statement Red Flags

Developed by Professor Messod Beneish, the M-Score uses a set of eight financial ratios to assess whether a company is likely to be manipulating its earnings. These ratios examine areas like asset quality, sales growth, depreciation, and leverage.

$$M = -4.84 + 0.92 \cdot \text{DSRI} + 0.528 \cdot \text{GMI} + 0.404 \cdot \text{AQI}$$
$$+ 0.892 \cdot \text{SGI} + 0.115 \cdot \text{DEPI} - 0.172 \cdot \text{SGAI}$$
$$+ 4.679 \cdot \text{TATA} - 0.327 \cdot \text{LVGI}$$

A score above -2.22 suggests possible earnings manipulation, prompting deeper investigation. The model famously identified Enron and other fraudulent firms prior to their collapse.

Benford's Law for Fraud Detection

Benford's Law predicts the frequency of digits in naturally occurring financial datasets. When real-world accounting numbers significantly deviate from this expected distribution, it can be a red flag for fabricated data.

$$P(d) = \log_{10}\left(1 + \frac{1}{d}\right) \quad \text{for } d = 1, 2, ..., 9$$

The technique is particularly effective in examining expense reimbursements, vendor invoices, or general ledger entries where manual data fabrication is suspected.

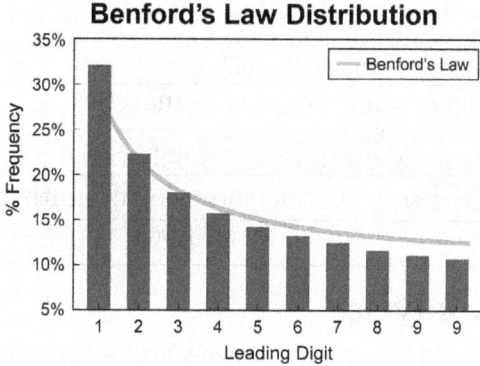

Figure 21.2: Expected Leading Digit Frequencies (Benford's Law)

21.3   Advanced Techniques

Transaction Mapping and Flow Reconstruction

Financial forensics often entails tracing the path of money through multiple entities, accounts, and jurisdictions. This process is critical in cases involving:

- **Money laundering:** Especially with international wires and shell corporations.

- **Asset dissipation:** In family law, where one party hides or liquidates marital property.

- **Off-book accounting:** Such as parallel ledgers,

phantom vendors, or ghost employees.

- **Cryptocurrency tracing:** Reconstructing flows via public ledgers and blockchain analytics.

Transaction mapping often requires subpoenaed bank records, international cooperation, and forensic accounting software that visually reconstructs financial flows.

Forensic Analytics

Modern forensic investigations leverage machine learning and data science techniques to sift through vast quantities of structured and unstructured data:

- **Clustering algorithms (e.g., k-means):** Identify patterns in vendor payments or employee reimbursements.

- **Outlier detection:** Highlights unusual transactions or payments that warrant investigation.

- **Network analysis:** Unveils relationships between actors, accounts, and entities, often visualized through graph theory.

- **Time series anomaly detection:** Identifies periodic reporting spikes or off-cycle payments used to conceal fraud.

These techniques are particularly useful in securities fraud, corporate internal investigations, and public corruption cases.

Digital Forensics Integration

Financial analysis increasingly intersects with digital evidence. Forensic economists and data analysts now work alongside digital forensics experts to analyze:

- **Email metadata:** To establish timing, intent, or coordination.

- **Accounting software audit trails:** For example, tracking changes to invoices or journal entries in QuickBooks.

- **Encrypted documents and hidden file partitions:** Which may contain concealed ledgers or transaction logs.

- **Mobile payment systems and cloud logs:** Especially relevant in decentralized finance and mobile app fraud.

21.4 Real-World Applications

- **Ponzi Schemes:** Reconstruction of investor flows to determine who received fictitious profits and who suffered net losses.

- **Business Divorce:** Evaluation of concealed distributions, personal expenses booked to corporate accounts, and improper asset transfers.

- **Tax Evasion:** Use of indirect methods such as the Net Worth Method, Bank Deposit Method, or Expenditure Method to uncover unreported income.

- **Insurance Fraud:** Statistical consistency tests across claims, as well as comparisons to actuarial expectations or known recovery timelines.

- **Shareholder Derivative Actions:** Identifying improper executive compensation, insider enrichment, or corporate waste.

21.5   Suggested Readings

- Silverstone, H., & Sheetz, M. S. (2007). *Forensic Accounting and Fraud Investigation for Non-Experts.* Wiley.

- Crumbley, D. L., Heitger, L. E., & Smith, G. S. (2017). *Forensic and Investigative Accounting.* CCH.

- Singleton, T. W., & Singleton, A. J. (2010). *Fraud Auditing and Forensic Accounting.* Wiley.

- Albrecht, W. S., Albrecht, C. C., Albrecht, C. O., & Zimbelman, M. F. (2018). *Fraud Examination.* Cengage Learning.

- U.S. Department of Justice. *Asset Forfeiture and Money Laundering Section (AFMLS) Manuals.*

21.6   Conclusion

Financial forensic tools empower litigators, regulators, and courts to detect the invisible architecture of economic misconduct. Whether dissecting fraudulent transactions, tracing asset concealment, or challenging fictitious valuations, forensic economics exposes deception with precision, translating numerical patterns into legally admissible truth.

But more than a technical discipline, forensic economics is a vigilant craft—a confluence of skepticism, logic, and analytical courage. It is the quiet sentinel behind the scenes of justice, giving voice to the voiceless data that lies buried in spreadsheets, balance sheets, and bank records. Its practitioners do not merely crunch numbers—they restore equilibrium, turning uncertainty into inference, suspicion into structure, and injury into quantifiable remedy.

This book has journeyed from foundational principles to complex litigation, from historical theory to modern investigative tools. Each chapter has sought to equip the reader with both the conceptual framework and the applied methodologies needed to navigate the evolving landscape of legal economics.

And now, as we close this volume, we affirm what the evidence has long shown: truth leaves a trail. For those with the discipline to follow it, the tools to decode it, and the resolve to testify to it, forensic economics will always illuminate the path toward justice.

Lex veritasque per numeros—Through numbers, truth and law.

21.7   End of Chapter Exercises

1. Define and explain the purpose of the Beneish M-Score. What are its limitations?

2. Calculate the expected frequency of the leading digit "1" using Benford's Law. Why is this useful?

3. You are asked to evaluate whether a restaurant is underreporting cash revenue. What forensic techniques would you apply?

4. Draw a transaction flowchart for a suspected fraudulent conveyance case.

5. How might data mining techniques enhance traditional financial statement analysis?

Suggested Readings

- Crumbley, D. L., Heitger, L. E., & Smith, G. S. (2015). *Forensic and Investigative Accounting.* CCH Incorporated.
  A comprehensive guide to the principles and practices of forensic accounting, including litigation support and expert testimony.

- Singleton, T. W., & Singleton, A. J. (2010). *Fraud Auditing and Forensic Accounting* (4th ed.). Wiley.
  A widely respected reference on uncovering and analyzing financial fraud across various industries.

- Wells, J. T. (2014). *Principles of Fraud Examination* (4th ed.). Wiley.
  Provides frameworks for detecting and deterring fraud using case studies and modern investigative tools.

- Golden, T. W., Skalak, S. L., Clayton, M. M., & Pill, J. C. (2020). *A Guide to Forensic Accounting Investigation*

(2nd ed.). Wiley.
Practical manual focusing on corporate investigations and regulatory compliance.

- Albrecht, W. S., Albrecht, C. C., Albrecht, C. O., & Zimbelman, M. F. (2018). *Fraud Examination* (6th ed.). Cengage Learning.
  Integrates theory, method, and legal application in examining different types of financial fraud.

- Association of Certified Fraud Examiners (ACFE). *Fraud Examiners Manual.*
  The industry-standard guide for CFEs, providing detailed methodologies for investigating and documenting fraud.

- Coffee, J. C. (2007). "Gatekeepers: The Professions and Corporate Governance." *Columbia Law Review*, 107(7), 1549–1611.
  Examines the role of accountants and legal professionals as gatekeepers in detecting corporate malfeasance.

- Squires, G. D., & O'Connor, S. (2001). "Color of Money: Racial Disparities in Economic Transactions." *Rutgers Race & the Law Review*, 3(1), 1–23.
  Explores forensic economic approaches to systemic financial inequality and fraud in lending.

- Deloitte Forensic Services. (2016). *Financial Forensics: Unlocking the Value.* Deloitte Insights.
  Describes real-world applications of forensic accounting in litigation, M&A disputes, and fraud investigations.

- PwC. (2020). *Global Economic Crime and Fraud Survey.*

PricewaterhouseCoopers.
Offers a data-rich overview of corporate fraud trends and detection mechanisms across jurisdictions.

- ACFE. (2022). *Report to the Nations: Global Study on Occupational Fraud and Abuse.*
An empirical analysis of thousands of fraud cases from around the world, with insight into detection methods and economic impact.

- U.S. Department of Justice. (2013). *Financial Investigation: A Financial Crimes Enforcement Network (FinCEN) Guide for Law Enforcement.*
A comprehensive federal guide to tracing money, banking analysis, and identifying fraudulent schemes.

- U.S. Securities and Exchange Commission (SEC). (2021). *Financial Reporting Manual.*
Contains detailed procedures and red flags related to forensic reviews of corporate financial statements.

- Internal Revenue Service (IRS). *Forensic Audit Techniques Guide.*
Guidance for identifying fraud and income concealment in civil tax proceedings and criminal prosecutions.

Chapter 22

Conclusion

From the outset, this book set out to demonstrate something both simple and ambitious: that law and economics—two disciplines often treated as separate intellectual provinces—are, in fact, deeply interdependent. The Introduction proposed that legal rules cannot be understood without appreciating how they shape incentives, allocate risk, transmit information, and influence behavior. It further suggested that economic reasoning, when applied with sensitivity to normative values and institutional realities, sharpens legal analysis rather than displacing it. This concluding chapter reflects on that mission and shows how the journey through the preceding chapters accomplishes precisely what was promised.

Earlier chapters began by laying the conceptual foundation for this fusion. They explained how legal systems succeed when they reduce uncertainty, lower transaction costs, and facilitate cooperation. The rule of law was reframed not only as a moral good but as an economic infrastructure—one that allows markets to function, promises to be enforced, and citizens to coordinate with confidence. This initial framework provided the lens through which the remainder of the text unfolded.

The chapters on contract, tort, property, and criminal justice demonstrated how classical legal doctrines align with economic principles, often more closely than traditional legal education admits. Contract law emerged as an institution designed to manage expectations and minimize the frictions of exchange. Tort law became a system for encouraging optimal care, deterring inefficient risk-taking, and internalizing externalities. Property law revealed itself as a scaffolding for markets, transforming scarcity into clarity by defining rights, reducing information costs, and creating stable platforms for investment. Even criminal justice—typically framed in moral, procedural, or constitutional terms—proved intelligible through the economic analysis of deterrence, error costs, incentives, and institutional design.

These doctrinal explorations were followed by more specialized applications of economic reasoning, including forensic economics, damages valuation, antitrust analysis, expert testimony, and econometric methods. These chapters fulfilled another part of the book's foundational promise: to show how quantitative tools inform litigation, regulatory policy, and the evidentiary battles that shape outcomes in modern courts. The integration of statistical inference, modeling, and empirical validation reaffirmed that legal argumentation is increasingly inseparable from data-driven reasoning.

One of the most significant expansions in this edition—the
chapter on asset management—illustrated the book's
interdisciplinary ambition at its fullest. By synthesizing
behavioral economics, portfolio theory, fiduciary law, market
microstructure, and agency costs, it demonstrated how the
management of capital cannot be understood through any
single lens. Instead, asset management operates at the very
intersection this book was designed to illuminate: where
incentives, psychology, and law converge to shape decisions
that influence both markets and society. This chapter, more
than any other, expressed the core theme of the text—that
law and economics are not parallel disciplines but interlocking
components of the same analytical system.

Throughout the book, the integration of behavioral science
added further depth. By acknowledging that neither judges
nor litigants nor investors behave as perfectly rational actors,
the text showed how legal rules must account for predictable
human tendencies such as overconfidence, loss aversion,
anchoring, herd behavior, and narrative-driven judgment.
Behavioral economics did not replace traditional models; it
enriched them, ensuring that the fusion presented in these
chapters reflects the real-world complexities of
decision-making.

Taken together, the chapters form a coherent whole that
speaks directly to the aspiration set forth in the beginning: to
provide an accessible, rigorous, interdisciplinary account of
how law and economics illuminate one another. Each section
built upon the last, progressing from conceptual foundations
to doctrinal applications, from theoretical analysis to
empirical tools, and from classical topics to modern

institutional systems. The book has shown that the law is neither a purely moral enterprise nor a purely procedural one; it is an economic institution that channels human behavior toward social order, cooperation, and flourishing. It has likewise shown that economics is not merely an abstract science of numbers and models; it is an interpretive framework that becomes most powerful when it engages with the institutional, ethical, and human realities embodied in law.

As this work concludes, the promise of the Introduction has been realized. The fusion of law and economics presented here is not an academic curiosity but a practical lens for understanding courts, markets, institutions, and the incentives that govern human life. The goal of this book was not to answer every question but to equip the reader with tools—conceptual, analytical, and empirical—that allow those questions to be engaged with clarity and confidence. If the reader now sees legal rules as economic structures, sees economic models as legal tools, and recognizes that both disciplines speak to the same fundamental challenges of risk, cooperation, justice, and institutional design, then the project has achieved what it set out to do.

This is not the end of the conversation but the beginning of more informed inquiry. The fusion explored here opens new paths for research, policymaking, litigation strategy, and judicial reasoning. It invites lawyers to think more like economists, economists to think more like jurists, and students of both disciplines to appreciate the profound unity between them.

The journey of this book, therefore, concludes where it

began—with a conviction that understanding law and economics together makes each clearer than when understood apart. The chapters that preceded this one demonstrate the richness of that union and affirm that the fusion of these fields is not merely useful, but essential for navigating the increasingly complex world in which law, markets, and human behavior continuously shape one another.

Chapter 23

Future Directions

The conclusion of this book marks not an ending, but an inflection point—a moment to look beyond the present synthesis and toward the emerging questions that will define the next generation of law and economics. As law confronts new technologies, new markets, and new forms of human behavior, the analytical tools explored throughout this text will become increasingly indispensable. Yet they will also require refinement and expansion. The future of the discipline will be shaped by developments in data science, behavioral psychology, financial innovation, institutional design, and global regulatory coordination. Each of these domains presents opportunities for deeper inquiry, as well as challenges that demand interdisciplinary thinking.

One immediate direction for future research lies in the expanding world of digital assets, algorithmic trading, and decentralized finance. Legal institutions were built for physical property, traditional markets, and identifiable actors; economic incentives now operate in digital environments where transactions occur across borders, pseudonymously, and at speeds that test the limits of human oversight. Questions of enforcement, deterrence, consumer protection, and systemic risk take on new dimensions when markets are governed by code rather than conventional intermediaries. A law-and-economics framework must adapt to these dynamics, developing models for how incentives, information, and governance operate in digital ecosystems.

Behavioral economics will also demand renewed attention. As predictive technology, nudging architectures, and behavioral design become embedded in everyday platforms, the interface between law, psychology, and economics will grow more complex. Regulators must grapple with the ethical and economic implications of systems that influence choice at scale. Lawyers will confront cases involving algorithmically shaped behavior, asymmetric information between humans and machines, and new forms of cognitive manipulation that traditional doctrine does not fully anticipate. Economic analysis must evolve to incorporate these behavioral realities, recognizing that rationality is not merely bounded but increasingly engineered.

The management of large-scale capital will likewise confront new pressures. As pension systems mature, sovereign wealth expands, and market cycles become more synchronized globally, fiduciary law will play an even greater role in shaping investment behavior. The intersection of asset management with climate risk, sustainability objectives, and

geopolitical uncertainty will require new legal tools and new
economic models. The stewardship obligations of institutional
investors—once narrowly conceived in financial terms—will
broaden into questions of long-term welfare, intergenerational
equity, and the appropriate role of private capital in public
governance. A future edition of this book may devote entire
chapters to these themes, as the role of institutions in shaping
markets becomes even more prominent.

Litigation and forensic economics will also evolve in response
to technological change. Courts will encounter new kinds of
damages claims involving data breaches, algorithmic bias,
autonomous systems, and losses that arise from interactions
between humans and artificial intelligence. Quantitative
methods will grow more sophisticated, drawing on machine
learning, causal inference, and real-time analytics. As
modeling becomes more complex, questions of admissibility,
reliability, and interpretability will grow in importance. The
legal system must ensure that analytics illuminates the truth
rather than obscuring it, and that the power of quantitative
evidence is balanced by appropriate safeguards.

Another promising frontier is the economics of institutional
integrity—how courts, administrative agencies, legislatures,
and regulatory bodies maintain legitimacy in environments of
political polarization and information saturation. Incentive
design, transparency mechanisms, and procedural fairness will
become essential economic levers for sustaining public trust.
Law-and-economics research will play a key role in diagnosing
failures of governance, proposing reforms, and evaluating
which institutional structures promote stability, accuracy, and
accountability.

Finally, the globalization of legal and economic systems demands more cross-border analysis. Markets are increasingly integrated, but laws remain largely national. This mismatch creates frictions, arbitrage opportunities, and regulatory gaps that sophisticated actors exploit. Future work must examine how international coordination, treaty frameworks, conflict-of-law principles, and harmonized standards can promote efficiency while respecting local values. The fusion of law and economics will be central to navigating these global tensions.

The path forward is rich with possibility. This book has provided foundations—conceptual, analytical, and practical—but the evolution of law and economics will require ongoing dialogue among scholars, practitioners, judges, policymakers, and students. The questions that lie ahead are too complex for any single discipline to answer alone. Yet the tools that emerge from their collaboration will shape the legal, economic, and institutional landscape for decades to come.

If the reader leaves this text with curiosity about these new frontiers, then the mission of this book extends beyond its final page. The fusion of law and economics is not merely a framework for understanding the present; it is a method for engaging the future with rigor, insight, and imagination.

Author's Note

Books have beginnings that rarely appear on the page. This one began many years ago—in courtrooms, in late-night conversations, in graduate seminars, and in the quiet spaces where complicated ideas refuse to stay separate. *The Fusion of Law and Economics* was never meant to be a technical manual or a purely academic exercise. It grew out of lived experience: from trying cases where incentives mattered as much as doctrine, from studying mathematics and economics with the curiosity of someone who wanted to understand why systems behave the way they do, and from the realization that law and economics are not parallel paths but intertwined ways of seeing the world.

Writing this book required revisiting the assumptions I carried into my legal career. It meant admitting where traditional legal reasoning needed the clarity of economic analysis, and where economic models needed the grounding of doctrine, fairness, and institutional reality. It meant confronting not only the rational structures of law and markets, but also the human tendencies—our fears, our biases, our hopes—that influence how those structures operate. The process was as much reflective as it was analytical.

I am deeply aware that no single volume can capture the full richness of two vast disciplines. What I have tried to do instead is offer a coherent map: a way of understanding how legal systems allocate risk, shape behavior, and promote cooperation; and how economic reasoning provides the tools to interpret those functions with precision. If this map helps readers navigate difficult questions in their own work—whether in litigation, policy, scholarship, or investment—then the effort behind these pages has achieved its purpose.

Certain people deserve acknowledgment beyond what a Preface can comfortably hold. My brother and friend, GERALD ALAIN P. CHEN-YOUNG, has been a partner in intellectual exploration for more than two decades. His insights into economics, finance, and human behavior helped shape the very architecture of this project. Professors and mentors across mathematics, economics, and law likewise influenced the path that led here; their lessons echo throughout the chapters even when unmentioned.

Most importantly, this book is dedicated to readers who are willing to think across boundaries. The world does not present us with problems neatly labeled "legal" or "economic." Courts, markets, governments, and private actors all respond to incentives, information, principles, and human psychology. Understanding those interactions requires curiosity and intellectual openness—qualities I hope this book both rewards and encourages.

As I close this project, I do so with gratitude: for the opportunities that made the work possible, for the teachers who shaped my thinking, and for the readers who will carry the ideas forward. Whether you are a student discovering these concepts for the first time, a practitioner refining your craft, or a scholar building on this foundation, I am honored to share this journey with you.

—Woody R. Clermont

Biography & Curriculum Vitae of Gerald Alain P. Chen-Young

Gerald Alain P. Chen-Young

Principal, Chief Investment Officer, Corporate Director & International Institutional Investment Advisor & Consultant

Since 2016, Gerald has served as principal of GCY Associates LLC. GCY Associates LLC is a small, independent, global institutional advisory and consulting firm whose clients have ranged from an Ivy League university, to a small private HBCU university, to a multi-billion euro multilateral scientific research organisation based in Geneva, Switzerland, and to multiple international periodicals. Gerald also serves on various boards, including working as an independent director to a hedge fund and as an advisory board member to an insurance group, where he also serves as Chair of the Investment Committee. Most recently (effective 8 December 2024), Gerald was named Chief Investment Officer of the National Public Pension Funds Association (NPPFA) and an advisor/consultant to a major global law firm's dedicated Securities Practice Group. Finally, and on a more personal note, Gerald has served in the past as Special Advisor to the Ambassador of Jamaica.

From 2002–2016, Gerald served as Vice President & Chief Investment Officer for the United Negro College Fund (UNCF), where he actively managed three investment portfolios through a constellation of outside consultants, managers, custodians, and related institutions. At their peak, these three portfolios totalled approximately $1 billion. One portfolio was a dedicated fixed-income portfolio for a special scholarship programme created in conjunction with the Bill & Melinda Gates Foundation, designed to use a dedicated defeasance strategy to immunise programme liabilities by matching cash flows and durations, akin to pension plans. The second portfolio was a traditional, fully diversified, long-term endowment portfolio. The third was a short-term portfolio that staggered maturities across various short-term instruments.

Prior to his tenure at UNCF, Gerald worked with UBS as a retail broker (2000). Before that, he spent several years with PaineWebber (1995) in institutional fixed-income sales covering government issues, corporates, Eurobonds, and later transitioned into retail brokering. He also worked in both the retail and commercial banking divisions of Riggs National

Bank of Washington (1990) in multiple capacities.

Gerald holds postgraduate degrees in Economics from the London School of Economics & Political Science and from York University, as well as a postgraduate degree in Law from both the University of Miami and the Washington College of Law. His undergraduate degree is in Economics from the American University, where he graduated with honours. Gerald has served on multiple advisory boards, committees, and related professional bodies. He has been nominated for multiple industry awards and most notably received the Institutional Investor "Investor Intelligence Awards – Endowments & Foundations, Thought Leadership" (2016). He was nominated twice to the global "ai-CIO, Power 100 CIOs" list (2012 & 2013) and has spoken on many global institutional investor panels around the world.

Most recently, Gerald agreed to serve as an Adjunct Professor on a part-time basis to teach a course on "Asset Management" at Georgetown University in Washington, D.C. Gerald is a dual Jamaican–American citizen, married, and currently resides in Washington, D.C. He is partly bilingual (English and French) and is also an avid recreational *chef de cuisine*. Gerald is a sportsman, a voracious reader, and a global traveller.

Biography of Woody R. Clermont

Woody R. Clermont, is a multidisciplinary attorney, author, and educator whose career reflects a rare fusion of legal practice, economic analysis, data science, theology, and public service. Over more than two decades, he has worked across nearly every dimension of the justice system—criminal prosecution, juvenile advocacy, administrative adjudication, municipal law, complex business litigation, and appellate practice, while simultaneously pursuing rigorous academic study in mathematics, economics, analytics, and public policy. His work is grounded in a belief that law is most powerful when it is informed by quantitative reasoning, historical awareness, and an unwavering commitment to human dignity.

Clermont's public-sector career reflects the depth of that commitment. He served the City of Miami Beach as an Assistant City Attorney, where he prosecuted criminal violations, represented the municipality in therapeutic courts, and ensured that victims received restitution and

accountability. He was appointed as a Special Assistant
United States Attorney for the Southern District of Florida,
an honor that demonstrated the trust placed in his
professional judgment. As a Medicaid Fair Hearing Officer
with Florida's Agency for Health Care Administration, he
presided over evidentiary hearings, issued written final orders
subject to appellate review, and provided legal and regulatory
analysis to state leadership. For more than a decade, he
served as a Senior Trial Court Staff Attorney in the Eleventh
Judicial Circuit of Florida, assisting judges across divisions
including appellate, criminal, family, probate, zoning, land
use, and complex business litigation. In that role, he drafted
proposed opinions, evaluated extensive trial records,
conducted deep statutory and constitutional research, and
assisted in matters involving the most serious stakes,
including death warrant litigation.

His earlier service as an Assistant State Attorney in
Miami-Dade County further shaped his prosecutorial and
courtroom experience. There he tried numerous bench and
jury trials, supervised divisions, trained young prosecutors,
and handled cases ranging from DUI and juvenile matters to
high-level felonies and life offenses. Before entering
government, he built practical skill in private practice
representing personal injury plaintiffs, and spent more than a
decade in the insurance industry as an independent all-lines
claims adjuster, where he investigated losses, resolved
coverage disputes, and developed the analytical discipline that
later defined his litigation approach.

Clermont's teaching career reflects a parallel passion for
education. He has taught business statistics, macroeconomics,

and microeconomics at Miami Dade College; courses in administrative law, American government, contracts, criminal procedure, property, and legal practice at Key College; and justice studies, including administrative law, criminal law, criminal procedure, and juvenile justice, at Southern New Hampshire University. His classroom work integrates doctrinal clarity with quantitative analysis, mirroring the interdisciplinary approach that defines his authorship.

As a writer, Clermont has earned national recognition, receiving the distinction of "Best Multidisciplinary Author and Thought Leader in the United States of 2025." Through Woody Clermont Book Publishing, he produces works that bridge law, economics, spirituality, history, and cultural analysis. His books span nonfiction, legal scholarship, forensic economics, and imaginative historical critiques, resonating with a diverse readership on Amazon and beyond. His work blends narrative, empirics, and accessible scholarship, reflecting a belief that knowledge should serve both the public and the profession.

His commitment to community extends beyond the courtroom and classroom. Clermont is a lifetime member of Omega Psi Phi Fraternity, Inc., a Silver Life Member of the NAACP in Broward County, an active member of Kiwanis International, and a lifelong mentor to young people across South Florida. He is also a lifetime member of the Circle of Brotherhood, an organization dedicated to service, justice, and community uplift.

Clermont's educational journey reflects the same interdisciplinary breadth as his career. He earned his Juris

Doctor from the University of Miami School of Law, where he and Gerald Chen-Young won the Moot Court Competition. He completed multiple graduate degrees, including an MBA and a Master of Science in Economics from Florida Atlantic University; a Master of Science in Data Analytics and a Bachelor of Science in Business IT Management from Western Governors University; and a Bachelor of Science in Mathematics from Mayville State University. His earlier academic work includes a Bachelor of Arts in Political Science from Binghamton University and associate degrees in computer science and information systems from SUNY Empire State College and the University of the People. His secondary education at Regis High School in New York, one of the nation's most prestigious Jesuit institutions, provided early training in classical thought, ethics, and intellectual discipline.

He is admitted to practice in Florida, New Jersey, and New York, and has been honored with numerous distinctions, including multiple Literary Titan Gold Book Awards, recognition from The BookFest, an Avvo "Superb" 10.0 rating, and membership in honor societies such as Phi Theta Kappa and Omicron Delta Epsilon. He is the proud father of two children.

Woody R. Clermont's professional identity is defined not by titles but by a consistent philosophy: that law, economics, and human stories cannot be separated. His work—whether in the courtroom, classroom, or his writing—seeks to illuminate how institutions shape lives, how data clarifies truth, and how justice requires both intellectual rigor and compassion. His multidisciplinary perspective continues to influence legal scholarship, public policy discourse, and the lives of readers and students across the country.

Appendix A

Selected Answers

Ronald Coase and the Problem of Social Cost

1. **Coase Theorem and Its Assumptions:** The Coase Theorem states that if property rights are well-defined and transaction costs are zero, parties will bargain to an economically efficient outcome regardless of the initial allocation of rights. The key assumptions, zero transaction costs, full information, and rational actors, are rarely satisfied in the real world. In practice, legal fees, holdouts, coordination problems, and asymmetric information often make bargaining infeasible or inefficient.

2. **Nightclub vs. Condo owner(s):** Under a pure Coasean analysis, the party who values the activity more (either quiet or noise) should prevail, as they will be willing to pay the other to tolerate or stop the externality. If only one condo owner is involved, low transaction costs might allow efficient bargaining—e.g., the nightclub pays the owner or vice versa. However, with 50 owners, transaction costs skyrocket, making coordination nearly impossible. In such a case, the initial allocation of rights (e.g., zoning law or noise ordinances) will heavily influence outcomes.

3. *Boomer v. Atlantic Cement Co.* **(1970):** The court allowed the cement company to continue operations but ordered it to pay permanent damages. This reflects a Coasean sensitivity: rather than halt a socially valuable operation with an injunction, the court enabled an economically efficient outcome by awarding compensation. The decision implicitly acknowledged that transaction costs prevented efficient private bargaining between the cement company and the plaintiffs.

4. **Real-World Dispute:** Consider a dispute between a wind farm and nearby homeowners complaining about turbine noise. Coasean bargaining could involve the wind farm paying affected homeowners, or the homeowners paying for mitigation measures. Efficient bargaining would aim to reach a mutually agreeable trade-off—such as installing noise barriers or compensating residents—if transaction costs (e.g., collective action problems) can be kept low.

5. **Diagram Illustration:** In the Coasean bargaining
   zone, the overlap between the marginal cost of
   abatement and marginal benefit from externality
   reduction represents the potential for a deal.
   Introducing transaction costs shifts or eliminates this
   overlap. A diagram should show:

   - X-axis: Units of externality reduction

   - Y-axis: Cost and benefit in dollars

   - Downward-sloping marginal benefit curve (to
     victim)

   - Upward-sloping marginal cost curve (to injurer)

   - Transaction cost zone shown as a wedge reducing
     or eliminating overlap

   (See Figure A.1)

Transaction Costs Narrow the Bargaining Zone

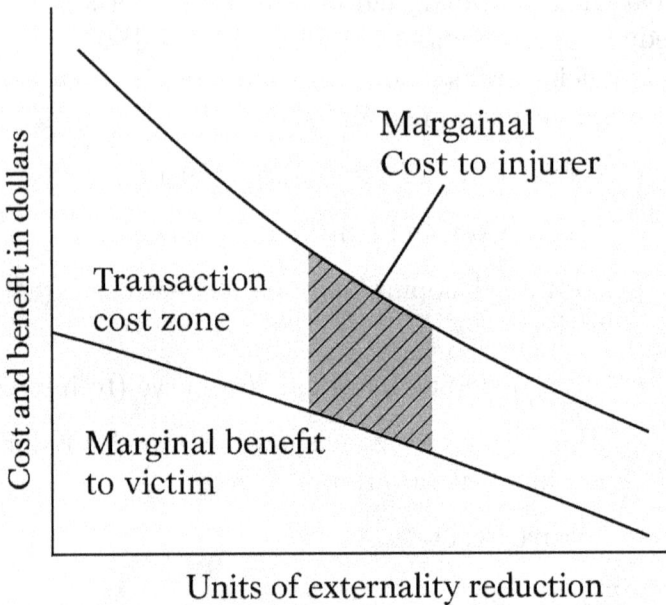

Figure A.1: Transaction Costs Narrow the Bargaining Zone

Anti-Competitive Answers

1. **Market power** is the ability of a firm to raise prices above competitive levels for a sustained period without losing customers. Forensic economists measure market power by analyzing:

- Market share of the firm;
- Elasticity of demand;
- Entry barriers;
- Profit margins and pricing behavior;
- Pricing above marginal cost.

Economists may also use regression analysis and event studies to quantify the exercise of market power.

2. The **Herfindahl-Hirschman Index (HHI)** is a commonly used measure of market concentration, calculated by summing the squares of the market share percentages of all firms in the market:

$$\text{HHI} = \sum_{i=1}^{n} s_i^2$$

where s_i is the market share of firm i.

- An HHI below 1,500 indicates a competitive market.
- An HHI between 1,500 and 2,500 indicates moderate concentration.
- An HHI above 2,500 suggests high concentration and potential antitrust concern.

3. In *United States v. Microsoft Corp.*, the government argued that Microsoft engaged in exclusionary conduct by bundling Internet Explorer with Windows to suppress browser competition. Economic theories applied included:

- **Network effects** — where a product becomes more valuable as more people use it;

- **Path dependence** — once a firm secures a dominant position, alternatives are hard to adopt;

- **Barriers to entry** — created through software compatibility and bundling strategies;

- **Predatory behavior** — foreclosing rival browsers without lowering prices.

4. A diagram of monopolistic pricing typically shows:

- The demand curve (downward sloping);

- Marginal revenue curve (beneath the demand curve);

- Marginal cost curve;

- Quantity produced at the point where MR = MC;

- Price charged (from demand curve at that quantity);

- Deadweight loss — the triangle between the demand curve and MC to the right of the monopoly output level.

This area represents the lost social welfare due to the reduced output and higher prices under monopoly compared to perfect competition.

5. In the AT&T breakup case, economic testimony was pivotal. Economists:

- Demonstrated how vertical integration deterred market entry and suppressed competition;

- Provided models showing how rate structures and long-distance access were manipulated to disadvantage rivals;

- Persuaded the court that structural remedies (divestiture into Baby Bells) would enhance competition more effectively than behavioral restrictions;

- Contributed to the framing of consent decrees and post-divestiture oversight mechanisms.

This was a landmark in U.S. antitrust enforcement, showcasing how forensic economists can influence remedy design.

Answers to Chapter 16 Problems

1. **What were the economic conditions that led to the passage of the Sherman Antitrust Act?**
   In the late 19th century, the U.S. economy experienced rapid industrialization and the rise of powerful monopolies and trusts, especially in sectors like oil, steel, and railroads. These conglomerates often colluded to fix prices, eliminate competition, and restrict supply. Public outcry over higher prices and unfair business practices led Congress to enact the Sherman Antitrust Act in 1890, which outlawed monopolistic conduct and conspiracies that restrained trade.

2. **Define market power and explain how forensic economists help courts measure it.**
Market power is the ability of a firm to set prices above competitive levels for a sustained period. Forensic economists assess market power by analyzing pricing behavior, elasticity of demand, barriers to entry, concentration ratios, and profit margins. Tools such as the Lerner Index, cross-price elasticity, and Herfindahl-Hirschman Index (HHI) help quantify the extent to which a firm can influence market outcomes.

3. **In the AT&T case, what economic arguments were used to justify the breakup of the company?**
The DOJ argued that AT&T used its monopoly over local phone service and infrastructure to suppress competition in long-distance service and telecommunications equipment. Economists presented evidence of vertical integration, discriminatory access pricing, and cross-subsidization that impeded entry by rivals. The breakup, achieved through divestiture of regional Bell operating companies in 1984, was intended to restore competition and prevent abuse of bottleneck control.

4. **Draw a diagram showing how a monopoly restricts output and increases price compared to a competitive market.**

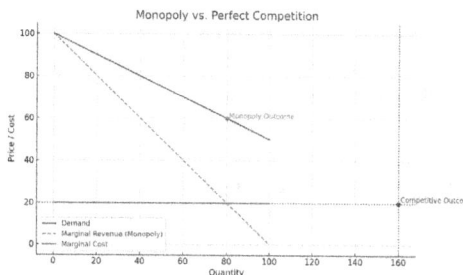

Figure A.2: Monopoly Outcome vs. Competitive Outcome

A monopolist reduces output to Q_M, raising price to P_M, compared to the competitive equilibrium at Q_C, P_C. The area between these curves represents the deadweight loss to society.

5. **Explain the Herfindahl-Hirschman Index and its use in merger analysis.**
   The Herfindahl-Hirschman Index (HHI) is calculated by summing the squares of each firm's market share:

$$HHI = \sum_{i=1}^{N} (s_i \times 100)^2$$

Where s_i is the market share of firm i. The U.S. Department of Justice uses the HHI to assess market concentration:

- HHI < 1500: Unconcentrated

- HHI 1500–2500: Moderately concentrated

- HHI > 2500: Highly concentrated

Mergers that significantly raise the HHI in already concentrated markets may be challenged as anticompetitive.

Chapter 17 Answers

1. **Describe the hedonic valuation technique and explain how it can be used in a wrongful death case.**
   Hedonic valuation estimates the implicit value of non-market goods or attributes—such as quality of life, environmental amenities, or risk—by analyzing how these factors influence market prices (e.g., wages or housing). In a wrongful death case, economists may use hedonic wage regressions to estimate the monetary value that individuals implicitly place on life by comparing wages across occupations with differing risk levels. This allows courts to assign value to lost enjoyment of life or the decedent's quality-of-life contributions beyond economic productivity.

2. **What are the key inputs needed to calculate lost future earnings in a personal injury case?**
   Key inputs include:

   - Projected annual earnings (wages, bonuses, commissions)

   - Work-life expectancy or retirement age

   - Discount rate for present value calculation

   - Fringe benefits (e.g., health insurance, retirement

contributions)

- Expected career progression and promotions
- Life expectancy (if permanent injury or wrongful death)

3. **How can regression analysis reveal wage discrimination in employment lawsuits?**
   Economists use regression models to isolate the effect of protected characteristics (such as gender or race) on wages, controlling for other factors like education, experience, job title, and tenure. A statistically significant negative coefficient on the gender or race variable—after accounting for legitimate factors—may indicate discrimination. For example:

$$\text{Wage}_i = \beta_0 + \beta_1 \cdot \text{Male}_i \\ + \beta_2 \cdot \text{Experience}_i \\ + \beta_3 \cdot \text{Education}_i + \epsilon_i$$

If $\beta_1 < 0$ and statistically significant, it suggests female employees earn less than males with similar credentials.

4. **Why is it important to consider fringe benefits in total earnings calculations?**
   Fringe benefits can account for 20–40% of total compensation. Ignoring them would underestimate the economic loss in personal injury or wrongful termination cases. These benefits include:

- Employer-provided health insurance

- Retirement plan contributions
- Paid leave and holidays
- Stock options and bonuses

Including them ensures a more comprehensive and accurate valuation of lost compensation.

5. **Given the following data (provided in Appendix X), compute a simple wage regression model.**
   Let the data in Appendix X include variables for wage, experience, and education. A simple OLS regression using statistical software such as R or Stata may yield an output such as:

   $$\text{Wage}_i = 12.3 + 1.5 \cdot \text{Education}_i + 0.7 \cdot \text{Experience}_i$$

   Interpretation:

   - Each additional year of education increases predicted wages by $1.50/hour.

   - Each additional year of experience increases wages by $0.70/hour.

   - The intercept suggests a base wage of $12.30/hour with zero education and experience (useful only within observed range).

Answers to Chapter 18 Problems

1. **Construct a regression model using hypothetical data to detect wage discrimination. Interpret your coefficients.**

Model:

$$\text{Wage}_i = \beta_0 + \beta_1 \cdot \text{Female}_i + \beta_2 \cdot \text{Experience}_i + \epsilon_i$$

Suppose the estimated model is:

$$\text{Wage}_i = 42{,}000 - 3{,}500 \cdot \text{Female}_i + 1{,}200 \cdot \text{Experience}_i$$

Interpretation:

- $\beta_0 = 42{,}000$: The baseline wage for a male employee with zero experience.

- $\beta_1 = -3{,}500$: On average, females earn \$3,500 less than males, controlling for experience.

- $\beta_2 = 1{,}200$: Each additional year of experience increases wage by \$1,200.

The negative coefficient on *Female* suggests potential gender-based wage discrimination.

2. **Explain why multicollinearity can undermine damage estimation models.**

Multicollinearity occurs when two or more explanatory variables are highly correlated. This leads to:

- Inflated standard errors for coefficients.

- Unstable coefficient estimates that vary with minor data changes.

- Reduced statistical significance, making it hard to isolate the effect of individual variables.

In forensic damage estimation, it may cause courts to

question the reliability or objectivity of the expert's valuation.

3. **What standards must a forensic economist meet for survey evidence to be admitted under the Daubert standard?**

   Under Daubert, survey evidence must meet four criteria:

   - **Testability:** The survey method must be empirically verifiable.

   - **Peer Review:** The methodology should be published or recognized in the field.

   - **Error Rate:** The survey must disclose margins of error and confidence levels.

   - **General Acceptance:** Techniques must be widely accepted among forensic economists.

   Additionally, the survey must avoid bias, use valid sampling, and ask neutral, reliable questions.

4. **Describe a case where instrumental variables would be necessary. What instrument would you propose?**

   Case: Suppose we wish to estimate the effect of education on earnings. Education may be endogenous due to omitted variables (e.g., motivation or innate ability).
   Instrument: Proximity to a college at age 18. It influences education level but is plausibly uncorrelated with earnings potential, conditional on other factors.

IV regression helps recover the causal effect of education while avoiding bias from endogeneity.

5. **Use a chi-square test to assess whether a company's promotion rate is independent of gender (data provided in Appendix Y).**

   Method:

   (a) Construct a contingency table with observed counts of promoted and non-promoted employees by gender.

   (b) Calculate expected frequencies under the null hypothesis of independence.

   (c) Compute the test statistic:

   $$\chi^2 = \sum \frac{(O - E)^2}{E}$$

   (d) Compare to the critical value from the χ^2 distribution with the appropriate degrees of freedom.

   Interpretation: If χ^2 exceeds the critical value (e.g., at 0.05 significance), reject the null hypothesis. This suggests that promotion rates depend on gender.

Answers to Chapter 19 Problems

1. **Define the SSNIP test and apply it to a hypothetical cell phone market.**
   The SSNIP test (Small but Significant and

Non-transitory Increase in Price) asks whether a
hypothetical monopolist could impose a price increase of
5–10% without losing sales to substitutes. If so, the
defined market is considered valid.

Example: In a local cell phone market, suppose Firm A
offers 4G data plans in City X. Analysts consider
whether consumers would switch to Wi-Fi, landlines, or
other carriers if prices increased by 5%. If most
consumers remain with Firm A, the 4G market in City
X passes the SSNIP test and can be treated as a distinct
market.

2. **Compute the HHI for a market where four firms
   hold 40%, 30%, 20%, and 10% shares. Interpret
   the result.**

   The Herfindahl-Hirschman Index (HHI) is computed by
   squaring each firm's market share and summing:

$$HHI = 40^2 + 30^2 + 20^2 + 10^2$$
$$= 1600 + 900 + 400 + 100$$
$$= 3000$$

According to U.S. DOJ guidelines:

- HHI < 1500: Unconcentrated market

- HHI 1500–2500: Moderately concentrated

- HHI > 2500: Highly concentrated

Thus, an HHI of 3000 indicates a highly concentrated
market—potentially raising antitrust concerns for

mergers or anticompetitive behavior.

3. **Explain how moral hazard can affect the behavior of insured parties in litigation.**
Moral hazard arises when insured parties take greater risks because they are shielded from the consequences. In litigation, this may manifest as:

- Inflated claims for medical treatment or income loss

- Less incentive to return to work promptly

- Filing of questionable or fraudulent lawsuits

Economists evaluate these effects by comparing observed behaviors to actuarial baselines and pre-incident conduct.

4. **Design a basic Monte Carlo simulation model to forecast lost income due to injury.**
A Monte Carlo model simulates possible income paths based on random sampling from a probability distribution.
Steps:

(a) Define the expected income range: e.g., Normal distribution with mean \$75,000 and standard deviation \$10,000.

(b) Generate 10,000 simulations of future annual earnings over a projected worklife (e.g., 20 years).

(c) Apply injury impact as a reduction in mean income or increased variance.

(d) Discount each income stream to present value.

(e) Aggregate simulations to compute expected value and confidence intervals.

Result: A distribution of present values that reflects uncertainty in recovery, employment trajectory, and macroeconomic volatility.

5. **Analyze how the discount rate changes when a risky future income stream is involved.**
   The discount rate increases with the riskiness of the income stream. Instead of using a risk-free rate (e.g., 3%), economists add a risk premium:

   $$r_{\text{total}} = r_{\text{risk-free}} + \rho$$

   Where ρ reflects job instability, health uncertainty, or industry volatility. Higher risk reduces the present value of future income, aligning valuation with potential variability and loss.

Answers to Chapter 20 Problems

1. **A plaintiff earned \$75,000/year and was projected to work 20 more years. If the discount rate is 4%, estimate the present value of lost earnings.**
   This is a standard present value of annuity problem:

   $$PV = \sum_{t=1}^{20} \frac{75{,}000}{(1 + 0.04)^t}$$

Using the present value of an ordinary annuity formula:

$$PV = 75{,}000 \cdot \left(\frac{1 - (1 + 0.04)^{-20}}{0.04} \right)$$

$$\approx 75{,}000 \cdot 13.5903$$

$$= 1{,}019{,}272.50$$

Thus, the estimated present value of lost earnings is approximately \$1,019,273.

2. **Explain the differences among cost, market, and income approaches to IP valuation.**

   - **Cost Approach:** Estimates value based on the cost to reproduce or replace the intellectual property. Appropriate when direct market data is unavailable or the IP has not yet been monetized.

   - **Market Approach:** Compares the subject IP to similar assets that have been bought, sold, or licensed in the marketplace. Useful when transaction comparables exist.

   - **Income Approach:** Projects future income attributable to the IP and discounts it to present value. Most common in litigation, particularly for patent and copyright cases.

3. **In a copyright infringement case, what data would you request to conduct a DCF analysis?** A robust Discounted Cash Flow (DCF) analysis requires:

   - Historical sales and profit margins tied to the

copyrighted work.

- Forecasted revenue from the work absent infringement.

- Estimated market share erosion due to infringement.

- Incremental costs and tax assumptions.

- Discount rate reflecting risk and time value of money.

- Royalty rate benchmarks, if using a relief-from-royalty method.

4. **In a breach of contract case, how would a but-for scenario be structured?**
   The but-for scenario reconstructs the economic position the plaintiff would have enjoyed had the breach not occurred. It involves:

   - Forecasting profits or revenues expected under contract performance.

   - Subtracting actual outcomes post-breach.

   - Adjusting for mitigation efforts, alternative opportunities, and external market forces.

   The resulting calculation quantifies the economic loss directly attributable to the breach.

5. **Construct a graph showing lost profits over time and mitigation efforts.**
   While a visual is ideal, a conceptual description follows:

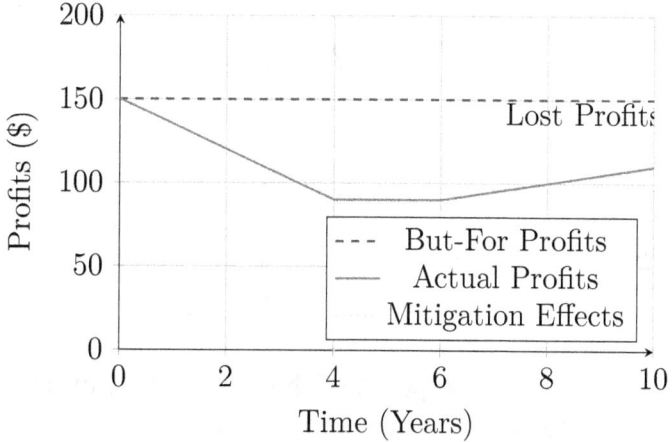

This chart illustrates declining actual profits (red line) post-breach, compared to the stable but-for scenario (blue line). The green line reflects gradual recovery or mitigation over time.

Answers to Chapter 21 Problems

1. **Define and explain the purpose of the Beneish M-Score. What are its limitations?**
   The Beneish M-Score is a mathematical model developed by Professor Messod Beneish to detect whether a company has manipulated its earnings. It uses eight financial ratios to calculate a score that indicates the likelihood of earnings manipulation. A score greater than -2.22 suggests possible fraud. The formula includes metrics such as Days Sales in Receivables Index (DSRI), Gross Margin Index (GMI), and Total Accruals to Total Assets (TATA).

Limitations: The model may produce false positives or miss manipulation if the financial indicators used are being obscured by other accounting tricks. It also assumes data integrity in the reported financials and was calibrated using historical data from a specific time period.

2. **Calculate the expected frequency of the leading digit "1" using Benford's Law. Why is this useful?**

Benford's Law predicts the distribution of first digits in naturally occurring numerical datasets. The expected frequency of the leading digit "1" is:

$$P(1) = \log_{10}(1 + \frac{1}{1}) = \log_{10}(2) \approx 0.3010$$

This means that about 30.1% of the numbers in such a dataset should begin with the digit 1.

Usefulness: Significant deviations from this expected frequency can suggest potential manipulation or fraud in accounting records, tax returns, or financial reports.

3. **You are asked to evaluate whether a restaurant is underreporting cash revenue. What forensic techniques would you apply?**

Several forensic methods are appropriate:

- **Bank Deposit Analysis:** Compare deposits to reported sales.

- **Lifestyle Analysis:** Evaluate whether owner expenditures align with reported income.

- **Industry Ratios:** Compare cost of goods sold

(COGS) and revenue ratios to benchmarks.

- **Invigilation Techniques:** Monitor operations during a "clean" period to compare actual sales to declared amounts.

- **Z-Score or Benford's Law Analysis:** Detect statistical anomalies in daily receipts.

4. **Draw a transaction flowchart for a suspected fraudulent conveyance case.**
   While a graphic is ideal, a textual flowchart is presented here:

   - Step 1: Company A sells assets to Affiliate B below market value.

   - Step 2: Affiliate B transfers funds offshore to Account C.

   - Step 3: Account C wires money to Trust D under control of Company A's owner.

   - Step 4: Funds are used to acquire personal property unrelated to company interests.

   This flowchart traces the conveyance of assets through intermediaries designed to shield ownership and avoid creditor claims.

5. **How might data mining techniques enhance traditional financial statement analysis?**
   Data mining adds predictive and diagnostic power through:

   - **Anomaly Detection:** Algorithms can flag

unusual transactions or patterns.

- **Cluster Analysis:** Grouping transactions by similarity may reveal hidden relationships or shell entities.

- **Text Mining:** Extract insights from unstructured data (e.g., footnotes, emails).

- **Machine Learning Models:** Train classifiers to distinguish between fraudulent and legitimate filings.

These techniques complement standard ratio and trend analysis by enabling pattern recognition at scale.

Diagrams

Negotiation Outcomes Under the Coase Theorem

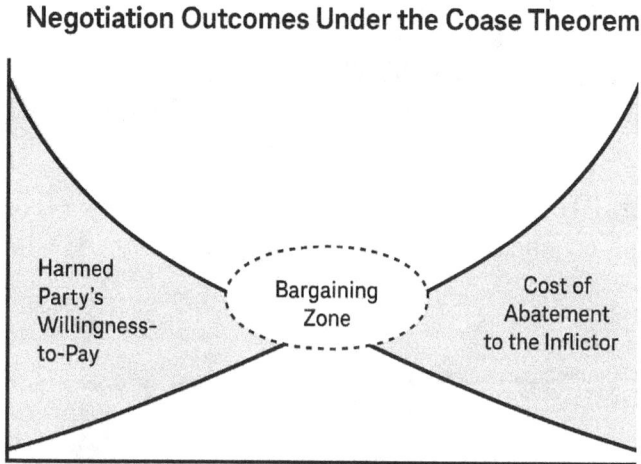

Figure A.3: Negotiation Outcomes: Bargaining Possibilities under the Coase Theorem

Interpretation: This diagram illustrates a simplified two-party negotiation scenario. The area where the cost to the polluter (or injurer) is less than or equal to the benefit to the harmed party (or victim) creates a *bargaining zone* in which voluntary agreements are Pareto optimal. The Coase Theorem predicts efficient outcomes within this zone when transaction costs are low and rights are clearly defined.

Additional Notes

- **Transaction Costs:** If bargaining is costly (e.g., legal fees, delays), the efficient outcome may not be reached.

- **Property Rights Matter:** Initial entitlement determines who must be compensated—but not the efficiency of the final allocation.

- **Legal Implications:** Courts may implicitly recognize these economic effects when shaping nuisance or liability rules.

©2025 Woody R. Clermont. All rights reserved. Please make sure to leave a Review of this work, on the marketplace you obtained it from as well as Goodreads. It would mean a lot to me, alls this work to reach more people, and gives good feedback. A full listing of all my books is available at: https://woodycbooks.com.

www.ingramcontent.com/pod-product-compliance
Lightning Source LLC
Chambersburg PA
CBHW061229220326
41599CB00028B/5374